BBC

Speak‹out›

3RD EDITION

B1+

Student's Book and eBook

CONTENTS

LESSON	GRAMMAR/FUNCTION	VOCABULARY	PRONUNCIATION	READING
LEAD-IN p6				
1 me & mine BBC VLOGS | What's the best present you've ever received?				
1A The story of me p8	Narrative tenses	Describing possessions; materials	Auxiliary verbs: weak forms	
1B Less is more? p11	Verb patterns	Personal preferences	Stress in prepositional phrases	Read an article about minimalism vs. maximalism
1C Don't forget to … p14	How to … leave phone messages	Phrasal verbs: housework	Intonation in polite requests	
1D Your gadgets p16	*except for, apart from, (not) even*			
UNIT 1 REVIEW p18				
2 behaviour BBC VLOGS | What good habits do you have?				
2A Change of habit p20	Present perfect continuous	Making changes	Weak form of *been*	Read an article about how to change habits **FUTURE SKILLS** Critical thinking
2B People pleaser p23	Relative clauses	Collocations: feelings and behaviour	Chunking in relative clauses	
2C That's annoying! p26	How to … talk about things that annoy you	Pet hates	Stress and intonation to show annoyance	
2D Planet Earth II: Jungles p28				
UNIT 2 REVIEW p30				
3 working life BBC VLOGS | Where do you prefer to work or study?				
3A Working from home p32	Conditional structures: *unless, even if, in case (of)*	Work phrases	Stress in phrases	Read an article about famous authors working from home
3B Gig work p35	Necessity, obligation and permission	Work	Elision of /t/	
3C Good question p38	How to … take part in an interview **FUTURE SKILLS** Job interviewing	Personality adjectives (1); negative prefixes	Word stress in personality adjectives	
3D This or that? p40	Expressing preferences			
UNIT 3 REVIEW p42				
4 fact or fiction? BBC VLOGS | Do you prefer true stories or fiction?				
4A Hoax! p44	Past plans and intentions	Truth and lies	Silent consonants	Read about a hoax
4B Documentary p47	Indirect and negative questions	Adjectives to describe films; films and film-making	Intonation in indirect and negative questions	
4C News p50	How to … talk about the news	News headlines; the news	Word stress in adverbs for summarising	
4D Fake friends p52				
UNIT 4 REVIEW p54				

LISTENING/VIDEO	SPEAKING	WRITING
Listen to a podcast about people's possessions	Tell 'a story of me in three objects'	Write an advert to sell an item online
	Discuss a questionnaire about preferences **FUTURE SKILLS** Communication	
	Leaving phone messages **FUTURE SKILLS** Communication **MEDIATION SKILLS** Agree on the best way to fix a work problem	
BBC Street Interviews about gadgets and screen time	Discuss a questionnaire about gadgets	Write an online forum comment
	Talk about ways of changing habits	
Listen to people talking about being a 'people pleaser'	Talk about ways of saying no	Write emails to decline invitations
	Talk about things that annoy you	**MEDIATION SKILLS** Summarise an article
BBC Programme *Planet Earth II: Jungles*	Discuss difficult situations	Write about a personal experience
	Talk about your approach to working or studying from home	
Listen to people talking about the gig economy	Talk about what's important in a job	Write a cover email for a job application
	MEDIATION SKILLS Choose a candidate for a position	
BBC Street Interviews about people's preferred jobs	Talk about 'This or That?' questions	Write a discussion board post
	Retell the story of a hoax **FUTURE SKILLS** Communication	
Listen to people talking about favourite documentaries	Present a pitch for a documentary	Write a review
	Discuss a news story	**MEDIATION SKILLS** Report a news story
BBC Programme *Ordinary Lies*	Have a conversation with an old friend	Write a personal email/letter

CONTENTS

LESSON	GRAMMAR/ FUNCTION	VOCABULARY	PRONUNCIATION	READING
5 consumer BBC VLOGS | When was the last time you had a problem with a product or service?				
5A The customer is always right? p56	Clauses of purpose: *to, so as to, in order to/that, so that*	Personality adjectives (2)	Word stress in adjectives	
5B Too good to be true p59	Comparative and superlative structures	Advertising; money	Linking *r* in phrases	Read an article about marketing tricks
5C Which should I buy? p62	**How to …** summarise information from different sources	Describing products	Intonation in summarising phrases	
5D I do it myself p64	Causative *have* and *get*; reflexive pronouns			
UNIT 5 REVIEW p66				
6 places BBC VLOGS | What's your favourite city?				
6A In the city p68	*so* and *such*	Areas of a city	Intonation for emphasis with *so* and *such*	
6B Great journeys p71	*be/get used to*	Challenges; idioms	*be/get used to*	Read an article about epic journeys
6C City transport p74	**How to …** ask for and confirm information	City transport	Fast speech: *just*	
6D A city of tomorrow p76				
UNIT 6 REVIEW p78				
7 connect BBC VLOGS | What's your favourite word?				
7A Mix-up p80	Reported speech	Reporting verbs; ways of speaking	Stress in reporting verbs	
7B Oversharing p83	Passives	Computer use; internet words	Stress and weak forms in passives	Read an article about oversharing online **FUTURE SKILLS** Critical thinking
7C 7C Conversation savers p86	**How to …** keep a conversation going	Adverbs	Intonation in short questions	
7D A good communicator p88	Avoiding repetition: *so, to, not, be*			
UNIT 7 REVIEW p90				
8 wisdom BBC VLOGS | What's the best piece of advice you've ever been given?				
8A Wise words p92	Third conditional and *should have*	Phrases of advice	Contractions in complex sentences	Read an article about advice from people of different ages **FUTURE SKILLS** Critical thinking
8B Life lessons p95	*would*	Learning; phrasal verbs	Contracted *would*	
8C One thing I know … p98	**How to …** give a presentation	Presenting	Stressing words in key phrases	
8D Dragons' Den p100				
UNIT 8 REVIEW p102				

GRAMMAR BANK p104   **VOCABULARY BANK** p132   **COMMUNICATION BANK** p138   **MEDIATION BANK** p145

LISTENING/VIDEO	SPEAKING	WRITING
Listen to people making complaints	Roleplay making complaints	Write a complaint email
	Discuss a marketing campaign **FUTURE SKILLS** Communication	
	MEDIATION SKILLS Explain something clearly to sell an idea to other people	
BBC Street Interviews about what people do themselves/have done	Talk about planning an event	Write a meeting summary
Listen to people talking about their favourite neighbourhoods	Describe your favourite neighbourhood **FUTURE SKILLS** Collaboration	Write instructions for how to get somewhere
	Describe a challenging experience	
	Roleplay asking for and confirming information **MEDIATION SKILLS** Discuss a proposal	
BBC Programme *Reggie in China*	Talk about what a place is famous for	Write a description of a business idea
Listen to a podcast about misunderstandings	Talk about recent conversations	Write a story about an event
	Discuss issues connected to online privacy	
	Two-minute conversations	**MEDIATION SKILLS** Explain a chatbot flowchart
BBC Street Interviews about communication	A discussion about communication	Write an an email giving advice about a problem
	Describe a situation, then give advice	
BBC Radio Listen to an account of the origins of one man's curiosity	Discuss the most important qualities of a mentor **FUTURE SKILLS** Collaboration	Write a short biography
	Give a five-minute presentation **FUTURE SKILLS** Communication **MEDIATION SKILLS** Ask follow-up questions	
BBC Programme *Dragons' Den*	Pitch a business idea	Write an email giving work-related news

AUDIOSCRIPTS p157   **VIDEOSCRIPTS** p170   **IRREGULAR VERBS** p175

LEAD-IN

GRAMMAR

1 A Work in pairs. Read the text and discuss. Do you have anything in common with Alejandra?

My name is Alejandra Morales. I'm an exchange student. I'm originally from Granada, which is in the south of Spain, but I currently live in Manchester, UK. I'd never travelled outside my country before this. I love music and I was told that Manchester is a great city for music. I've been to lots of excellent gigs and seen some amazing new bands. I also like sport, especially football, so I hope to see one of the Manchester teams in action. My other hobby is reading, particularly fiction. As for Manchester, I love everything except the climate. My flatmate told me it was the wettest city in the country!

B Read the text again and find an example of:
1 a superlative.
2 reported speech.
3 the passive.
4 the present perfect simple.
5 a non-defining relative clause.
6 the past perfect.

COMMON ERRORS

2 Correct the mistakes in the sentences.
1 Where I can buy a phone?
2 Yesterday I've visited the castle.
3 I've known her since fifteen years.
4 I will to work from home next year.
5 If I'll have time, I'll come to the party.
6 What means this?

VOCABULARY

3 A Choose the correct words to complete the questions.
1 Have you studied with any of your **classmates** / **class-colleagues** before?
2 Do you work or are you a **whole-time** / **full-time** student?
3 Where do you note **up** / **down** new words? Do you use a notebook?
4 Have you ever watched a TV **series** / **sequence** in English?
5 Are you interested in current **news** / **affairs**, like politics and cultural topics?
6 Have you ever **made** / **done** a phone call in English?
7 Have you **loaded** / **downloaded** any apps to help you study recently?
8 Are there any languages that you tried to study, but you gave **over** / **up**?

B Work in pairs. Choose five of the questions from Ex 3A to ask your partner.

PRONUNCIATION

4 A Match (1–6) with (a–f) to make pairs that rhyme.
1 should   a show
2 weight   b filled
3 build   c fur
4 white   d wood
5 though   e height
6 were   f late

B 🔊 L.01 | Listen and check your answers.

C Work in pairs. Think of other words in English that rhyme with words 1–6.

REGISTER

5 Are the sentences (1–5) formal or informal? Where might you hear or read them? Compare your ideas with a partner.
1 I look forward to hearing from you at your earliest convenience.
2 Wow! That's fantastic news!
3 Gone into town. Be back at 3.
4 One of the main advantages of this programme is that it is less expensive than its competitors.
5 Guess what!

COLLOCATIONS

6 A Complete the word webs with the words and phrases in the box.

| a break | fired | a good memory | lost |
| a mess | a mistake | on holiday | viral |

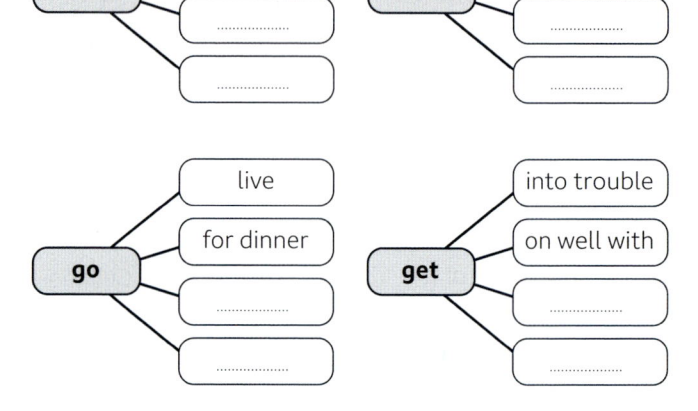

have: lunch, trouble, ..., ...
make: an excuse, a plan, ..., ...
go: live, for dinner, ..., ...
get: into trouble, on well with, ..., ...

B Work in pairs. Take turns to say true sentences using one collocation for each of the four verbs in Ex 6A.
A: Yesterday I **had lunch** in a French restaurant.
B: I always **have trouble** finding a place to park my car.

# me & mine 1

GSE LEARNING OBJECTIVES

1A LISTENING | Understand people talking about their possessions: describing possessions; materials
Tell 'a story of me in three objects': narrative tenses
Pronunciation: auxiliary verbs: weak forms
Write an advert to sell an item online

1B READING | Read an article about minimalism vs. maximalism; verb patterns
Answer a questionnaire about preferences: personal preferences
Pronunciation: stress in prepositional phrases

1C HOW TO … | leave phone messages: phrasal verbs: housework
Pronunciation: intonation in polite requests

1D BBC STREET INTERVIEWS | Understand people talking about gadgets and screen time: *except for, apart from, (not) even*
Answer a questionnaire about gadgets
Write an online forum comment

VLOGS

Q: What's the best present you've ever received?

1 ▶ Watch the video. Which do you think is the best present?

2 What's the best present you've ever received?

Unit 1 | Lesson A

1A The story of me

GRAMMAR | narrative tenses
VOCABULARY | describing possessions; materials
PRONUNCIATION | auxiliary verbs: weak forms

LISTENING

1 A Think of three people you know and two or three objects connected with each person. Make notes.

B Work in pairs and tell each other about the people and the objects. How are the objects connected to their personalities?

2 A Read about *A story of me in three objects* and look at the photos. Why might these objects be important to the speakers?

B 🔊 1.01 | Listen to the podcast and number the objects in the order you hear them.

coffee pot	leather jacket
lemon tree	silver rings
Spanish guitar	walking boots

C Work in pairs. What information can you remember about each object?

3 A 🔊 1.01 | Listen again. Are the statements True (T) or False (F)?

1 Marta inherited a valuable ring from her mother.
2 Marta borrowed a jacket from a friend.
3 One of Marta's friends helped her dream to come true.
4 The owner of the guitar shop asked Tim if he was a professional.
5 Tim enjoys walking with friends.
6 Tim always made good coffee when he was at university.

B Work in groups. Discuss the questions.

1 Do you have anything in common with either Marta or Tim? What?
2 'If you can't enjoy little things, then you will never be happy.' What do you think this means? What are some 'little things' that make you happy?

A story of me in three objects

The objects that we choose to have around us reflect our personalities in different ways. Our possessions contain our memories; they remind us of people and places in our lives. Do you ever think about why you choose to keep some objects and not others? The objects we keep often reflect who we were, who we have become and who we want to be. In this podcast we ask people to choose three objects from their life that they would never throw away, and tell us about them.

Marta

Tim

8

1A

VOCABULARY

describing possessions

4A Read the extracts (a–b) from the podcast. Match the words and phrases in bold with the meanings (1–8).

   a I've worn silver rings all my life. … This one **belonged to** my mother and I **inherited** it when she died. It's **not worth a lot**, but it's very **special** to me.

   b I borrowed this **leather** jacket from a friend when I was studying at university … It's a **genuine** 1980s leather jacket … When I was wearing it, I always thought it looked really **cool**. It's a bit **damaged** now, but I still love it.

   1 If something was owned by someone else, we can say it .... them.
   2 If something is not valuable, it's ....
   3 If it's made of animal skin, it's ....
   4 If you received a possession (or money) from someone after the person died, you .... it.
   5 If something is real, an original and not a copy, it's ....
   6 Something which is broken in some way is ....
   7 If something has emotional importance for you, it's ....
   8 If we think something looks good in a fashionable way, we can say it's ....

B Work in pairs. Ask and answer the questions.
   1 Do you have any possessions which previously belonged to your parents, grandparents or friends? What are they? Who did they belong to?
   2 Do you have a possession which is not worth a lot, but is special to you?
   3 Do you own a lot of things made from the same material, e.g. silver, denim, leather?

C Learn and practise. Go to the Vocabulary Bank.

▶▶ page 132 **VOCABULARY BANK** materials

GRAMMAR

narrative tenses

5A Match the sentences from the podcast (a–d) with the rules (1–2). Choose the correct words to complete the rules.

   a I bought these boots while I **was travelling around** New Zealand.
   b I got this ring in a street market when I **was living** in Italy for a few months.
   c I bought it to replace a similar one that I**'d lost**.
   d The shopkeeper **had listened** to me playing and he asked me, 'Are you a professional?'

   1 We use the past continuous to refer to **temporary** / **fixed** or changing states and situations.
   2 We use the past perfect to describe an action which happened **before** / **after** another action in the past.

B Learn and practise. Go to the Grammar Bank.

▶▶ page 104 **GRAMMAR BANK**

PRONUNCIATION

6A 🔊 **1.02** | auxiliary verbs: weak forms | Listen and complete the sentences.

   1 I .... around Australia.
   2 We .... in China.
   3 He .... at university.
   4 I bought a new leather jacket to replace the one I ....
   5 My mother .... the ring to me.
   6 He .... me making coffee.

B 🔊 **1.02** | What do you notice about the auxiliary verbs? Are they stressed? Listen again and repeat the sentences.

C Work in pairs. Make sentences about one or two of the options to tell your partner.

Think of a time when:
   1 you had to replace something you had lost. What happened?
   2 a friend or relative gave you something special. What was the occasion?
   3 someone made something and gave it to you. What was it? Did you like it? Why/Why not?
   4 you were living or studying in a different place to now. Why were you there?

SPEAKING

7A Prepare to talk about three important objects that say something about you and your life. Make some notes to answer the questions.

   1 What are the objects? How would you describe them?
   2 Tell a story about each of the objects. Where did you get them? Why are they important to you?

This old leather biker's jacket belonged to my dad. He wore it a lot when he was living and working in London. He'd finished university and was working as a motorcycle courier. It's a bit damaged now, but it's very special to me, even if I don't actually wear it much anymore.

B Work in groups. Tell each other your 'story of me in three objects'. Ask and answer any questions about the stories.

C 📷 Take a photo of the three objects you discussed, or make a photo collage. Bring the photo and show it to the class. Look at your partner's photos. Can you remember what the objects are and why they are important?

Unit 1 | Lesson A

WRITING

an advert to sell an item online

8 A Work in pairs and discuss. Do you ever buy or sell items online? What kinds of thing? Which platform do you use?

B Complete the descriptions of items for sale in the photos with the words in the box.

| condition | good | includes |
| Italian | leather | new | used |

9 A Look at the sentences from the adverts. Which types of word are missing: nouns, articles, pronouns or other grammatical words?

1 The price of the bike includes front and back lights, a bike lock and keys. → Price includes front and back lights, bike lock and keys.

2 They are new and they are in perfect condition. → New and in perfect condition.

B How are the sentences (1–5) reduced in the adverts?

1 This bike was bought earlier this year but it was never used.
2 It is in the same condition as it was when it was new.
3 The coffee pot serves four people.
4 The back of the guitar is slightly damaged.
5 They come in the original box.

C Reduce the sentences (1–4) to note form.

1 It has been slightly damaged.
2 The price includes a spare set of strings.
3 This has never been used.
4 It is in very good condition.

D Choose three possessions that you could sell on a trading website or app. Write short descriptions of the different items for sale, with prices, using note form.

men's jacket – medium

1980s vintage denim jacket. In perfect [1] ....

Price: £75

Size: Medium

♡ 12

bicycle

Brand new men's bike. Bought earlier this year but never [2] ....
[3] .... front and back lights, bike lock and keys.

Price: £350

Location: Manchester, UK

Condition: As [4] ....

♡ 8

moka coffee pot

Cool [5] .... moka coffee pot. Serves 4.

#espresso #coffee

Price: £18

BUY NOW

♡ 3

Spanish guitar

Spanish classical guitar. In [6] .... condition, back slightly damaged.

Comes complete with spare set of strings.

Price: £120

♡ 10

for sale

Ladies' walking boots, size 40

[7] .... boots. New and in perfect condition. In original box.

Price: £40

♡ 5

1B Less is more?

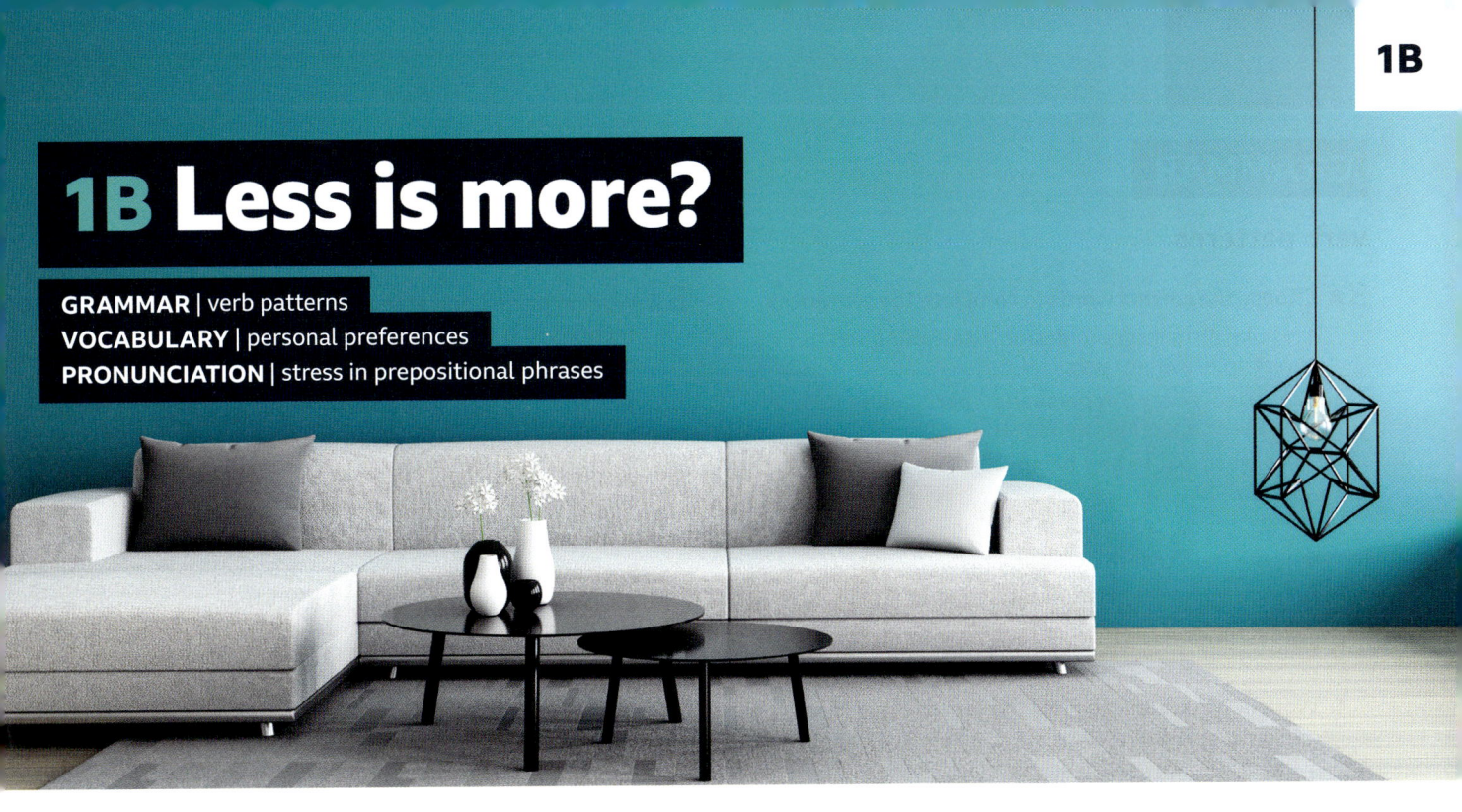

GRAMMAR | verb patterns
VOCABULARY | personal preferences
PRONUNCIATION | stress in prepositional phrases

READING

1 A Look at the photo and discuss the questions.
   1 What kind of person do you think lives in a place like this? Why?
   2 What would/wouldn't you like about living in this place? Why?

B Read the introduction to a magazine article about maximalism and minimalism. Are you surprised by any of the facts in the first paragraph? Why/Why not?

C Work in pairs. Turn to page 139. Student A: Read what Zuleya says about minimalism. Student B: Read what Richard says about maximalism. Tell each other an interesting fact from your part of the article.

D Swap texts with your partner and read the rest of the article. Who do you think makes the stronger argument: Zuleya or Richard? Discuss in pairs.

2 A Work in pairs. Can you remember what the full-length article says about these things? Check your answers.
   1 a crazy number
   2 twelve toys
   3 the world's number of phones
   4 a simpler world
   5 who Joshua Fields Millburn and Ryan Nicodemus are
   6 appreciating the things that really matter
   7 objects that give visitors pleasure

B Are the ideas in Ex 2A facts or opinions? Think about where the information comes from. Read the examples to help you.
   1 The idea that it's 'crazy' is the writer's opinion, not a fact. There is no source except the writer's thoughts.
   2 The number twelve is from research quoted in the newspaper *The Daily Telegraph*. It is a fact, not an opinion.

C Work in pairs and discuss. Which opinions in the article do you agree with?.

Minimalism vs. Maximalism

According to the *Los Angeles Times*, the average American home contains 300,000 items. It's a crazy number, even if it includes everything from pencils to beds. A British newspaper, *The Daily Telegraph*, reported that the average British 10-year-old owns 238 toys but plays with only twelve daily. *The Story of Stuff*, a documentary, tells us we consume double the number of things that we did half a century ago and there are more phones in the world than people.

All of this might explain why minimalism – the idea of living more simply – has become a trend. Minimalism began as an artistic movement in the 1950s. Artists like Donald Judd and Agnes Martin produced paintings and sculptures reduced to bare, pure lines. Now it's not art but the environmental impact of our lifestyles that has seen minimalism return.

Maximalism also has its roots in the art world, especially the French Rococo style of the eighteenth century and a 1920s movement called Art Deco. It involves bright colours and interesting patterns like zebra stripes and leaf prints. Fans of maximalism say it's not only for eighteenth century French kings, but for anyone who enjoys having lots of beautiful objects in the house.

So, space and simplicity or colour and craziness? Here, two designers share their views on the issue: minimalism or maximalism.

Unit 1 | Lesson B

GRAMMAR

verb patterns

3 A Choose the correct words to complete the sentences.
1. Minimalism refers to **design / designing** things in a simple, elegant way.
2. They succeeded in **persuade / persuading** people to stop collecting useless stuff.
3. It turned out to **be / being** the most important trip of my life.
4. I went on to **become / becoming** a designer.
5. I believe in **create / creating** joyful designs.
6. I look forward to **visit / visiting** more street markets.

B Check your answers in the article on page 139.

C Work in pairs. Look again at the sentences in Ex 3A and answer the questions.
1. What usually follows verb + preposition: the -ing form or the infinitive?
2. Which two sentences in Ex 3A do **not** follow this pattern?

4 A Match the words in bold in sentences 1–2 with the definitions a–b.
1. They persuaded people to **stop collecting** useless stuff.
2. If we **stop to think** about what's really important …
a. Stop + to infinitive means pause an action so that you can do a different action.
b. Stop + -ing means change a habit.

B Learn and practise. Go to the Grammar Bank.

➤➤ page 105 **GRAMMAR BANK**

VOCABULARY

personal preferences

5 A Work in pairs. Look at the words in bold in the two sections of the article about Minimalism vs. Maximalism on page 139. Answer the questions.
1. Which two adjectives mean 'perfect for me'?
2. Which two phrases mean 'I don't like …'?
3. Which phrase means 'don't need'?
4. Which word means 'enjoy or be thankful for something'?
5. Which phrase means 'make someone happy'?
6. Which word means 'the kind of things you like'?

B Choose the correct words to complete the summaries.

Zuleya says that, for creative people, the homes she designs are ¹**pleasure / ideal**. She thinks minimalism allows us to ²**stand / appreciate** the important things in life. She believes we can ³**do without / give pleasure** so many things.

Richard is doing his ⁴**dream / first** job. Minimalism isn't ⁵**for him / the taste** because he ⁶**dreams of / is not a big fan of** blank, empty spaces. He says his objects give ⁷**taste / pleasure** to his visitors. He also says people have different ⁸**hopes / tastes** and you can live a simple life and still enjoy colours and patterns in your home.

C Complete the sentences with your own ideas. Read your sentences to other students and compare ideas.
1. One sound or smell that gives me pleasure is …
2. My dream job would be … , and the ideal place for it would be …
3. I have very different tastes from … . For example, …
4. I always appreciate … . In fact, I can't do without …
5. … isn't for me because I'm not a big fan of …

PRONUNCIATION

6 A 🔊 **1.03 | stress in prepositional phrases** | Read the sentences (1–4). Which words in bold are not stressed: the verbs or the prepositions? Listen and check.
1. I **believe in living** a simple life.
2. He **succeeded in finding** his dream job.
3. You should **think about tidying** your stuff.
4. **Concentrate on appreciating** the simple things.

B 🔊 **1.03** | Listen again and repeat the sentences.

C Change the phrases in bold by adding your own ideas. The first word you write should be an -ing form.
1. I don't care about **being famous**.
   I don't care about owning lots of things.
2. I sometimes dream about **escaping to another country**.
3. I never think about **going to nightclubs**.
4. I believe in **helping others**.
5. I never apologise for **being myself**.

D Read your sentences to a partner. Make sure you stress the verbs. Are the sentences true for both of you?

12

SPEAKING

7 A Read the questionnaire and think about your answers. What explanations and examples can you think of?

B Read the Future Skills box and do the task.

C Work in groups. Ask and answer the questions in the questionnaire. Give examples and use emphatic language.

D Work with another group. Guess what their answers were. Are there any surprises?

FUTURE SKILLS
Communication

To show a strong attitude towards a topic, we often use emphatic language, e.g. 'I definitely …', 'I definitely don't …'. Can you think of any other emphatic phrases?

Before you do the activity in Ex 7C, look at the questions and think about which emphatic phrases you can use in your answers to show your attitude.

WHO ARE YOU?

social butterfly or 'stay-at-home'
Is your ideal evening spent alone or do you look forward to spending time with other people?
> I like …
> I enjoy …

messy or tidy
Does it give you pleasure to keep rooms, desks, tables, etc. tidy or are you happy to live or work in an environment with lots of stuff everywhere?
> I'm (not) a big fan of …
> I prefer …

social media fan or non-user
For how long could you give up checking your phone messages and social media? One hour? One day?
> I can/can't do without …

multitasker or 'one-thing-at-a-time'
Do you prefer to concentrate on doing one thing at a time or do you do lots of different tasks at the same time?
> I prefer …

future dreamer or happy with 'now'
Do you dream about achieving amazing things (like getting a dream job) or do you appreciate the things you have now and feel content?
> I dream about …
> I care about …

follower of tradition or independent
Do you care about following your family's traditions in habits, beliefs, clothes, education, etc., or do you have different tastes?
> I believe in …
> I (don't) care about …

planner or non-planner
Are you the type of person who thinks about planning their holidays at the last minute or do you prefer to plan everything months before?
> I (don't) put off …
> I like …

Unit 1 | Lesson C

1C Don't forget to …

HOW TO … | leave phone messages
VOCABULARY | phrasal verbs: housework
PRONUNCIATION | intonation in polite requests

VOCABULARY

phrasal verbs: housework

1 A Work in pairs. Name as many household tasks as you can in one minute. Then compare with other students.

washing the dishes …

B Work in groups. Discuss the questions.
1 Which of the tasks in Ex 1A do you do?
2 Which do you dislike the most?
3 Are there any that you like?

2 A Match the 'to do' lists (1–3) with the situations (a–c).
a someone moving house
b someone organising a party
c someone going away for the winter

1
- throw out food from the fridge
- take out the rubbish
- pack suitcases
- set house alarm

2
- pick up cake from bakery
- tidy up living room
- buy snack food
- clean bathrooms
- hang up clothes lying around in bedroom
- turn up heating

3
- finish packing boxes
- phone new owners – go over instructions for alarm system
- sweep floor
- complete 'new address' form for post office
- lock up the house

B Look at the lists in Ex 2A and find phrasal verbs to match with meanings (1–8).
1 put something outside
2 increase
3 something you do with doors and windows to stop people getting in
4 put something in the rubbish because you don't want it
5 get/buy something (can be collecting something you arranged to buy earlier)
6 put things on a hook or other object
7 explain instructions to make sure someone understands
8 make somewhere neater by putting things in the right place

C Match the questions (1–8) with the answers (a–h).

What do you do when:
1 your clothes are lying all over the floor?
2 you're going home and you remember you need to buy milk?
3 your desk papers, books and cups are all over the room?
4 you need to explain complicated instructions to your flatmate?
5 food goes bad?
6 the temperature changes and the heating is too low?
7 you're leaving the house to go on holiday?
8 the bin is full of rubbish?

a lock it up
b throw it out
c tidy it up
d hang them up
e pick some up
f go over them
g take it out
h turn it up

D Work in pairs. Student A: Close the book. Student B: Test Student A. Then swap roles.

B: What do you do when your clothes are lying all over the floor?
A: Hang them up.
B: Correct!

14

How to ...
leave phone messages

3 A Work in pairs and discuss the questions.
1 Do you ever have to leave or listen to phone messages in English?
2 Do you find this difficult? Why/Why not?

B 🔊 1.04 | Listen to the phone messages. Number the items in the box in the order you hear them.

| alarm system   broken pipe   folder   garage door |
| leather jacket   pizzas   plants |

C Complete the phrases (1–10) with the words in the box.

| back   call   calling   find   here   message |
| number   reached   this   you'll |

Things you'll hear on a recorded message:
1 You've .... Café Roma.
2 Please leave a message and we'll get .... to you.
3 Thank you for .... Smiths and Co. Our office hours are 8 a.m. to 6 p.m.
4 I can't take your call right now, but if you leave a .... with your name and number, I'll get back to you as soon as I can.

Starting a message:
5 .... is Marcelo Fagundes calling about …
6 It's Patricia .... …

Giving detailed information:
7 .... need to unlock the …
8 You'll .... it on the table next to the …

Asking for further phone actions:
9 Can you .... me back?
10 You can reach me on this ....

D 🔊 1.05 | Listen and check.

4 A Complete the requests with the words and phrases in the box.

| could you please   do you think |
| I wonder if you   wonder   would |

1 .... you explain the alarm system to her?
2 .... could bring my folder to the meeting?
3 .... let me know that you've got this message?
4 .... you'll be able to pick up some pizzas on the way home?
5 I .... if you'd mind watering the plants for me.

B 🔊 1.06 | Listen and check.

C Are the polite requests in Ex 4A direct or indirect requests? How do you know?

D Learn and practise. Go to the Grammar Bank.
▶▶ page 106 **GRAMMAR BANK**

PRONUNCIATION

5 A 🔊 1.07 | **intonation in polite requests** | Listen to the requests (1–4). Does the speaker start with a high or low pitch to sound polite?
1 I wonder if you could bring my folder, please?
2 Would you walk the dog, please?
3 Do you think you'll be able to come today?
4 Will you pick up some food on the way home?

B 🔊 1.07 | Listen again and say the sentences with the recording.

C Complete the requests using your own ideas. Read them to a partner using a high intonation to sound polite.
1 I wonder if you could …
2 Would you tell me …
3 Do you think …
4 Will you …

SPEAKING

6 A Work in pairs. You are going to practise leaving some phone messages. Read the Future Skills box and plan your messages for the situations in Ex 6B.

FUTURE SKILLS
Communication

Before leaving a phone message in English, it helps to plan and write down the main points. Think about how to:
- start the message,
- say why you're calling,
- explain details clearly (if necessary),
- end the message.

B Work in pairs. Prepare voicemail messages. Student A: Go to page 138. Student B: Go to page 141.

C Take turns to leave your messages by saying them in your pairs. Student B: Start with a recorded message.
B: You've reached [name]. Please leave a message.
A: …

MEDIATION SKILLS
inviting contributions
agree on the best way to fix a work problem
▶▶ page 145 **MEDIATION BANK**

1D BBC Street Interviews

Your gadgets

GRAMMAR | except for, apart from, (not) even
SPEAKING | a questionnaire about gadgets
WRITING | an online forum comment

Joshua

Catherine

PREVIEW

1 A Are you a technophile or technophobe? Which statement is closest to the truth for you?
  1 I love technology and try to be as up-to-date as possible.
  2 I use technology, but I don't need to have all the latest gadgets.
  3 I'm not very interested in new technology and think it's a waste of money.

B Work in pairs and compare your answers. Say what gadgets you use the most and how you use them.

Q1: Which gadgets do you love, and which could you live without?

Q2: Do you think people spend too much time looking at screens?

VIEW

2 A ▶ Watch the interviews and answer the questions.
  1 Which of the items below do the speakers mention?
   - coffee maker
   - home computer
   - smart speaker
   - gaming console
   - iPad
   - smartwatch
   - guitar pedals
   - phone
   - VR headset
  2 How many of the speakers think that people spend too much time looking at screens?

B ▶ Watch the first part of the interviews again. Write the name of the speaker who:
  1 uses their phone in bed.
  2 could live without their smartwatch.
  3 could live without all their gadgets except for their phone.

C ▶ Watch the second part of the interviews again. Complete the things the speakers say.
  1 You lose the .... contact and that emotion that you get from that interaction.
  2 I think people are .... to screen time, needing information or entertainment more immediately.
  3 I think people probably spend .... on their phone.
  4 It prevents you from being able to talk to people in ....

D Do you agree with the statements (1–4) in Ex 2C? Discuss in pairs.

GRAMMAR

except for, apart from, (not) even

3 A Look at the sentences from the video (a–d) and complete the rules (1–3) with *except for*, *apart from* or *even*.
  a I think I could live without all my gadgets **apart from** my phone, because it's so important to me.
  b I love a range of gadgets from my Xbox and my laptop, but I could live without all of them **except for** my phone.
  c I love my phone. I use it all the time. I **even** use it in bed.
  d People certainly look at their phones too much. It might **even** be the first thing in the morning.

  1 We use .... to show something is surprising or unusual, and we want to emphasise the point.
  2 We use .... and .... to say that something is not included.
  3 We usually follow .... and .... with a noun.

B Learn and practise. Go to the Grammar Bank.

▶▶ page 107 **GRAMMAR BANK**

1D

BBC

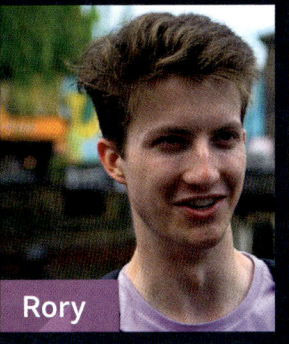

Shannon

Rory

Marc

Josh

Connor

SPEAKING

a questionnaire about gadgets

4 A Write down all the gadgets you use on an average day in the order you use them. Compare with other students. Are your lists similar or different?

My phone first, for my alarm and checking social media, then my coffee maker, …

B Read the questionnaire and make a note of your answers.

You and your gadgets

1. How old were you when you got your first phone? What do you remember about getting it?
2. Apart from your phone, what gadgets do you love, and which could you live without? Why?
3. Are there any gadgets that you would like to have?
4. What gadget would you like to have that hasn't been invented yet?
5. Think of three gadgets that were invented during your lifetime. Which is the best and why?
6. Do you think you spend too much time looking at screens? Why/Why not?

C Work in groups. Ask and answer the questions in the questionnaire. Use your notes and the Key phrases to help you. Respond to your partners' opinions.

KEY PHRASES

Apart from my phone/laptop, I'd say that …
I could easily live without …
One thing I'd love to have/I could do without is …
In my honest opinion, …
I would say I definitely …
Absolutely! Me too.
Really? Are you sure … ?
Do you really/honestly think that … ?
I don't believe it!

WRITING

an online forum comment

5 A Read the online forum discussion. Do you think the suggestions are good or bad? Why?

MA **Mairat21** 1 h
What gadget would you like to have that hasn't been invented yet?
4 Comments | 5 Share | 11 Likes

B8 **Beatrice86** 52 mins | One thing I would love to have that hasn't been invented yet is a pet translator. It could tell you what your pet is saying, and could even translate what you say to the pet. I would love to know what my cat is thinking.
Comment | Share | Like

MX **Marcx991** 47 mins | Really? Are you sure? You look at all the problems in the world that could be solved with technology and you want to invent a pet translator? I don't believe it!
Comment | Share | Like

SM **Smithsy42** 36 mins | I would say that apart from flying cars, one of the best gadgets would be something that can change the size and shape of your vehicle at the push of a button. You would never have to sit in traffic again!
Comment | Share | Like

DD **DarrenDarren** 31 mins | Absolutely! This is a great idea.
Comment | Share | Like

B Work in pairs. Think of a gadget you would like to have that hasn't been invented yet. Write a post describing the gadget and the problem it would solve.

C Read other people's suggestions. What do you think of the ideas? Write comments on each one giving your opinion and explaining it.

1 REVIEW

GRAMMAR
narrative tenses

1 A Choose the correct words to complete the text. What do you think the idiom in the final sentence means?

The Story of Me ... on Wheels!

The first mode of transport that I remember was my tricycle. My parents gave it to me the year after I ¹**was learning / had learnt** to walk, and I loved it. Then came my famous red bike. My dad ²**was teaching / taught** me how to ride it. I was ten years old and I ³**was riding / rode** down the main road when something ⁴**had happened / happened** that I'll never forget. It ⁵**had rained / was raining** heavily so I could barely see, and I skidded in a puddle and lost control. Luckily, the road was empty and I ⁶**wasn't getting / didn't get** hurt. Later, I bought a motorbike. I ⁷**was wanting / had wanted** one for years, but I ⁸**hadn't been / wasn't being** able to afford it until my twenties. I rode it everywhere. In my thirties, I got married and started a family, so I ⁹**was having / had** to sell my motorbike and buy a car. Yesterday I ¹⁰**watched / had watched** my three-year-old learning to ride his tricycle. You could say the wheel has come full circle!

B Work in pairs and discuss. Do you have stories to tell about yourself on wheels?

verb patterns

2 A Make sentences about yourself using the words and phrases in box A and the verbs in box B. Use the correct form of the verbs in box B: -ing or to infinitive.

A	care about dream about give up look forward to plan on remember stop

B	be do eat go help relax travel watch work

I dream about travelling to West Africa.

B Work in groups. Take turns to read your sentences. Did you have any similar ideas?

3 A Add the words in the box to complete the sentences. One word isn't used.

apart   even   except   from   not

1 I'm the quietest person in my family, apart my father.
2 Everyone in my family dances, my grandparents, who love it.
3 No one in my family knows how to cook from my mother.
4 Everyone I know plays video games, for me.

B Are any of the sentences true for you? Tell a partner.

VOCABULARY

4 A Choose the correct words to complete the sentences.
1 It's a beautiful old **cotton / silver** ring which **belonged to / owned** my grandmother.
2 They're my favourite pair of **denim / diamond** jeans. They're quite **leather / damaged**, but I would never throw them away.
3 It's a lovely **stone / rubber** vase that a friend gave me as a birthday present. It's **cool / not worth a lot** but it's very **special / gold**.
4 It's a **steel / genuine** Italian suitcase, made of **leather / stone**. It belonged to my father.

B Work in pairs. Do you have any objects which you would never throw away? Describe them to your partner and say why they are special to you.

5 A Choose the correct option (A–C) to complete the extract from a story.

The House that Jock Built

When Elizabeth finally saw the house, it ¹_____ part of her family legend for 200 years. It had been built by Jock Phillip, her distant ancestor who ²_____ Scotland for America aged sixteen with nothing but the clothes on his back. Five years after arriving, he discovered a hidden treasure in California: a seam of gold, which he later mined. He had succeeded in ³_____ his fortunes, and with his earnings he built his ⁴_____ home.

It was the ⁵_____ house, large and beautiful, a house to pass down from generation to generation. It belonged to his children, then his grandchildren, and so on. When Elizabeth was young, she remembered ⁶_____ stories about it. For this reason she had always dreamed about ⁷_____ the house. Finally, her chance came.

While she ⁸_____ there, she suddenly felt a sense of sadness. She arrived and saw immediately that the house was badly ⁹_____ . The walls, made of ¹⁰_____ , were falling down, and the windows were long gone. Birds had made their homes in the roof.

1	A was being	B had been	C had
2	A had been leaving	B was leaving	C had left
3	A changing	B to change	C change
4	A taste	B dream	C treasure
5	A ideal	B big	C great
6	A hearing	B to hear	C hear
7	A visit	B to visit	C visiting
8	A was driving	B had driven	C drove
9	A damaging	B damaged	C damage
10	A glass	B silver	C stone

B 🔊 R1.01 | Listen and check your answers.

18

behaviour 2

VLOGS

Q: What good habits do you have?

1 ▶ Watch the video. What habits do they talk about?

2 What good habits do you have? Talk about one or two of them.

GSE LEARNING OBJECTIVES

2A READING | Understand an article about how to change habits: making changes

Talk about ways of changing habits: present perfect continuous

Pronunciation: weak form of *been*

2B LISTENING | Understand people talking about being a 'people pleaser': collocations: feeling and behaviour

Talk about ways of saying 'no': relative clauses

Pronunciation: chunking in relative clauses

Write emails to decline invitations

2C HOW TO ... | talk about things that annoy you: pet hates

Pronunciation: stress and intonation to show annoyance

2D BBC PROGRAMME | Understand a TV wildlife programme about an exciting escape

Discuss difficult situations

Write a story about a personal experience

Unit 2 | Lesson A

2A Change of habit

GRAMMAR | present perfect continuous
VOCABULARY | making changes
PRONUNCIATION | weak form of *been*

VOCABULARY

making changes

1 A Work in pairs. Which bad habits (1–6) are in the photos (A–C)?
1. 'I spend over three hours on social media every day.'
2. 'I leave the tap running when I clean my teeth.'
3. 'I sometimes binge-watch TV series for hours at a time.'
4. 'I often leave the lights on when I go out of a room.'
5. 'I throw away quite a lot of food.'
6. 'I never stop work for lunch.'

B Work in pairs and discuss. Do you do any of the things in Ex 1A?

2 A Work in pairs and look at the statements (1–6). Which are true for you?
1. I **make an effort** to walk away from my screen every hour, but I don't always succeed.
2. I often **put off** important jobs if they're difficult and do easy tasks instead or just check my messages.
3. I've tried to stop biting my nails, but I **keep on** doing it.
4. I **can't resist** coffee. I drink about eight cups a day. I want to **give up** drinking coffee, but I can't.
5. Every time I **take up** a sport, for example swimming, or something like that, I only **manage** to do it for a few weeks.
6. I'm good at **setting goals** for changing my habits, but I'm not very good at **sticking to** them, so I rarely **achieve** my **goals**.

B Complete the sentences (1–10) with the correct form of the phrases in bold in Ex 2A.
1. I decided what I want to do – I ...set... a ...goal... .
2. She's talking and talking and talking – she just .... talking.
3. I can't say no to it, I .... it.
4. I wanted to stop doing it, so I tried to .... it ....
5. I've started something new – badminton. I .... it .... last month.
6. I practise the guitar every day. If I don't .... it, I'll never get better at it.
7. He tried to finish it on time, but it was too difficult so he didn't .... to do it.
8. I don't want to do it now, but I should. I'll do it later. I'm .... it ....
9. I've done many things in my life, but I still haven't .... my .... of becoming a lawyer.
10. I'm trying, I'm trying – I'm .... to do it.

C Work in pairs. Look at Ex 2A and 2B and answer the questions.
1. Which phrases are followed by *to* + infinitive?
2. Which phrases are followed by verb + *-ing*?
3. Which phrases are phrasal verbs?

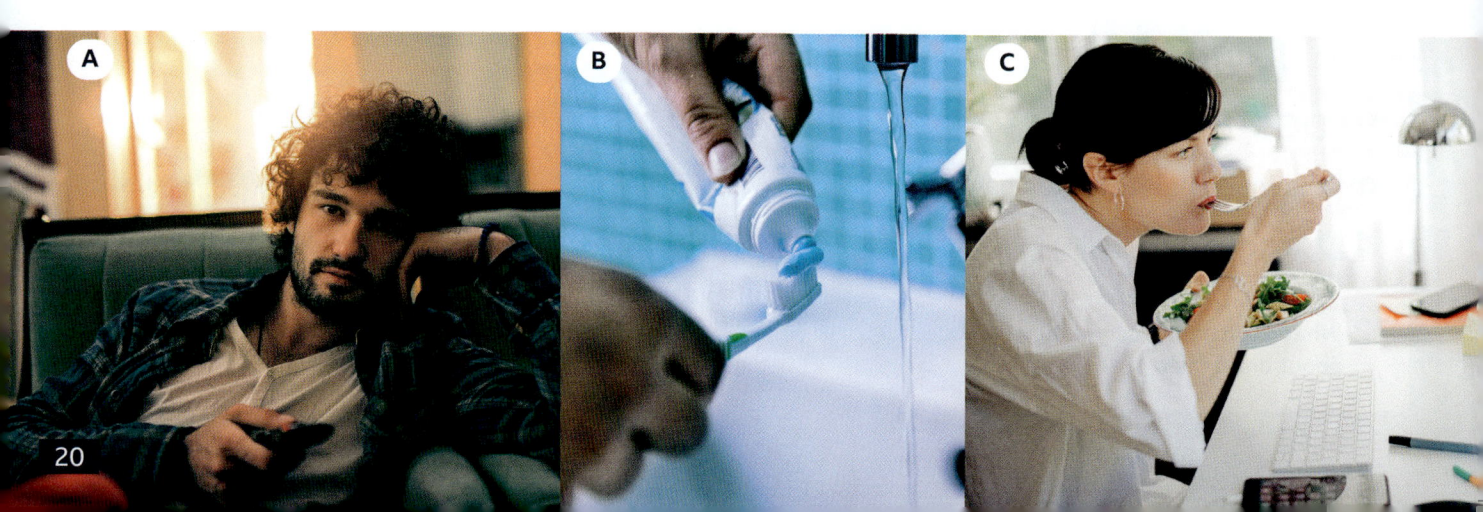

READING

3 A Work in pairs. Discuss the questions.

1 Have you ever tried to stop a bad habit or build a new positive habit? What happened?
2 Why is it difficult to break bad habits, do you think?

B Read the article and choose the best summary (1–3).

1 If you understand how habits work, you'll be better able to change them.
2 Changing bad habits and forming good habits are more or less the same thing.
3 Everyday mistakes are the reason why people often fail to break a habit.

C Read the article again and answer the questions.

1 What three reasons does the writer give for being qualified to write on this topic?
2 What are the four main tips?
3 What are two types of triggers?
4 Which words best describe the style of this article: factual, formal, helpful, humorous, informal, scientific?

4 A Read the Future Skills box and do the task.

FUTURE SKILLS
Critical thinking

Writers use many different techniques to connect with and influence their readers. It is useful and important while you are reading to notice these techniques and reflect on the writer's purpose in using them. One technique is the use of quotes.

Complete Exercise 4B to find out the writer's purpose in using these quotes.

B Look at the article. What is the writer's purpose for using the quotes (1–5) in bold? Choose at least two purposes (a–e) for each quote.

a to create a connection with the reader – the reader can imagine saying or thinking this
b to make the passage more interesting, the way dialogue does in a story
c to give the reader an idea of what to do in the situation
d to give an example of the suggestion that was just made, to make it clearer
e to help show how the tip might work in practice

5 Work in pairs and discuss the questions.

1 Which of the tips in the article do you think are the most and least useful? Why?
2 What other advice would you give someone who is trying to break a bad habit?

Make or Break:
the habits we'd like to change

I've been a life coach for the past seven years, and before this I worked as a psychologist for over ten years. I've been helping people to change their habits since the start of my career, and yes, I've been trying to change my own habits recently, so I know how hard it is. Time and time again, people have asked me questions like [1]**'I want to stop looking at my phone all the time. Why is it so difficult?'** and [2]**'I've been working seven days a week since I was twenty-two. Can I really change that?'**

To answer these questions, let's look at an example. Suppose you want to give up coffee and you currently drink eight cups a day. All that coffee makes you feel nervous and you know it's bad for you. So, you decide to drink water instead of coffee. Everything's fine for the first four days and you manage to follow your plan. But then on the fifth day you come home late and tired – that tiredness is one of your 'triggers' – and you head straight for the coffee. You tell yourself, [3]**'Just this one time. I'm definitely going to stick to my plan after this.'** But that one cup turns into two and then before you know it, you're back to eight cups a day.

So, what's happening here? Well, you've given yourself an impossible task. You can't go from eight cups to zero overnight. You've probably been drinking coffee for a long time and you didn't go from zero cups to eight overnight either! So, tip number one: give yourself mini-goals that you can achieve on a daily basis. Going from eight cups to seven, then six and so on brings you the satisfaction of achieving a new goal almost every day.

Another mistake you've made is that you haven't prepared for the triggers – the things that make you want to 'do' the bad habit, which can be a feeling (e.g. tiredness) or something external (e.g. the smell of coffee). When changing a habit, you need to be ready for these moments, which brings us to tip number two: when a trigger makes your brain scream for coffee (or whatever), just stop and focus on that feeling. Tell yourself [4]**'Yes, I knew there would be moments like this.'** Then pour yourself a glass of water.

And that leads to the next point: just do it! Your brain says coffee and you have a water. Skip the argument (with yourself), just do it, just pour yourself that glass of water. Do you keep putting off a difficult task that is actually important, and take the easy way instead? Tell yourself, [5]**'I have one task, one goal. Just do it.'** Do you look at your phone too much at night? Well, turn it off, put it in another room and go to bed. Just do it.

Finally, from time to time it's important to remind yourself of why you're doing this. Remember, all that coffee makes you feel nervous and you know it's bad for you; your goal is to be a healthier person. Say it to yourself, out loud. You'll be surprised how much motivation you'll feel.

Unit 2 | Lesson A

GRAMMAR

present perfect continuous

6A Find the time phrases at the end of the sentences (1–5).
1 Before this I worked as a psychologist for over ten years.
2 I've been helping people to change their habits since the start of my career.
3 I've been trying to change my own habits recently.
4 I've been working seven days a week since I was twenty-two.
5 You've probably been drinking coffee for a long time.

B Work in pairs. Choose the correct words to complete the rules. Use the sentences in Ex 6A to help.
1 We use the past simple for actions or situations that are **finished** / **unfinished**.
2 We use the present perfect continuous for actions or situations that are **finished** / **unfinished**.
3 We form the present perfect continuous with *have* + *been* + **-ing form** / **past participle**.
4 We use *since* to talk about a **period of** / **point in** time.
5 We use *for* to talk about a **period of** / **point in** time.

C Learn and practise. Go to the Grammar Bank.

▶▶ page 108 **GRAMMAR BANK**

PRONUNCIATION

7A 🔊 2.01 | weak form of *been* | Listen to the sentences (1–4). Underline the main stresses in each sentence. How do we pronounce *been*?
1 How long have you been studying English?
2 I've been studying since I was ten.
3 Have you been living in the same place for a long time?
4 I've been living there for five years.

B 🔊 2.02 | Listen and repeat.

SPEAKING

8A Make a list of three to five lifestyle habits you want to change, and how long you've had each habit. Include bad habits that you want to stop and good habits that you want to start. Use the pictures for ideas.

B Next to each item on your list, make notes about the steps you can take to change or start the habit.

C Work in pairs. Talk about each habit, what you've been doing to change it and what you're going to do to change or start it. Give each other advice on steps to take.

> I've been … for years. Now I'd like to …

> I've been trying to stop/start … and now it's time to …

> I haven't been making an effort to …

> I'd like to take up …

> I've set myself a goal of … and I'm going to try to stick at it for …

D Talk to other students. Find goals that you have in common. Tell each other your ideas for those goals.

9 At home, choose one habit from your list in Ex 8A. Do research about how to change that habit, or how to start it if it's a good habit. Make notes of the new ideas you find and prepare to tell other students in the next lesson.

2B People pleaser

GRAMMAR | relative clauses
VOCABULARY | collocations: feelings and behaviour
PRONUNCIATION | chunking in relative clauses

VOCABULARY

collocations: feelings and behaviour

1 A Work in pairs. What do you think a 'people pleaser' is? How much of a 'people pleaser' are you? Give examples.

B Do the quiz and read the key. Discuss your results.

2 A Choose the correct option (a or b). Use the quiz to help.
  1 When you **make a comment** about something,
    a you say something negative about it.
    b you say something positive or negative about it.
  2 When you **get upset** about something,
    a you become unhappy, hurt or angry.
    b you become very worried and scared.
  3 When you **avoid an argument**,
    a you try not to disagree with people.
    b you don't join in any discussions.
  4 When you **do a favour** for someone,
    a you do something that they ask you to do.
    b you ask them to do something for you.
  5 When you**'re in a bad mood**,
    a you feel unhappy or angry all the time.
    b you feel unhappy or angry, usually for a limited period.
  6 When you **feel guilty** about something,
    a you are understanding about someone's problem.
    b you feel bad because you think you have done something wrong.
  7 When something **is your fault**,
    a you are the person who is responsible for the problem.
    b you feel there is something wrong with you.
  8 When you **feel comfortable** being or doing something,
    a you strongly want to be or do it.
    b you feel calm and relaxed about it.
  9 When you **feel like doing** something,
    a you enjoy doing it.
    b you want to do it.
  10 When you**'re happy to do** something,
    a you don't mind doing it.
    b it makes you feel very positive and good.

B 🔊 **2.03** | Work in pairs and listen. Say what's happening in each situation. Use the correct form of the phrases in bold in Ex 2A.
  1 He's happy to help.

Are you a people pleaser?

Read each sentence. Put two ticks (✓✓) if it's completely true for you, one tick (✓) if it's partially true and a cross (✗) if it's not true.

1 When I get dressed, I think about the comments that people will make about my clothes.
2 When I post something on social media and it doesn't get many 'likes', I get upset.
3 I avoid arguments. When I'm with a group and I disagree with everyone, I keep quiet.
4 I hardly ever say no if a colleague or friend asks me to do them a favour, for example, to give them a lift somewhere or lend them money for lunch.
5 If someone is in a bad mood, for example, angry or sad, I feel guilty about it even if it's not my fault!
6 For me, it's better to be a host than a guest. I feel more comfortable.
7 A positive comment from a stranger feels better than one from a close friend.
8 If I don't feel like doing something but my friend really wants to, I'm happy to do it.

KEY

Count the ticks, and find out if you're a people pleaser.

12 or more ticks: You're a true people pleaser. Maybe you need to think more about yourself and less about other people.

8–11 ticks: Sometimes it's a bit too important what people think about you, but you seem to take care of yourself.

7 or fewer ticks: You're not a people pleaser. You don't let other people's expectations and feelings direct your actions.

Unit 2 | Lesson B

LISTENING

3 A ◆ 2.04 | Listen to the podcast. Are all three speakers, Greta, Colin and Anna, 'people pleasers'?

B Work in pairs and look at the examples the speakers give in the podcast. How is each one connected to the idea of 'people pleasing'?
1 working late
2 a new dress
3 pizza or sushi
4 a film
5 a negative comment on social media
6 a terrible idea at a meeting

C ◆ 2.04 | Listen again and check your ideas in Ex 3B.

4 A Look at audioscript 2.04 on page 158. What phrases do the speakers use to introduce the examples in Ex 3B?

B Work in pairs and discuss. How would you behave in the situations in the podcast? Give examples of any similar situations you have experienced.

GRAMMAR

relative clauses

5 A Choose two correct alternatives for each sentence.
1 I think people **which / who / that** care too much about other people's opinions are wasting their time.
2 I don't pay attention to comments **which / who / that** are negative.
3 We were talking about a film **which / who / that** we'd just seen.
4 And it's even better if I don't know the person **who says / says / saying** it.
5 He isn't the first person **who has told / tells / to tell** me that.

B Work in pairs and answer the questions about the sentences in Ex 5A.
1 In each sentence what do the words and phrases in bold refer to?
2 In which sentence can you leave out the relative pronoun: *who, which* or *that*? Why?
3 In sentences 4 and 5, what can we use instead of a relative pronoun + verb?

C Learn and practise. Go to the Grammar Bank.

▶▶ page 109 **GRAMMAR BANK**

PRONUNCIATION

6 A | **chunking in relative clauses** | Work in pairs and look at the sentence below. Find a relative clause and the noun it refers to.
I try to avoid people who lie.

B ◆ 2.05 | Listen to two different ways of pronouncing the sentence. Which one is correct?

7 A ◆ 2.06 | Listen and write the sentences.

B Work in pairs. Find the relative clauses and the nouns they go with.

C ◆ 2.06 | Listen and say the sentences at the same time as the speaker. Pay attention to chunking the noun and relative clause.

8 A Change the sentences in Ex 7A so they are true for you.

B Work in pairs and tell each other your ideas. Ask one question for each sentence. Remember to say the nouns and relative clauses without pausing between them.
A: I try to avoid people who have very strong opinions.
B: Why do you do that?

SPEAKING

9 A Look at the list of ways to say no. Tick the ones that you think are good ideas.

People pleaser no more! Tips for saying NO!

The party you want to avoid ... The overtime work you don't want to do ... The lunch invitation from an old friend you don't want to see ... You **can** say no!

1 Prepare in advance. Practise what you're going to say.
2 Say something nice first. A positive comment first makes it easier to hear and accept the no.
3 Don't delay. Don't be the one to say yes because you took too long to say no.
4 Give a reason, but don't explain in detail.
5 Suggest an alternative, e.g. think of another time to meet.
6 Understand the tricks people use to turn your no into a yes.
7 Be gentle but firm. A message making it clear how you feel is easier to understand.
8 If the person doesn't take no for an answer, **don't** say yes. Say nothing.

B Work in pairs and discuss the questions (1–3).
1 Which of the things in Ex 9A do you normally do?
2 Which ones don't you do?
3 Which ideas would or wouldn't work for you? Why/Why not?
A: I think preparing in advance would work because it would give you time to think about what to say.
B: I don't think it would work for me. I'd forget what I'd planned to say!

WRITING

emails to decline invitations

10 A Work in pairs. Look at the events in the box and answer the questions.

> concert   conference   meal out   meeting
> party   sports event   wedding   work trip   other

1 Do you often get invitations to these events?
2 Do you usually accept or decline them?

B Read the email and answer the questions.

1 What event is the invitation for?
2 What will happen there?

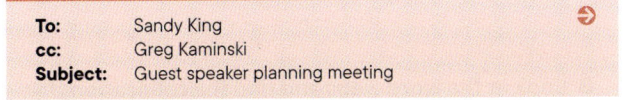

To: Sandy King
cc: Greg Kaminski
Subject: Guest speaker planning meeting

Sandy, we need to meet to discuss arrangements for our guest speaker programme this year. We're planning to choose the speakers and to suggest topics for the lectures. We also want to decide on the dates. I'm attaching the provisional agenda. Could we meet on Thursday morning? Let me know if that works for you.

Regards,
Pat

C Read two answers from Sandy. Which one is more suitable for a work situation? How do you know?

1

To: Pat Summers
cc:
Subject: Re: Guest speaker planning meeting

Dear Pat,
Thursday is no good for me. I'm very busy! 😞 Do we really need to meet? If we do, let's meet next week some time.
Sandy

2

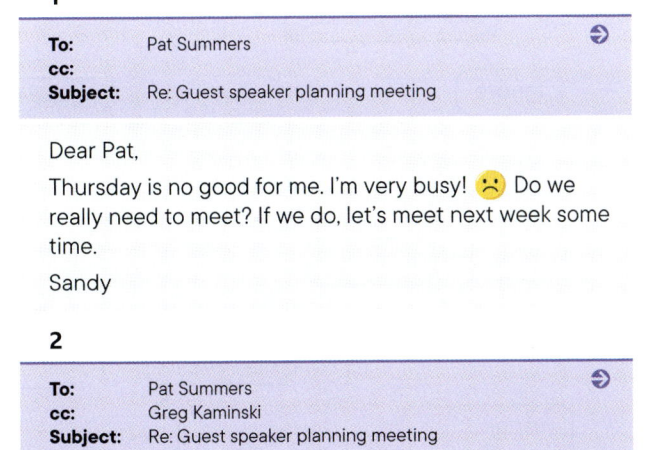

To: Pat Summers
cc: Greg Kaminski
Subject: Re: Guest speaker planning meeting

Pat, I'm sorry, but I can't make Thursday. There's another meeting which I have to go to. Would you mind if we put the meeting off until the following week? I'm free most mornings except Wednesday.
Best wishes,
Sandy

D Number the items (a–d) in the correct order. Use the second email in Ex 10C to help you.

a Sign off politely.
b Make a suggestion for an alternative.
c Give a reason.
d Use a subject line that is the same as the invitation.

11 A Look at the sentences from emails (1–8). Are they saying no (N), giving a reason (R) or giving an alternative suggestion (A)?

1 I'm out of the office all day. R
2 I'm afraid that Thursday isn't convenient for me.
3 Afraid I can't. Will get back to you with another time.
4 I'm sorry, I can't make Wednesday evening.
5 I'm in classes all afternoon.
6 Sorry, I'm doing something else then.
7 I wonder if we could arrange it for Monday instead?
8 I have something else on.

B Work in pairs and look at the sentences in Ex 11A. Find two which are very formal and two which are very informal.

12 A Read the invitations. Write an email to decline each one. Follow the order in Ex 10D and use the sentences in Ex 11A for ideas. Think about whether each reply should be formal or informal.

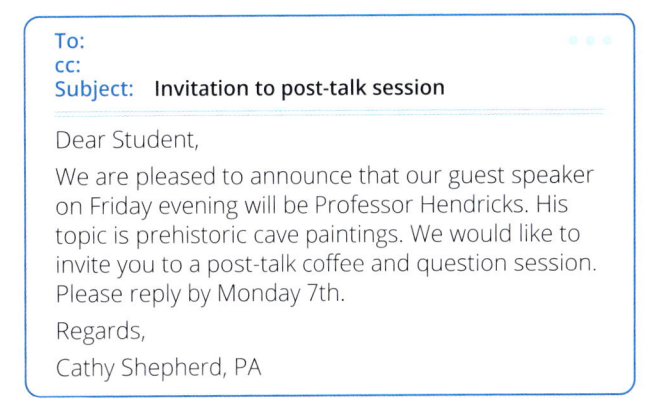

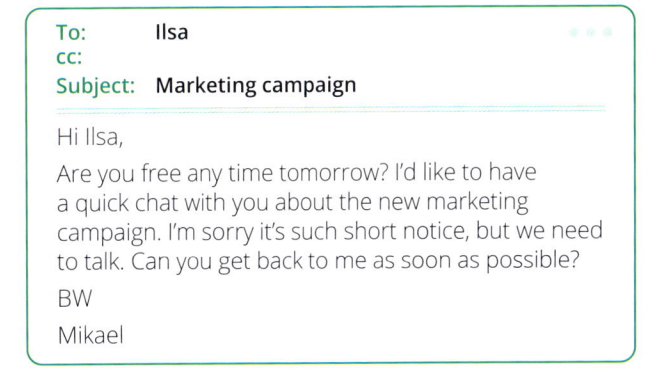

To:
cc:
Subject: Invitation to post-talk session

Dear Student,
We are pleased to announce that our guest speaker on Friday evening will be Professor Hendricks. His topic is prehistoric cave paintings. We would like to invite you to a post-talk coffee and question session. Please reply by Monday 7th.
Regards,
Cathy Shepherd, PA

To: Ilsa
cc:
Subject: Marketing campaign

Hi Ilsa,
Are you free any time tomorrow? I'd like to have a quick chat with you about the new marketing campaign. I'm sorry it's such short notice, but we need to talk. Can you get back to me as soon as possible?
BW
Mikael

B Work in pairs. Read each other's emails and answer the questions.

1 Do they follow the order in Ex 10D?
2 Decide if each email is formal or informal enough.
3 Which is the most polite?
4 Which is the least polite?

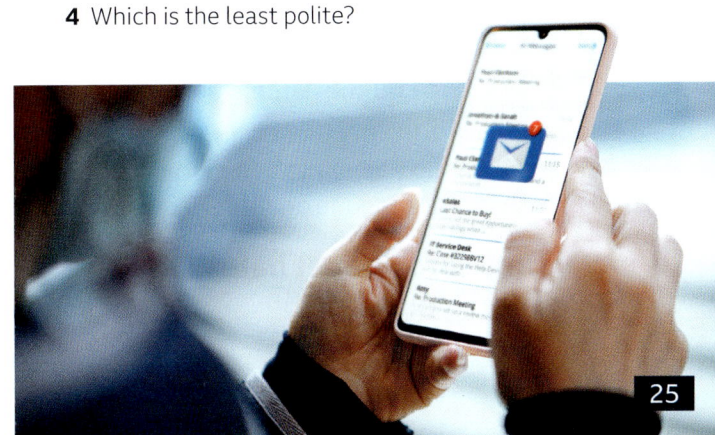

Unit 2 | Lesson C

2C That's annoying!

HOW TO ... | talk about things that annoy you
VOCABULARY | pet hates
PRONUNCIATION | stress and intonation to show annoyance

VOCABULARY

pet hates

1 A Read the article. Work in pairs and discuss the questions.
  1 How do you feel about each of the pet hates in the article?
  2 What are your pet hates?

> **What's your pet hate about behaviour in public?**
>
> Everybody has one or more things that really annoy them in public. Here are some classics:
>
> ❗ when I'm in a hurry and the people in front of me walk slowly and get in the way
> ❗ when public announcements in stations are impossible to hear
> ❗ when I'm in a shop and the customer ahead of me is on their phone and ignores the sales assistant
> ❗ when I'm waiting for a bus and people jump the queue
> ❗ when people throw litter out of car windows
> ❗ when children behave really badly in a public place and the parents don't react or do anything
> ❗ when I'm next to someone and they argue loudly with someone on their phone
>
> So, those are our pet hates. What are yours?

B Look at the word webs and find the collocation that does NOT belong. Use the article in Ex 1A to help.

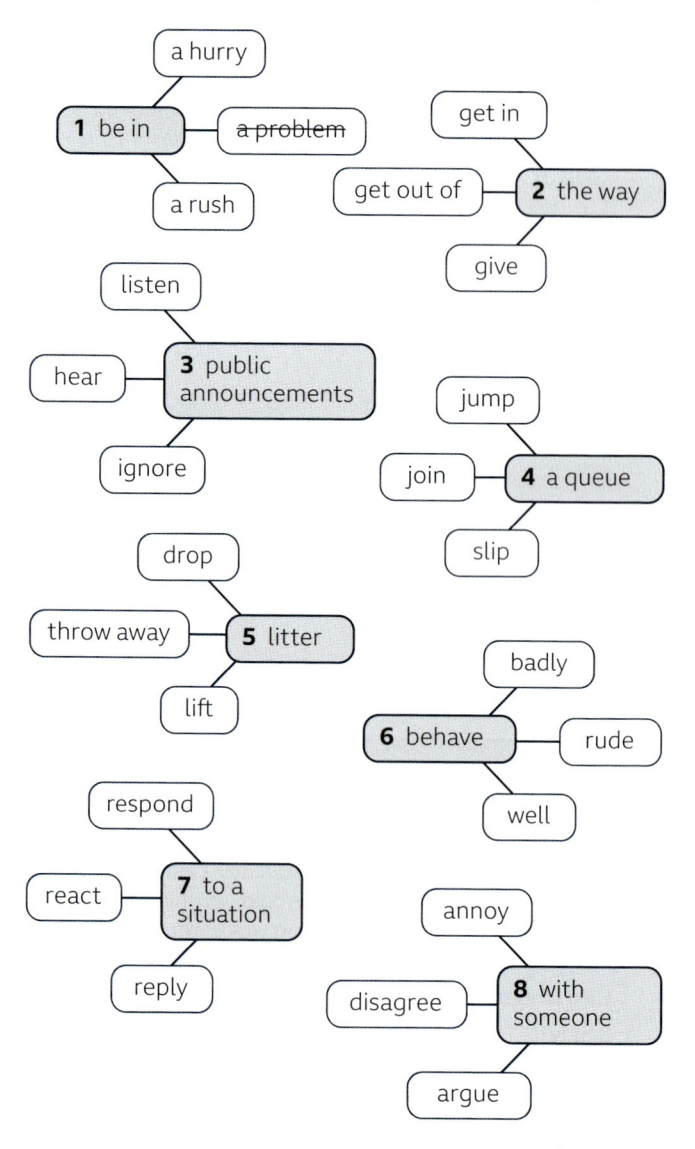

1 be in — a hurry / ~~a problem~~ / a rush
2 the way — get in / get out of / give
3 public announcements — listen / hear / ignore
4 a queue — jump / join / slip
5 litter — drop / throw away / lift
6 behave — badly / rude / well
7 to a situation — respond / react / reply
8 with someone — annoy / disagree / argue

C Work in pairs. Tell your partner about something that annoys you on the street. Use the collocations in Ex 1B.

  A: I hate it when I can see someone who needs help and no one else reacts to the situation.
  B: Yes, I hate that, too. They just ignore the person and pretend they don't see or they're too busy.

2C

PRONUNCIATION

4 A | **stress and intonation to show annoyance** | Work in pairs and read the sentences (1–6). What place are the people talking about?

1. I can't stand it when people take a long time to pay.
2. It annoys me when they try to sell me something I don't want.
3. It drives me crazy when people eat food while shopping.
4. I hate it when I can't reach something on the top shelf.
5. I can't bear it when food is packaged in too much plastic.
6. People are always jumping the queue.

B 🔊 **2.09** | Listen to the sentences in Ex 4A and underline the word with the most stress in each sentence. Is the speaker's voice higher or lower on the key stressed word?

C Work in pairs. Student A: Say one of the sentences in Ex 4A. Pay attention to stress. Student B: Say how you feel using one of the responses below.

Yes, that annoys me, too.

Yes, I hate that, too.

Yes, that gets on my nerves, too.

I don't mind that.

That doesn't bother me.

How to ...
talk about things that annoy you

2 A Work in pairs and discuss. What things annoy you about people's behaviour on public transport? Make a list.

B 🔊 **2.07** | Listen to the conversation. What things do they talk about that are on your list?

3 A Work in pairs and complete the sentences with two or three words.

1. B: Were there a lot of people on the train?
   A: No, not many, but it's just the way some people behave. I _____ it.
2. A: First I had to queue to buy a ticket because the ticket machines were broken.
   B: I hate _____ happens.
3. B: People _____ doing that on trains! I expect it smelled bad.
   A: Yeah, the smell was terrible! It really _____ nerves.
4. B: I know what you mean, without asking anyone?
   A: Yeah, it _____ me when they do that.
5. B: You're _____ so upset about things. And you're here now.
   A: But that sort of behaviour _____ me.

B 🔊 **2.08** | Listen and check.

C Learn and practise. Go to the Grammar Bank.

▶ page 110 **GRAMMAR BANK**

SPEAKING

5 A Work in pairs. Choose three of the situations. Think of three or more things that annoy you in each situation. Say why they annoy you. Use the phrases in Ex 3A.

- on social media
- in a cinema
- with neighbours
- with a flatmate or roommate
- on an online video call
- on a plane
- in a restaurant

B Work with other students. Choose one of the situations. Tell each other what annoys you and why. Listen to other students and say how you feel.

C Tell the whole class which situations came up the most in your discussions.

MEDIATION SKILLS
summarising skills
summarise an article

▶ page 146 **MEDIATION BANK**

Speak anywhere Go to the interactive speaking practice

Unit 2 | Lesson D

2D BBC Documentary
Planet Earth II: Jungles

SPEAKING | discuss difficult situations
WRITING | a personal experience

PREVIEW

1 A Work in pairs and answer the questions.
1 What wildlife programmes are popular in your country?
2 Why do you think people enjoy these kinds of programmes?
3 In what ways do they affect our attitudes to the natural world?

B Read the programme information and answer the questions.
1 What is the animal in the photo on page 29?
2 What does it want to do?
3 How do you think it can escape?
4 What 'extraordinary ability' do you think it has?

Planet Earth II: Jungles

David Attenborough celebrates the amazing variety of the natural world in this epic documentary series, filmed over four years across sixty-four different countries. This episode takes us to the jungles of Malaysia, inhabited by creatures with extraordinary abilities, such as the Draco lizard. Watch as a Draco lizard faces danger and has to choose between fighting to make his home in a tree or finding a way to escape. Will he survive?

VIEW

2 A Watch the BBC video clip. Check your ideas in Ex 1B.

B Work in pairs. What does the speaker say? Choose the correct words. Then watch again and check.
1 He's only the size of a **pen / pencil** and he eats ants.
2 This one tree could provide him with all he will ever **need / eat**, a conveyor belt of food.
3 The owner's not only intimidating, he's prepared to **fight / battle**.
4 Now he must choose – fight or **flee / run away**.
5 Only in the jungle do you find lizards that can **soar / fly** like dragons.
6 Maybe this new tree will have food and no **present / resident** owner.

C Work in pairs and discuss the questions.
1 What do these animals do to escape from danger?

| bird   chameleon   deer   mouse |
| skunk   spider   wasp |

2 What do you think the 'fight, flight or freeze responses' to danger mean?

2D

SPEAKING

difficult situations

3 A Work in pairs and discuss. What response would you have in these situations: fight, flight or freeze?
1 You see a snake in your bedroom.
2 You're alone at a friend's house and it's winter. Someone knocks on the door. It's ten o'clock at night.
3 You're walking along a street and a big dog is coming towards you. It's growling. You can see the owner in the distance.
4 You're on a train and the person opposite you drops their empty drink can on the floor.

B 🔊 **2.10** | Listen to the conversation and answer the questions.
1 Which situations in Ex 3A do they talk about?
2 What does the woman say she would do in the situations?

C 🔊 **2.10** | Listen again and tick the phrases you hear.

KEY PHRASES
And then what?
How do you mean?
That's a tricky one.
I'd like to say that I'd …
I don't quite get what you mean.
Could you say more about that?
I think that in real life I'd hesitate.
Why's that?
Do you mean that … ?
Oh, no question in my mind. I would definitely …

D Which of the Key phrases ask someone to give more detail about what they have just said?

4 Work in pairs. Look at the situations on page 140. Use the Key phrases to say what you would do in each situation or to ask your partner to give more detail.

WRITING

a personal experience

5 A Read the story. What would you do in the same situation?

Not what it seemed to be

A few years ago, I was living in New York City and I took the subway to work every day. One morning I was on a crowded train, [1]......... sitting and reading when I heard some shouting near me. Two women were having an argument. They stood up and started really yelling at each other. A couple of people near the two women moved away [2]......... . All the other people were looking at the women.

At that point I noticed a third woman trying to take a wallet out of a man's pocket without him knowing and I realised that the argument was fake. Everyone was listening and not paying attention to their own belongings, so they were easy targets for the pickpocket. I shouted loudly, 'Watch out, the fight's a trick, hang on to your wallets!' Well, the two women stopped right away and the third woman walked [3]......... over to me and kicked me in the knee. She got off at the next stop, along with the two other women. [4]......... The next station was my stop, too, but I decided to wait a few more stops before I got off!

B Look at the words and phrases (a–d) about people's feelings. Find the place in the story (1–4) where each one fits.
a nervously
b We all felt relieved.
c angrily
d feeling quite relaxed,

6 A Choose one of the situations on page 140 and make notes for a story about what happened – either a true story or one you make up. Use these questions to help.
• Where and when did it happen?
• What was the situation?
• What were the main events?
• How did people feel at different points in the story?
• How did it end?

B Write your story. Use your notes from Ex 6A to help.

C Work in pairs. Read each other's stories. Would you do the same as your partner in the situation they describe?

29

2 REVIEW

GRAMMAR
present perfect continuous

1 A Complete the sentences with the present perfect continuous form of the verbs in brackets.

1 I .... (try) some new ideas for recipes.
2 We .... (practise) the violin. We have a concert next week.
3 She .... (research) a story about how the government lost the election. She has a deadline tomorrow.
4 They .... (talk) with some new clients. They're interested in buying our products.
5 I .... (mark) exam papers, which I need to give back to my students this week.

B Think of a job to go with each sentence in Ex 1A. Write two or three sentences that this person could say at the end of a busy day. Use the present perfect continuous.

I've been interviewing politicians. I've been reading through reports.

C Work in pairs. Take turns to say your sentences. Can your partner guess the job?

relative clauses

2 A Complete the phrases with the words in the box. Put – if it's possible to leave the gap blank. More than one answer might be possible.

| that | to | when | where | which | who | whose |

1 the last book .... you read
2 a time of day .... you feel the most relaxed
3 someone .... you'd like to meet
4 the best places .... eat lunch near you
5 a person .... songs you love
6 a film .... almost made you cry
7 the first person .... teach you English
8 an ability .... you wish you had
9 a nearby café .... they make great coffee
10 a person .... makes you laugh

B Work with other students and take turns. Choose one of the topics in Ex 2A and ask the other students to talk about it for one minute.

VOCABULARY

3 A Add vowels to complete the phrases (1–12).

1 _ch_ _v_ goals
2 _rg_ _ with someone
3 _v_ _d arguments
4 be someone's f_ _lt
5 do someone a f_v_ _r
6 feel g_ _lty
7 _gn_r_ someone
8 k_ _p on doing
9 make a c_mm_nt
10 m_n_g_ to do
11 set g_ _ls
12 t_ k_ up something new

B Work in pairs. Choose one of the topics (1–3) and talk about it. Use at least three of the phrases in Ex 3A.

1 a change you've made in your life that was difficult to make
2 things that bother you when you're trying to sleep
3 a time that someone was angry with you, or you were angry with them

4 A Choose the correct options (A–C) to complete the text.

Taking the pain out of the wait

Waiting in a queue ¹.......... most people crazy, and that's bad for business. So businesses ².......... a lot of effort to solve this. When high-rise buildings became common, waiting for the lift was frustrating for anyone who was in a ³.........., and there were lots of complaints. So mirrors were put next to the lifts and complaints dropped because it gave people something to look at while waiting. An airport was ⁴.......... getting complaints about the long wait for baggage. When they moved the arrival gates further away, complaints about waiting stopped, and no one got ⁵.......... about the longer walk. When a new electronic product comes out, there can be long queues, and people ⁶.......... outside a shop can be a real problem. Danish researchers found a solution: serve the last people ⁷.......... first. That way there's no reason to show up early. As far as we know, no other countries are ⁸.......... to try out the Danish solution – we can guess how people might ⁹.......... to it. Most people would probably stick to their belief that first-come, first-served is fair, and anyone ¹⁰.......... the queue is just behaving rudely.

1	A causes	B gets	C drives
2	A make	B do	C have
3	A way	B hurry	C speed
4	A constantly	B ever	C continual
5	A far	B tired	C upset
6	A camping	B camp	C who
7	A arrived	B who	C to arrive
8	A thinking	B intends	C planning
9	A answer	B react	C argue
10	A jump	B jumping	C jumps

B 🔊 R2.01 | Listen and check your answers.

working life 3

VLOGS

Q: Where do you prefer to work or study?

1 ▶ Watch the video. Which places do people mention?

2 Where do you like working and why?

GSE LEARNING OBJECTIVES

3A READING | Understand an article about famous authors working from home: work phrases

Pronunciation: stress in phrases

Talk about your approach to work or study: conditional structures: *unless, even if, in case (of)*

3B LISTENING | Understand people talking about the gig economy: work

Talk about what's important in a job: necessity, obligation and permission

Pronunciation: elision of /t/

Write a cover email for a job application

3C HOW TO … | take part in an interview: personality adjectives (1); negative prefixes

Pronunciation: word stress in personality adjectives

3D BBC STREET INTERVIEWS | Understand people talking about their preferred jobs

'This or That?' questions: expressing preferences

Write a discussion board post

Unit 3 | Lesson A

3A Working from home

GRAMMAR | conditional structures: *unless, even if, in case (of)*
VOCABULARY | work phrases
PRONUNCIATION | stress in phrases

READING

1 A Work in pairs and discuss the questions.

1 Do you work or study at home?
2 What's good about it?
3 What are the main challenges?

B Read the article quickly and match the headings (a–d) with the sections (1–4).

a Another way (or ways)
b Classic authors' routines
c Writers' tips
d Then came the internet

2 A Look at the tips in the first section. Which tips does each author follow?

Start early – Hemingway, Le Guin, Murakami

B According to the article, are the statements True (T), False (F) or Not Mentioned (NM)?

1 Writers have more experience working from home than many other people.
2 Hemingway started early because he wanted to finish early.
3 Le Guin started writing at exactly 7.15.
4 Fleming tried to write at least 500 words a day.
5 Murakami doesn't use the internet.
6 Smith doesn't want to answer messages when she's writing.
7 Evaristo likes to find out what people think about the news.
8 Angelou lived in a hotel.

C Work in pairs and discuss.

1 Which ideas in the article are the most useful for you?
2 Which authors' routines and habits are the most balanced?
3 Which writer's routine is most like yours?

Working from home: How the great writers do it

Many of those who started working from home in the past few years have discovered that it can be incredibly difficult to work efficiently. Unless you're very focused, you'll find too many distractions and excuses NOT to work.

1 ....

If there's one group of people with extensive experience working from home, it's writers. Writers have long had to **deal with** the **challenge** of working from home, having to **meet a deadline** to finish a book and to **avoid distractions** that can make them **fall behind schedule**. And writers have been generous with their advice.

• Start early. If you **get** difficult tasks **out of the way**, you'll feel more relaxed later on.
• **Keep to a routine** and do the same things at the same time every day.
• Set daily goals. For a writer it can be a number of words, for you it might just be hours of work.
• Remove anything that takes your attention away from your work.
• Exercise regularly. Even if you live in a tiny apartment in the middle of the city, you need to do some physical activity every day.

2 ....

These tips could have been taken directly from the lives of great writers. Ernest Hemingway began writing at 6 a.m., because, he said, there was no one around to disturb him. Ursula K. Le Guin used to wake up at 5.30. She spent the first 45 minutes of the day lying in bed, thinking, and started writing by 7.15, finishing her day's work by lunchtime. James Bond author, Ian Fleming, started his day with a swim in the sea. Then he wrote from 9 till noon, had lunch and a nap and worked more from 5 p.m. He had a goal of 500 words per day.

VOCABULARY

work phrases

3 A Match the phrases in bold in the article with the meanings (1–8).

1 keep away from things which take your attention
2 follow a plan or timetable, without changing it
3 do a task by a particular time
4 finish a large amount of work
5 stop giving attention to something
6 be late in doing work or a task
7 manage a difficult situation successfully
8 finish something so you're free to do something else

3 ....

In the internet era, authors' routines aren't necessarily that different from previous times. Japanese novelist Haruki Murakami says he doesn't use social media at all, and describes his work day as going from 4 a.m. till about 10, followed by a run or a swim; after that he reads and listens to music, and goes to bed at 9 p.m. However, the digital world is a big factor for many authors. Novelist Zadie Smith doesn't have a smartphone and uses internet-blocking software on her laptop in case she feels like reacting to news or messages. Australian writer Benjamin Law recommends an app which turns off your social media and internet for certain lengths of time so you don't **lose concentration**.

4 ....

Not every author hides from the internet. Bernardine Evaristo starts her day with two cups of coffee, then goes online to catch up on the news and opinions about what's happening. She starts work after that and keeps at it till 9 p.m., but not without taking breaks to exercise and take a siesta.

And not every writer writes at home. Poet and novelist Maya Angelou couldn't. She used to check into a hotel room and put a 'Do not disturb' sign on the door before she started writing. But wherever you work, if you follow the advice of these writers and use your time wisely, you can **get a lot done**, or at least you can finish your work day faster and get away from your desk sooner!

B Complete the conversations with the correct form of phrases from Ex 3A.

1 A: This homework is really difficult. I'll do it later.
   B: No, do it now. You should .... it ....
2 A: How was your day?
   B: Great, I .... I finished my essay, had lunch with a friend, went to an online seminar and then played tennis.
3 A: What time will lunch be? I need to tell the people in the café.
   B: Sorry, we're a bit late, we've .... by about fifteen minutes. So I think it'll be at quarter past one.
4 A: Is your new job hard?
   B: Yes, but I enjoy .... with a ....
5 A: You look good. Where have you been?
   B: For a swim. I always .... : 6 o'clock get up, 6.30 go for a swim.
6 A: Is it OK if I turn the TV on?
   B: Well, not really. I'm trying to .... The sound of the TV would bother me.
7 A: What's wrong?
   B: It's that music from next door. It's making me .... I can't think!
8 A: We've only got two days to finish the report!
   B: Yes, do you think we'll .... ?

C 🔊 3.01 | Listen and check your answers.

PRONUNCIATION

4 A 🔊 3.02 | **stress in phrases** | Listen to the phrases from Ex 3B and underline the stressed words.

got a lot done

B 🔊 3.02 | Listen again. Which word in each phrase has the strongest stress?

got a lot done

C 🔊 3.02 | Listen again and repeat.

D Work in pairs. Student A: look at Ex 3B. Read out part A in each conversation. Student B: Answer using one of the phrases.

A: This homework is really difficult. I'll do it later.
B: No, you should get it done now.

5 Work in pairs and discuss the questions. When you answer, give extra information.

1 Do you usually get a lot done in the morning?
2 How do you feel when you fall behind schedule?
3 Do you try to get easier tasks out of the way before you start difficult tasks?
4 Do you easily lose concentration when you're working or studying?
5 What steps do you take to avoid distractions when you're working or studying?
6 Is it important to keep to a routine?
7 Are you good at meeting deadlines?
8 Do you usually deal well with unexpected problems?

Unit 3 | Lesson A

GRAMMAR

conditional structures: *unless, even if, in case (of)*

6 A Choose the correct words to complete the sentences.

1 **If / In case** you get difficult tasks out of the way, you'll feel more relaxed later on.
2 **Unless / If** you are very focused, you'll find too many distractions and excuses NOT to work.
3 **Even if / In case** you live in a tiny apartment in the middle of the city, you need to find a way to do some sort of movement every day.
4 She uses internet-blocking software on her laptop **in case of / in case** she feels like reacting to news or messages.

B Find words or phrases in Ex 6A which mean:

1 despite the fact that
2 if not
3 because (you/he/she) might

C Learn and practise. Go to the Grammar Bank.

▶▶ page 111 **GRAMMAR BANK**

7 A Complete the sentences with *unless, even if, in case (of)* or *if*.

1 I can't work .... I have people around me. I like being able to share ideas with others and I get lonely when I'm working by myself.
2 .... I turn off my phone, I still find a way to check my messages.
3 I always keep food at my desk .... I get hungry.
4 .... I have music on in the background when I'm working, I lose concentration. I don't like working in silence.
5 .... I could choose, I'd like to have a mixture of studying online and face to face.

B Change the sentences so that they are true for you.

I always keep a bar of chocolate in my bag in case I get hungry.

C Work in pairs and take turns reading out your sentences. Do you do the same things as your partner?

SPEAKING

8 A What is your approach to working or studying from home? Complete or change the sentences with your own ideas.

STARTING THE WORK/STUDY DAY
The first three things I do are ...

DAILY SCHEDULE
I keep to a routine and work/study from .... to ...., unless ...

EQUIPMENT (COMPUTER, PAPER, PEN, PHONE)
The most important things I have around me are ...

INTERNET AND PHONE ACCESS
I (would) only cut off the internet if ...
I never switch off my phone in case ...

TAKING BREAKS
I think you should take regular breaks even if ...
I take a ....-minute break every .... hours.

SOCIALISING
If I don't talk to someone every .... I ...

ENDING THE DAY
I stop working .... (when?) even if ...

B Work in pairs and take turns. Student A: Talk about your ideas for two minutes. Student B: Listen and ask questions. Which ideas would you like to 'borrow' from each other?

C Work with a new partner. Compare the different ideas you have each discussed. Choose the three ideas you like best.

3B Gig work

GRAMMAR | necessity, obligation and permission
VOCABULARY | work
PRONUNCIATION | elision of /t/

VOCABULARY

work

1 A Work in pairs and look at five people's statements about work. Which do you agree with? Which don't you agree with? Why/Why not?

1 I'd like to be my own boss.
2 I want to work at one company all my life.
3 It's important to me to choose when I work and when I don't.
4 For me it's good to have a steady job. I like knowing what to expect day to day.
5 I don't want someone telling me what to do all the time.

B Work in pairs and read the definition of 'gig work'. Which people in Ex 1A would prefer this way of working?

gig work = a job that usually lasts a short time; a gig worker is paid for doing that job only and is otherwise not employed by the company

2 A Read the text about a webinar on gig work and choose the best summary (1–3).

1 There are positive and negative sides to gig work.
2 Find out if gig work suits you first before you choose it as a way of working.
3 Gig work is a better way for young people to enter the working world.

B Read the text again. Which three questions in the text would you be most interested in hearing answers to?

C Replace the words in bold in the questions (1–8) with the correct form of words in bold in the text in Ex 2A.

1 Did you have any **chances** to visit a workplace when you were younger? Where was it?
2 How much **background** do you have in working in a team? What is the most challenging thing about it?
3 Have you ever **planned and arranged** an event like a party or a conference? How did it go?
4 Would you be OK **being in charge of** organising a friend's wedding?
5 Are you good at **dealing with** the conflicts in a work or school situation? Can you give an example?
6 What sort of **short-term** jobs are available in your country in the summer?
7 Would you like to make a **long-term** move to another country? Where to?
8 Do you think a company is **treating** workers **unfairly** if it makes them work overtime?

D Work in pairs and answer the questions (1–8) in Ex 2C.

Introduction to GIG WORK

Webinar: Introduction to Gig Work

Whether you're looking for your first job or looking for a new one, you'll find that many **opportunities** are actually gig work rather than **permanent** contracts. More and more people are working as **temporary** workers, choosing what they do and when they do it, often doing multiple gig jobs at the same time.

The idea of choosing when you work and when you don't can be exciting, but you may well wonder: Is gig work for me? How do I get started, and how do I **organise** my life? What do I have to be careful of, and will I earn enough to survive? Can I **take responsibility for** finding myself work from week to week? Can I **handle** the ups and downs of gig work? How do I avoid being **exploited** by an employer?

Join our webinar this Saturday at 3 p.m. EST to find out answers to these and many other questions. Our guest host is Andrea Butcher, an employment advisor, and two special guests who will share their years of **experience** as gig workers.

Click here to sign up.

Unit 3 | Lesson B

LISTENING

3 A Work in pairs and list the advantages and disadvantages of gig work.

B 🔊 **3.03** | Listen to part of the webinar on gig work from Ex 2A. How many of your ideas do the speakers mention?

C 🔊 **3.03** | Work in pairs. Write Paul (P), Cybil (C) or both (B) next to the phrases. Then listen again and check.

1 does gig work by choice
2 does gig work by necessity
3 isn't happy with the money
4 finds it difficult to say no to a job
5 sometimes enjoys the work
6 works long hours sometimes
7 would say 'There's more to life than work'.
8 would say 'I don't have time for anything but work'.

4 Work in pairs and discuss.

1 Is gig work common where you live? What sort?
2 If you chose to become a gig worker, what sort of gig work would you choose?

GRAMMAR

necessity, obligation and permission

5 A Work in pairs. Complete the sentences using the prompts in brackets.

1 Something _needs to be done_ about the rights of gig workers. (need / do)
2 I like it because you .... when you work. (allow / choose)
3 I feel as if I .... yes to every offer that comes along. (have got / say)
4 It .... a balance, to do enough work that you actually enjoy doing. (necessary / find)
5 It .... savings for times like this, for going on holiday or if I get ill. (essential / have)
6 People act like you .... a big goal in life. (suppose / have)

B 🔊 **3.04** | Listen and check your answers.

C Work in pairs. Answer the questions (1–4) about the sentences in Ex 5A.

1 Which phrases are about necessity, about something that is very important to do? _needs to,_
2 Which phrases are about obligation, about something you are expected to do?
3 Which phrase is about something you should do, but maybe you don't?
4 Which phrase is about permission?

D Learn and practise. Go to the Grammar Bank.

▶ page 112 **GRAMMAR BANK**

PRONUNCIATION

6 A | elision of /t/ | Work in pairs. Which phrases for necessity, obligation and permission in Ex 5A have a final 't' or 'd' followed by an initial 't'?

allowed to

B 🔊 **3.05** | Listen and check your answers.

C 🔊 **3.05** | Work in pairs and listen again. What happens to the final 't' or 'd' in the first word?

D Work in pairs. Tell your partner:
- two things you're not allowed to do at work or school, college or university.
- two things you've got to do today.
- two things you're supposed to do this week.

SPEAKING

7 A Read the statements about work and put ✓✓ if you strongly agree, ✓ if you agree and ✗ if you disagree.

> When you're young, it's not necessary to have job security, but later in life it's essential.

> People should be permitted to choose how much holiday they take each year.

> People should be allowed to work flexibly (choosing their own hours, location, etc.) when possible.

> People work better if they are paid more.

> Everyone needs to be paid the same no matter what work they do.

> It's good that computers and machines are replacing workers because people will have more free time.

B Work in pairs. Choose two statements to discuss in detail. Say what you think and why. Tell your partner what you think of their opinion.

I'm not sure about that.
I agree up to a point, but don't you think that …
I'm completely with you there.

C Choose one statement. Ask at least three other students their opinions and make notes.

D Work in groups. Take turns telling the group about other students' opinions on your statement. Use the phrases below to help.

Everyone agreed that …
I found it very interesting/surprising that …
Two people said they think that …
There were mixed opinions about …

WRITING

a cover email for a job application

8 Read the job adverts. Which job would be better for you?

Elaine Events Ltd.
Edinburgh

Events Assistant

We organise events including weddings, corporate functions and all kinds of parties, and we are looking for a friendly, reliable, flexible person to work on individual events in a variety of roles.

You will transport and set up equipment and furniture, prepare food and drink, serve clients, take part in the clean-up and help wherever it is needed.

No two days are the same!

Previous experience of working on similar events preferred.

Intermediate (or higher) level of English preferred.

Apply

KwikClickFood
Dublin

Delivery Rider

E-bike riders urgently wanted for fast delivery across Dublin.

KwikClickFood takes restaurant food to customers around central Dublin.

We are recruiting part-time staff right now for evening work.

Are you organised, reliable and independent?

Are you good at dealing with people?

Do you have a smartphone?

Training provided.

Apply

9 A Read the cover email for an application to one of the jobs in Ex 8. Which job is the person applying for?

Dear Ms Patel,

I am applying for the job as a … with your company.

I am very interested in this job. Your company looks like a good place to work and it has excellent feedback on your website. I am a student at college and am looking for a part-time job to fit in with my studies.

I beleive I am a good candidate because,
- I have recent experience of working in a hotel reception where I had to deal with many diferent guests.
- I am reliable and friendly.
- My English is level B1.
- I know the city very well. I live here for three years now.
- I have a smartphone.
- I could start immediately.

I have three questions. Is it necessary to have my own bike or will you provide that? Am I supposed to work every evening or am I allowed to choose the days I work? Do I need to wear a uniform?

I look forward to discuss my application and I will phone on Monday to check?

Best wishes,

Xavier DuPont

B Number the sections (a–e) in the correct order. Then look at the email and check.
- **a** Ask questions (if you have any).
- **b** Close the letter, saying when you'll contact them.
- **c** State the reason for writing. 1
- **d** Say why you think you're qualified.
- **e** Say why you're interested in the job.

C Look at the email again. Find and correct:
1. two mistakes in the grammar.
2. two mistakes in the punctuation.
3. two mistakes in the spelling.

10 A Write a cover email for the other job or for a job you would like to apply for. Pay attention to the organisation of the email.

B Check your email carefully for mistakes. Then swap with another student and check each other's emails.

C Read the emails of other students in the class. Then work in pairs and tell your partner about an email you read.

Unit 3 | Lesson C

3C Good question

HOW TO ... | take part in an interview
VOCABULARY | personality adjectives (1); negative prefixes
PRONUNCIATION | word stress in personality adjectives

VOCABULARY

personality adjectives (1)

1 A Work in pairs and discuss the questions.
  1 Have you ever had an interview for a college or university course, or a job? Were there any questions that surprised you?
  2 How would you answer the interview questions (a–c)?
    a Which magic power would you most like to have?
    b How do you fit an elephant into a fridge?
    c If you could rob a bank without being caught, would you do it?
  3 Why do you think interviewers might ask questions like this?

B Read about an interview and look at the questions the interviewee answered badly. How would you answer them differently?

My terrible interview

I had prepared answers to tricky questions that would show how creative and practical I am, but instead my interview was very straightforward. It went something like this.

Interviewer: Why do you want this job?
Me: Well, mainly because I need the money.

Interviewer: What three words would your closest friend use to describe you?
Me: Erm, I don't really know. I'll need to think about that.

Interviewer: How much of a team player are you?
Me: I'd say I'm very independent, I like to do things on my own. So I don't need to ask for help.

Interviewer: Why are you the best person for this job?
Me: Well, I don't know the other applicants, but it seems pretty easy, so I think I might be as good as anyone.

Interviewer: What's your biggest weakness?
Me: Maybe I'm too sensitive, I get very emotional when people give me negative feedback. And I'm not all that flexible. I like to do things my way. I don't like change, but I am enthusiastic. I get very excited and interested in new ideas.

Interviewer: How do you fit an elephant into a fridge?
Me: I'm so glad you asked that ...

Of course I didn't get the job, but I learned a few important lessons. Prepare for the basics. Remember why you're there. And be honest, but not too honest.

2 A Which four words in the box does the interviewee use?

> confident   enthusiastic   flexible
> independent   professional
> responsible   sensitive   willing

B Find the phrases in the text that give the meaning of those four words in Ex 2A.

C Complete the sentences (1–4) with the other four words in Ex 2A.
  1 If you are .... , you are sure you can do something very well.
  2 If you are .... , you do very high-quality work.
  3 If you are .... to do something, you will do it if someone else asks you.
  4 If you are .... , people can trust you. You behave in a sensible way.

PRONUNCIATION

3 A | **word stress in personality adjectives** |
Work in pairs and look at the words in Ex 2A. How many syllables are there in each word? Which syllable is stressed?

B 🔊 **3.06** | Listen and check your answers.

C 🔊 **3.06** | Listen again and repeat.

D Work in pairs and discuss.
  1 Which words in Ex 2A describe you best? Give examples for each.
  2 Which qualities would you like to develop most? Why?
  3 Think of a person you admire. Which of these qualities do they have?

4 A Which word in Ex 2A has a negative prefix? What prefixes do the other adjectives take to make them negative?

B Check your ideas in the Vocabulary Bank.

▶▶ page 133 **VOCABULARY BANK**
negative prefixes

38

How to ...
take part in an interview

5 A Look at the job advert. Work in pairs and answer the questions.

Programmer needed

We're looking for a programmer to join our team. This person will work on-site and remotely, and will be responsible for developing company software. Knowledge of JavaScript and two years' coding experience are required. Good communication skills and a high level of creativity are also essential.

Salary will depend on the level and type of experience. Full-time is preferred, but part-time may be considered.

1 What sort of person would answer this job advert?
2 Would this job interest you?
3 What questions might the interviewer ask?

B 🔊 **3.07** | Listen to the interview. Which of the questions in the text in Ex 1B does the interviewer ask?

6 A Work in pairs and complete the sentences by adding TWO words to each gap.

1 A: So, ¹**tell me** _____ about yourself.
   B: Oh, erm, ²**where should** _____ ?
   A: Let's keep it work-related.
   B: All right.
2 A: So why are you here today?
   B: ³**How do** _____ ?
   A: ⁴**Why do you want** _____ ?
   B: ⁵**I** _____ some research about the company and I think it's …
3 B: I want to be part of that, and ⁶**I think I have a lot** _____ .
   A: OK, so ⁷**what will you** _____ the company?
   B: ⁸**I think one of my** _____ is that I have a problem-solving mind …
4 A: I have more questions, but let's turn things around for a bit. ⁹**What questions do you have** _____ ?
   B: ¹⁰**About** _____ ?
   A: About the position, the company, anything.

B 🔊 **3.08** | Listen and check your ideas.

C Match the phrases (1–10) in Ex 6A with the correct category.

Interviewer's questions 1
Phrases to check
Interviewee's answers

7 A Read the Future Skills box and do the task.

FUTURE SKILLS
Job interviewing

In a job interview, as in any conversation, it's important to make completely sure you understand a question before you answer it. You can do this by asking for clarification, repeating the question in your own words or asking another question.

Look at audioscript 3.07 on page 160 and find three more examples of the interviewee doing this.

B Learn and practise. Go to the Grammar Bank.
⏩ page 113 **GRAMMAR BANK**

8 Work in pairs and take turns. Student A: Ask Student B one of the questions below. Student B: Use a checking phrase to clarify the question before you answer.

> How would a colleague or classmate describe you?

> What are your main strengths?

> Tell me about a time that you learnt from a mistake.

> What motivates you, and what makes you feel unmotivated?

> How well do you deal with stressful situations?

> What are your long-term goals?

SPEAKING

9 Work in pairs. You are going to roleplay two job interview situations. Student A: Go to page 138. Student B: Go to page 140.

MEDIATION SKILLS
asking people to explain their reasons

choose a candidate for a position

⏩ page 148 **MEDIATION BANK**

Speak anywhere — Go to the interactive speaking practice

3D BBC Street Interviews

This or that?

GRAMMAR | expressing preferences
SPEAKING | 'This or That?' questions
WRITING | a discussion board post

PREVIEW

1 Work in pairs and answer the questions.
1 What did you want to be when you were growing up?
2 Look at the jobs in the box. Which ones would suit you most now? Which would suit you least? Why?

> actor   astronaut   astronomer
> doctor   electrician   fashion designer
> footballer   lawyer   musician
> photographer

Q1: What did you want to be when you were growing up?

Q2: Which would you prefer to be …?
- a teacher or a chef?
- an actor or a journalist?
- an author or an engineer?
- a farmer or a politician?

VIEW

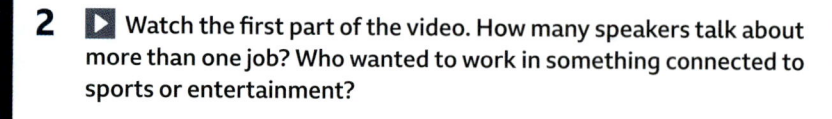

2 ▶ Watch the first part of the video. How many speakers talk about more than one job? Who wanted to work in something connected to sports or entertainment?

3 A ▶ Watch the second part of the video. Which job does each speaker prefer?
1 Dara   a teacher
2 Monica _____
3 Des   _____
4 Eva   _____
5 Tian   _____
6 Daniel _____
7 Sky   _____
8 Rohan   _____
9 Anais   _____

B ▶ Work in pairs. Complete the things that the speakers say. Then watch the second part of the video again and check.
1 Dara: I like _____ and I'm quite used to working with _____ .
2 Monica: I'm very interested with what's happening with the _____ .
3 Des: I think I could reach more _____ by writing books and I could work from _____ .
4 Eva: I don't like _____ with people.
5 Tian: I like _____ with people.
6 Daniel: I do my own _____ and I really enjoy it.
7 Sky: I like being outside in _____ .
8 Rohan: I love _____ and I would love to share a good _____ as well.
9 Anais: I think it would just be pretty cool to make some cool _____ .

GRAMMAR

expressing preferences

4 A Choose the correct words to complete the sentences.
1 I'd **prefer / rather** be a journalist.
2 I **would / had** rather be a teacher.
3 I'd **prefer / rather** to be a farmer.
4 I'd definitely **be for / go for** an author.

B Learn and practise. Go to the Grammar Bank.

▶▶ page 114 **GRAMMAR BANK**

3D

BBC

Des

Rohan

Sky

Daniel

Anais

Tian

Eva

SPEAKING

'This or That?' questions

5 A Work in pairs and look at the 'This or That' questions. Write a question for each one.

Dentist or vet? Which would you rather be, a dentist or a vet?
City or country?
Cats or dogs?
Mountain or beach?
Chocolate or vanilla?

B Look at the Key phrases. Ask each other the 'This or That' questions in Ex 5A. Use some of the Key phrases in your answers.

> **KEY PHRASES**
>
> I'd much rather/prefer to …
> I'd prefer to …
> I'd go for …
> I can't really explain why.
> I've always wanted to …
> It just suits me more.
> I wish I had that choice.
> If I had to choose, I would say …

6 Work in pairs. Ask and answer 'This or That' questions. Student A: Go to page 144. Student B: Go to page 139.

WRITING

a discussion board post

7 A Read the comments on a website. Which replies do you agree with the most?

Driver or passenger?
Which do you prefer?

I'd much rather drive than be a passenger. I get bored when I'm a passenger, and to be honest I don't like the way most people drive. I suppose I like to be in control.

Passenger. I much prefer looking out of the window at the scenery to staring at the road ahead of me. How much nicer to relax and watch the world going by. Driving actually makes me nervous, because I don't feel free to look around.

I drive for a living – I'm a taxi driver – so I feel pretty strongly about being the one in control. Driving is a big responsibility, and people see it as a game, like they don't have to concentrate. I'm extremely uncomfortable in a car with a driver like that. So I'd always choose to be the driver.

That's easy, because I don't have a choice. I want to learn how to drive, but it's too expensive, so I'm always the passenger. If I had the choice, I'd go for being the driver, but only because it would be a nice change for me.

B Work on your own. On a piece of paper, write a 'This or That' question using the ideas in the box or your own ideas. Then write an answer below it and give reasons.

> entertainment   food and drink   travel

C Now work in groups. Pass your piece of paper to other students to write their answers to your question.

D Take back your piece of paper and read out the answers to the question you wrote. Can you guess who wrote each one?

41

3 REVIEW

GRAMMAR

conditional structures

1 A Complete the sentences with *unless, even if, in case (of)*.

Next time I take a long trip:
1 I'll travel alone
   a .... I feel lonelier that way.
   b .... I can find the perfect travel companion.
2 I'm going to take a first aid kit.
   a .... our guide is carrying one; then I won't.
   b .... accidents.
3 I'll definitely study the local language first
   a .... no one speaks English or my mother tongue.
   b .... it's very difficult and I don't have time.
4 I'll certainly bring warm clothes
   a .... cold weather.
   b .... I go to a warm place and it's summertime. You never know!

B Work in pairs. Which sentences do you agree with? Say why or why not.

necessity, obligation and permission

2 A Choose the correct words to complete the sentences.
1 You are not **permitted** / **necessary** to use a smartphone, though you **are allowed** / **'ve got** to use a dictionary.
2 It's **permitted** / **necessary** to register if you want to borrow a book.
3 All liquids need to be **remove** / **removed** from your carry-on luggage.
4 You're **supposed** / **essential** to stay to the right except when passing.
5 You**'ve got** / **'re permitted** to show your passport or a national identity card.
6 It's **essential** / **supposed** to use a seatbelt at all times.

B Work in pairs. What is the situation or context for each sentence in Ex 2A?

expressing preferences

3 A Work in pairs. Read the sentences. Where is the speaker?
1 **Would you prefer** twin beds or a double bed?
2 **I'd rather** skip the starters and just have a main course.
3 **I prefer** cycling outside to an exercise bike in here.
4 **I'd rather not** wait now. Is there a doctor available tomorrow?

B Work in pairs. Think of a place. Make sentences using the phrases in bold in Ex 3A. Say your sentences. Can your partner guess the place?

VOCABULARY

4 A Complete the words.
1 She believes in herself. She's c............ .
2 He's always positive about new ideas. He's so e............ .
3 We work weekends in order to keep our jobs. The company is e............ us.
4 It's only lunchtime and I've done so many things. I got a l............ d............ this morning!
5 Let's do this first. It's not fun, but I just want to get it out of t............ w............ .
6 I quit my job. Too much responsibility. I couldn't h............ the pressure.

B Work in pairs and list four more personality adjectives and eight more work words and phrases from the unit.

5 A Choose the correct options (A–C) to complete the text.

Remote working on the rise

Working from home is no longer only for the self-employed. Based on the ¹............ of recent years, companies have discovered that some employees are happier when working remotely. The employee works from home, a favourite café, wherever they want, but it's ²............ that they're connected all the time, ³............ a colleague wants to reach them. They ⁴............ responsibility for keeping to a routine so that they ⁵............ their deadlines and don't fall ⁶............ schedule in their work. The company saves on the costs of renting office space and the employee saves the cost of commuting. There are downsides too, of course. Remote workers can feel isolated ⁷............ they have regular contact with someone. And they have to find ways to ⁸............ distractions. A person who isn't independent might ⁹............ working in an office, but if a person is flexible and willing to ¹⁰............ with the challenge of turning their home into their workplace, it's ideal.

1	A opportunity	B experience	C routine
2	A essential	B allowed	C rather
3	A unless	B in case of	C in case
4	A take	B make	C get
5	A stick	B meet	C do
6	A late	B between	C behind
7	A if	B unless	C in case
8	A avoid	B deal	C make
9	A prefer	B rather	C prefer to
10	A handle	B be	C deal

B 🔊 **R3.01** | Listen and check your answers.

42

fact or fiction?

4

VLOGS

Q: Do you prefer true stories or fiction?

1 ▶ Watch the video. Do more speakers prefer true stories or fiction?

2 Work in pairs. What about you? Tell a partner.

GSE LEARNING OBJECTIVES

4A READING | Read about a hoax: truth and lies
Pronunciation: silent consonants
Retell the story of a hoax: past plans and intentions

4B LISTENING | Understand people talking about favourite documentaries: adjectives to describe films; films and film-making
Present a pitch for a documentary: indirect and negative questions
Pronunciation: intonation in indirect and negative questions
Write a review

4C HOW TO ... | talk about the news: news headlines; the news
Pronunciation: word stress in adverbs for summarising

4D BBC PROGRAMME | Understand a TV programme about keeping secrets
Have a conversation with an old friend
Write a personal email/letter

Unit 4 | Lesson A

4A Hoax!

GRAMMAR | past plans and intentions
VOCABULARY | truth and lies
PRONUNCIATION | silent consonants

READING

1 A Read the definition of a hoax. Do you know of any hoaxes? Why do you think people create hoaxes?

hoax (n): an unreal story, event or situation that is presented as true in order to trick people into believing it

B Work in pairs. Read the text and answer the questions.

1. What was the lie that the two men from Scotland told?
2. What happened when they told this lie?
3. How did the story end?

C Number the sentences (a–h) in the correct order to complete a summary of the story.

a They decided to pretend they were US rappers from California.
b They had a lot of success (a record deal, appearing on television, a UK tour).
c The hoax was turned into a film.
d After three years, the two men decided to tell the truth.
e Gavin Bain and Billy Boyd dreamed of becoming successful rappers. 1
f Record companies became interested.
g They went to London to meet executives of a record company.
h The executives laughed at their Scottish accents and told them that rappers don't come from Scotland.

D Work in pairs and discuss the questions.

1. What do you think of the way Gavin and Billy behaved? Did they do something bad or just funny?
2. What talents did Gavin and Billy have? Were they just lucky?

The great Hip Hop hoax

Gavin Bain and Billy Boyd met at college in Dundee, Scotland. They shared a love of rap music and planned to become professional rappers, but things didn't work out as they'd intended. When they went to London to meet some record company executives, they were laughed out of the room. The executives listened to their music for about ten seconds, then told the duo that 'real' rappers don't have Scottish accents.

The pair decided to **pretend** to be 'Silibil' (Boyd) and 'Brains' (Bain), a pair of small-town Californians who'd met at a rap competition in San Francisco. They thought they'd have a better chance of being successful rappers if they were American, although Bain had never even been to America.

Their new identities suddenly attracted interest from a record company, but in order to become successful they would need to **live a lie**. And that's exactly what they did. Now living in London, they managed to **deceive** everyone – fans, fellow musicians and the record industry. They **made up** all kinds of stories about themselves, spoke and sang with American accents and started behaving like real Californian rappers. They weren't expecting to become global superstars, but soon a well-known music manager signed them up. After that, they got a record deal with Sony, appeared on MTV in the USA, partied with Madonna and played on a UK tour with rapper Eminem.

Boyd's girlfriend, who still lived in Dundee, was one of the few people who found out about their **scheme**. She noticed that when they answered a phone call from the 'office' back in Scotland, they would start speaking with an American accent. She said that after a while, the boys were finding it hard to keep up the lie. Every day for over three years, they had pretended to be American. Bain even had a girlfriend from Texas. Amazingly, she never **doubted** that Bain was who he said he was. The boys hadn't intended to lie for so long, but things had got out of control once they became successful.

Eventually, under all the stress of living a lie, the pair decided to **come clean**. They broke up the band, **told the truth** about who they were and went back to Scotland. The Great Hip Hop Hoax was over, but the story got a second life when it was made into a film.

44

4A

VOCABULARY

truth and lies

2 A Work in pairs. Look at the words in bold in the text. What do you think they mean? Use the context to help you.

B Complete the sentences (1–8) with the words in bold in the text. Change the verb forms where necessary.

1 If you .... someone, you make them believe something that isn't true.
2 When we ...., we behave as if something is true when we know it's not.
3 A .... is a plan that's intended to achieve something that may be illegal or wrong.
4 If you .... something, you think it might not be true.
5 When we .... something, we invent it, e.g. a story.
6 To .... means the opposite of to tell a lie.
7 When we ...., we decide to be honest about something we were hiding.
8 If you ...., you hide the truth about the way you live your life.

C Think of an example of at least four of the following. Then tell a partner.
- a time when people have to tell the truth
- something or someone that young children pretend to be
- a story that you doubt is true
- a scheme you read or heard about recently
- someone who makes up good stories
- someone who deceived a lot of people

PRONUNCIATION

3 A 🔊 4.01 | **silent consonants** | Read the words from the text in Ex 1B. Which letters are silent? Listen to check.
1 scheme
2 doubt
3 sign
4 answer
5 would
6 listen

B 🔊 4.01 | Listen again and repeat the words.

GRAMMAR

past plans and intentions

4 A Read the sentences (a–d) and answer the questions (1–2).
   a They **planned to become** rappers.
   b They hadn't **intended to lie** for so long, but things got out of control.
   c They **thought they'd** have a better chance of success if they were American.
   d They **weren't expecting** to become global superstars.
   1 Which two sentences are about personal plans made in the past?
   2 Which two sentence are predictions made in the past (things that someone thought might happen)?

B Answer the questions about the sentences in Ex 4A.
Which use:
1 the past continuous?
2 verb + the past form of *will*?
3 verb + *to* infinitive?

C Learn and practise. Go to the Grammar Bank.

⏵ page 115 **GRAMMAR BANK**

5 A Complete the sentences with your own ideas. Make some true and some false.
1 When I was a child, I planned to … but …
2 Years ago I thought I would … but of course …
3 When I first started learning English, I wasn't expecting …
4 One thing I intended to do last year was … but unfortunately …

B Read your sentences to a partner. Are your partner's sentences true or false?

45

Unit 4 | Lesson A

SPEAKING

6 You are going to retell the story of a hoax. First, read the Future Skills box and answer the question.

> **FUTURE SKILLS**
> **Communication**
>
> When we tell a story, we sometimes add our own comments. We often use short phrases with adjectives: 'The interesting/funny thing was …' or 'This was the strange/amazing part …'. What other adjectives can be used to create interest in a story?

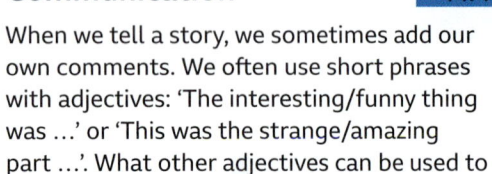

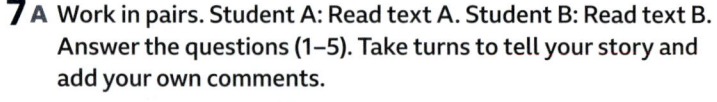

7 A Work in pairs. Student A: Read text A. Student B: Read text B. Answer the questions (1–5). Take turns to tell your story and add your own comments.
1 What did they pretend?
2 What was their plan?
3 Who did they deceive?
4 Did anything go wrong?
5 Did they decide to come clean and tell the truth in the end?

B Work in pairs and discuss the questions.
1 Which story did you find more interesting?
2 Do the two stories have anything in common or are they completely different?
3 Do you know of other stories like these?

Yes, I heard a story about … What about you?

A The greatest restaurant that never existed

For a while, The Shed at Dulwich was London's number one restaurant on Tripadvisor. It received outstanding reviews and was flooded with requests for a table. But it was impossible to get in because the restaurant was always fully booked months in advance.

However, The Shed was a hoax. The 'restaurant' was actually journalist Oobah Butler's garden shed. So how did it become number one? The Tripadvisor reviews were written by his family and friends. (There was a one-star review, which, he assumed, was written by a rival restaurant.) The restaurant had its own phone and a website with photos of modern cuisine, although Butler had made up the recipes, and the 'food' in the photos consisted of household products like shaving cream and paint. The website noted that the restaurant was 'appointment-only'.

The Shed at Dulwich only opened for one night, in which ten guests were blindfolded (so they couldn't see where they were going). They were led to the space outside Butler's shed, where he served them ready-made food. At least one customer enjoyed the experience and said he'd return.

Butler clearly wasn't expecting The Shed to become so successful, and in the end, after deceiving the public, he came clean: he wrote an article for *Vice* magazine, explaining that he'd planned to expose how ratings websites can't be trusted.

B The multi-millionaire with no money

For years Anna Sorokin pretended to be from an amazingly rich family worth about $60 million. She lived in expensive New York hotels, where she handed out $100 tips, wore designer clothes, and went to fashionable restaurants. She even persuaded a bank to lend her $100,000.

Sorokin succeeded in deceiving bankers, hotel owners, and new 'friends', who also lent her money that she never paid back. In truth, she wasn't rich at all and her adventures ended in a prison sentence.

Sorokin was originally from Russia but grew up in Germany. As a teenager, she went to live in Paris to do a fashion degree. But things didn't go as planned – she found it hard to make friends, and she never graduated. Next, she moved to New York and worked for a while at a fashion and culture magazine called *Purple*. She gave herself a new name – Anna Delvey – and began to live a lie.

How did she manage to deceive everyone? Sorokin used fake bank documents. It also appears she was an excellent actress. Certainly, she deceived dozens of New York's rich, who welcomed her into their social circle and believed her story that she was planning to start a $40 million private club. She later said she wasn't sorry for her actions, and claimed that she had intended to pay all the money back.

4B Documentary

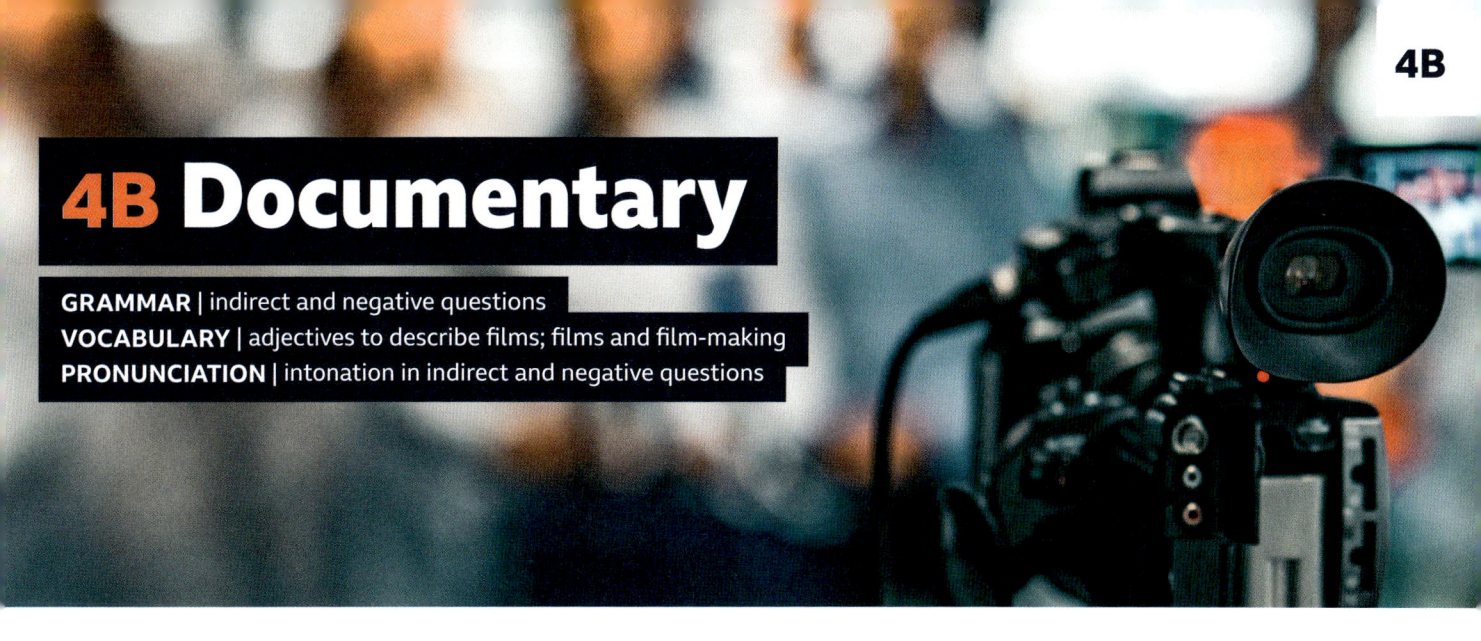

GRAMMAR | indirect and negative questions
VOCABULARY | adjectives to describe films; films and film-making
PRONUNCIATION | intonation in indirect and negative questions

GRAMMAR

indirect and negative questions

1 Work in groups. Discuss the questions.
   1 What are the differences between documentaries and other types of film?
   2 Do you like watching documentaries? If so, which types? If not, which subjects for a documentary would interest you?

2 A Read the '3-minute interview' with a film blogger. What does she say about documentaries compared to social media?

B Work in pairs. Do you agree with the blogger's opinions on documentaries compared to social media? In what ways do you think they are different?

C Look at the interviewer's questions in the interview. Answer the questions (1–3).
   1 Which question is a direct question with the verb *to be*?
   2 Which are 'negative questions': questions that start with a negative verb form and are used to check or confirm information?
   3 Which are indirect questions: questions that use an opening phrase to sound polite (*Could I ask you*, *Can you explain*, etc.)?

D Learn and practise. Go to the Grammar Bank.

➢ page 116 **GRAMMAR BANK**

PRONUNCIATION

3 A 🔊 4.02 | **intonation in indirect and negative questions** | Listen to the questions. Does the speaker's voice start high or low?
   1 Can I ask what you think of this documentary?
   2 Could you tell me when the film starts?
   3 Do you know where I can see it?
   4 Isn't that the documentary you were telling me about?
   5 Didn't you watch it?

B Work in pairs. Use the prompts to make indirect or negative questions to ask your partner. Use the correct intonation.
   • Can you tell me … ?
   • Could I ask you … ?
   • Do you know … ?
   • Didn't … ?

3-minute interview: JC, The Film Fan

What's your favourite documentary?
A film called *Undefeated*.

Could you tell us what it's about?
Sure. It's about a struggling inner-city high school American football team which can barely win a game. Then a new coach arrives and turns them into a team of winners on and off the field.

I remember it. Wasn't it an Oscar winner?
Yes, it won Best Documentary Feature. It's one of many brilliant documentaries of the last few years. It has that 'fly-on-the-wall' approach that you get a lot with social media and video taken on mobile phones.

Absolutely. Don't you think the popularity of documentaries right now is partly because of the rise of social media? Real events get filmed and watched all the time.
Yes, but there are differences. Social media is all about the quick exchange of ideas or information, but documentaries ask us to stay for a while. They take the time to go deeper into a story, to tell a story in ways that social media can't.

Do you know where we can find this film?
It's streaming on various different platforms at the moment.

Unit 4 | Lesson B

LISTENING

4A 🔊 **4.03** | You are going to listen to people discussing their favourite documentaries. Look at the photos below. What do you think the documentaries will be about? Listen and check.

B 🔊 **4.03** | Work in pairs. Answer the questions. Then listen again and check.

My Octopus Teacher
1 Why did Craig Foster decide to spend time freediving?
2 What did he learn from filming the octopus?
3 What does the documentary teach us about the oceans?
4 Did Dave enjoy *My Octopus Teacher*? Why/Why not?

The Salt of the Earth
5 Whose life does the documentary focus on?
6 Why does the documentary show people living in terrible conditions?
7 What does the documentary try to teach us about humanity?
8 Did Amy enjoy *The Salt of the Earth*? Why/Why not?

C Work in pairs and discuss the questions.
1 What do you think are the biggest threats to the natural world?
2 Do you think documentaries are an effective way to learn about issues like this? Why/Why not?

VOCABULARY

adjectives to describe films

5A Match the adjectives in bold with the best option (a or b).
1 It's the **extraordinary** story of a diver who makes friends with a wild octopus.
   a very unusual   b very difficult
2 The underwater filming is very **dramatic**. I'd never seen anything so beautiful on screen.
   a surprising   b exciting
3 It's a very **intelligent** film in that it makes you realise just how important our oceans are.
   a makes you think   b difficult to understand
4 The whole film is really **enjoyable**. My family loved it.
   a easy   b fun
5 I found it a bit **disappointing**.
   a similar to what you expected   b worse than what you expected
6 It was really **slow**. A lot of the film just shows footage of the octopus.
   a without interest or excitement   b long
7 It's a really **powerful** documentary about the life and work of photographer Sebastião Salgado.
   a it made a strong impression   b it has a lot of information
8 He tells the story of the **shocking** conditions that many people around the world often have to live in.
   a different   b surprising in a bad way

B Choose the best words to complete the sentences.
1 There was so much action at the end of the film – it was very **intelligent / dramatic / slow**.
2 If you watch this documentary, it'll change how you think about food forever. It has a very **powerful / disappointing / enjoyable** message about vegetarianism.
3 The idea is amazing, but I didn't like how it was filmed. It was a bit **slow / enjoyable / intelligent**.
4 It's a very **extraordinary / intelligent / shocking** documentary. The ideas are really clever.

C Work in pairs. Tell your partner about a film, documentary or TV programme you have watched recently using the adjectives in Ex 5A.

D Learn and practise. Go to the Vocabulary Bank.

▶▶ page 133 **VOCABULARY BANK** films and film-making

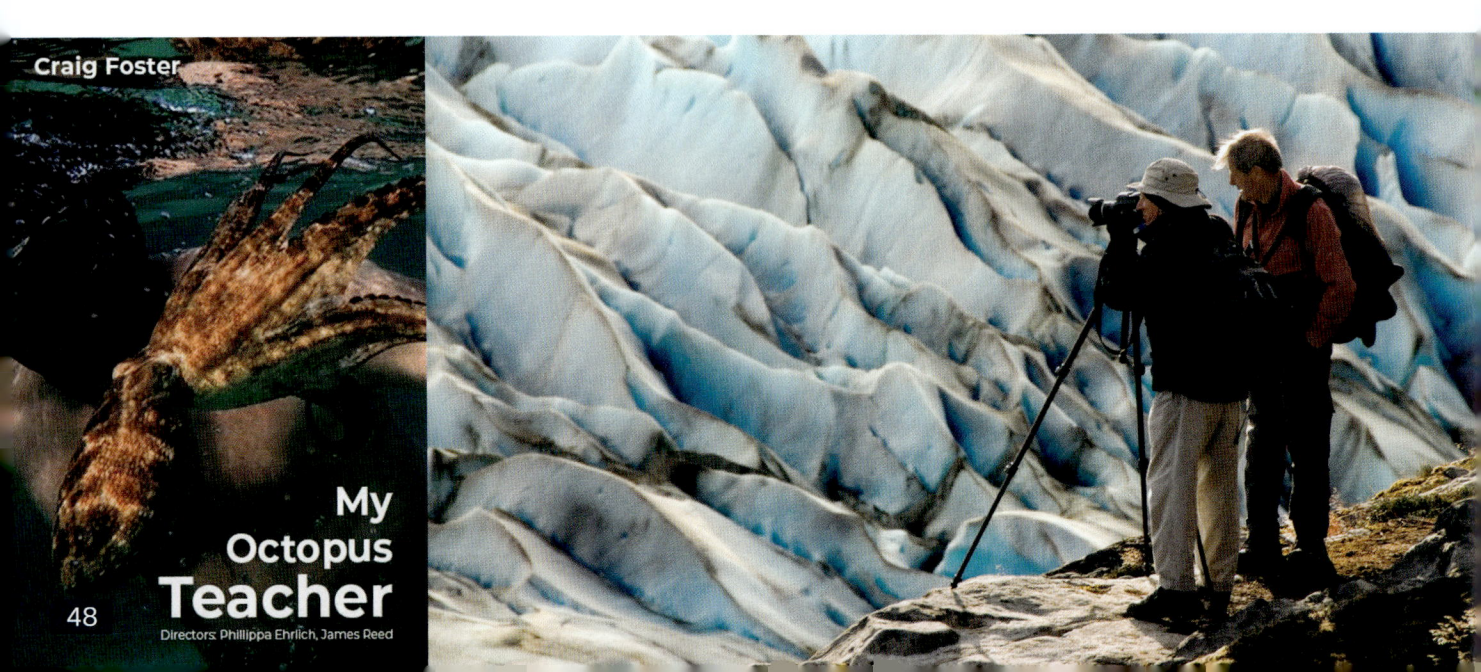

SPEAKING

6 A Imagine you have an idea for a documentary and you need to pitch your idea to the class to get funding. You are going to plan the documentary and make a presentation to the class. Think about these questions.

- What is the documentary about (a person, a place, an issue, etc.)?
- What is the title?
- Where will it be filmed?
- Who will you interview and who else will be involved?
- What will you try to teach people about the topic? How?
- How will you describe the documentary when you pitch it to the class? (Can you compare it to other films?)

B Work in groups. Agree on an idea and plan the details using the questions in Ex 6A.

Wouldn't it be good to film a documentary about … ?

Isn't there a … that's more … ?

Don't you think it might be better to … ?

C Present your documentary idea to the class. During other presentations, think of questions for the presenters. Ask them at the end.

Why do you think the subject is important?

Don't you think this has been done before?

Isn't there a way you could … ?

D Work in groups. Which documentary would you fund? Why?

WRITING

a review

7 A Read the film review. What four things does the writer like about the film?

B Which of these are included in the review of *Parasite*?

1. an introduction with background information (e.g., setting, actors, director, true story behind the film)
2. a summary of the story
3. the writer's opinions of the film (e.g., plot, acting, set, dialogue, themes, music)
4. opinions from other people saying what is good/bad
5. a conclusion saying if the film is worth watching

8 A Read the sentences (1 and 2) and underline the adverbs.

1. We first see the Kims as they desperately try to get an internet connection.
2. We watch the Kims cleverly deceive the Parks.

B Work in pairs and answer the questions.

1. Why do we use adverbs?
   a. to describe how someone does something
   b. to describe a person
2. What two letters do many adverbs end in?
3. What actions could you describe using these adverbs: *dramatically, intelligently, powerfully, slowly, wonderfully*?

C Complete the sentences with the adverbs in the box. Sometimes more than one adverb may be possible.

| dramatically   intelligently   powerfully   slowly   wonderfully |

1. The documentary has been very .... thought out.
2. As we watch, we .... realise the answer to the problem.
3. The films starts very .... with a man jumping out of an aeroplane.
4. The footage of the mountains is .... shot. It's spectacular.

9 Write a review of a film, documentary or TV programme. Use the list in Ex 7B to help.

REVIEWFILES.COM

Parasite ★★★★★

Posted on 27 May | Release date 21 May   ♥ 12   💬 13

Parasite is a 2019 South Korean film directed by Bong Joon-ho. A dark comedy, it became the first foreign-language production to win an Academy Award for Best Film.

The story follows two families, one rich (the Parks) and one poor (the Kims). We first see the Kims as they desperately try to get an internet connection from the horrible basement they call home. Then the teenage son gets lucky. A friend gives him the chance to teach English to the son of the Park family. Soon, the whole Kim family is employed by the Parks in various roles: driver, art tutor, and housekeeper. They pretend to be highly qualified and never reveal to the Parks that they are all from the same family.

There is a lot to like about this intelligent film. The plot is very original. We watch the Kims cleverly deceive the Parks, and this is the source of a lot of humour, although it eventually leads to an ending that is both shocking and dramatic.

The acting is brilliant, with Song Kang-ho particularly good as the father of the Kim family who ends up as Mr Park's driver. Also, the set is wonderful, especially the Parks's extraordinary hi-tech house with its secret spaces and huge windows.

Overall, *Parasite* is extremely enjoyable. While it has lots to say about modern society, with the rich and the poor living side by side, above all it's a lot of fun.

Unit 4 | Lesson C

4C News

HOW TO ... | talk about the news
VOCABULARY | news headlines; the news
PRONUNCIATION | word stress in adverbs for summarising

LIVE BREAKING NEWS

VOCABULARY

news headlines

1 A Work in pairs and discuss the questions.
1. Do you regularly share stories or videos on social media? Who with? What type of stories/videos?
2. Are there any types of story/video you really don't like?

B Read the headlines (1–5). Discuss which stories you might read and which you definitely wouldn't. Explain why.

1. Students **march** dressed as bears in **protest** against restaurant

2. Man **arrested** after dog **attacks** politician

3. FILM DIRECTOR **QUITS** AS ACTORS **STRIKE** BECAUSE OF BAD SMELL

4. **Celebrity** in financial **scandal** hid €500,000 under bed

5. Cat **escapes** flat, gets **rescued** from tree

C Match the headlines (1–5) in Ex 1B with the opening lines of the stories (a–e).

a. A movie production paused after actors refused to film on a farm because of the smell. The film-maker, Kitty Mendelssohn, walked away from the project saying, 'Actors these days just want an easy life. It drives me crazy'.

b. Plans to open a Big Bear restaurant on the campus of a university have been paused after angry students walked the streets yesterday. They say the restaurant chain has poor working conditions.

c. Musician Fantaye DeBruin told a court yesterday that she kept suitcases full of money in her home.

d. A pregnant Siamese cat named Zoe climbed out of a third-floor window and onto a tree, but got stuck. Firefighters came and brought Zoe down several hours later.

e. Police are holding a man whose dog turned violent in public. Bill Cheney, 33, lost control of his dog in a local park.

D Which of these stories might go viral? Why?

2 A Choose the correct word to complete the paragraph about news stories.

Making the News

A million cars on the road isn't a news story, but if two of them crash, it is. If a politician does a good job, that's not news, but if they [1]**quit** / **arrest** because of a [2]**strike** / **scandal**, it'll make the front pages. What about [3]**celebrities** / **strikes** behaving well? That's not a news story, but if they get [4]**escaped** / **arrested**, it is. 'News' usually means 'bad news'. Bad news travels fast, but so does cute news. Animals are particularly popular, especially if they get [5]**escaped** / **rescued**: GoPro's Fireman Saves Kitten video attracted 1.5 million views on YouTube in its first week. And famously, a few years ago, a story about a cow went viral. The cow [6]**escaped** / **quit** and ran down a New York street before being caught by the police. While it's usually events that make the news, at least one 'non-event' went viral. In 2015, when a group of environmental activists weren't allowed to [7]**escape** / **march** through the streets in France, they simply left their shoes – 10,000 of them – as a [8]**strike** / **protest**.

B Work in pairs. Say which of the words in bold in Ex 2A have been in the news recently.

march: There was a march in the capital last week.
quit: There was a story about a famous football manager who quit recently.

C Learn and practise. Go to the Vocabulary Bank.

▶▶ page 134 **VOCABULARY BANK** the news

How to ...
talk about the news

3 A Work in groups and discuss. Do you watch or listen to the news regularly? What are the latest news stories in your country or city/town?

B 🔊 **4.04** | Listen to people discussing some news stories and complete the headlines.

1 _____ lifts boy into the air
2 Huge _____ destroys supermarket
3 Sean Davies quits job as _____
4 _____ cancelled due to bad weather
5 _____ take over university buildings

C Work in pairs. What happened in each story?

4 A 🔊 **4.04** | Complete the extracts from the discussions. Then listen again and check.

1 A: **Have** ¹_____ that story about the kid in the zoo?
   A: **So,** ²_____, **what happened was** that he was feeding the giraffe and …
   B: Oh no! **That** ³_____ **scary**.

2 A: **Have you** ⁴_____ **about** the fire?
   B: What fire?
   A: In town. Didn't you see the smoke?
   B: No, ⁵_____?
   A: The supermarket caught fire. **It's** ⁶_____ **the news**.
   A: **It** ⁷_____ there might have been an electrical fault or something.

3 A: **Did you hear the news about** Sean Davies?
   B: No. What happened?
   A: He's quit his job as manager.
   B: **Really? I had no idea!**
   A: Yes. **I saw it** ⁸_____ **the news**. … **I** ⁹_____ **the details, but basically,** …

4 A: ¹⁰_____, thousands of people are stuck at the airport. **It's** ¹¹_____ **all the news channels**.

5 A: **Are you** ¹²_____ **the news about** the protests?
   B: Yes, **it's received a lot of coverage. It's terrible. Apparently,** …
   A: I know. It all happened so quickly. **I can hardly believe it.**

B Which of the phrases in bold in Ex 4A are good for:

1 initiating a discussion about a news story?
2 describing/summarising the news story?
3 commenting on where you saw the story?
4 responding to a news story?

C Learn and practise. Go to the Grammar Bank.

▶ page 117 **GRAMMAR BANK**

PRONUNCIATION

5 🔊 **4.05** | **word stress in adverbs for summarising** | Listen to how the speakers summarise. How many syllables do the words *basically* and *apparently* have? Which syllable has the main stress?

1 So, **basically**, what happened was …
2 **Apparently**, thousands of people are stuck at the airport.
3 **Basically**, it seems like he's going to manage a different team.
4 **Apparently**, the protesters have taken over the university buildings.

6 A Work in pairs. Discuss two news stories. Student B: Go to page 144 and follow the instructions. Student A: Read the story below and prepare to tell it to Student B. Use these phrases.

> Have you heard … ?   Apparently, …
> It seems that …   Basically, …

Dog under umbrella

A security guard was photographed standing outside a supermarket holding his umbrella over a dog. The dog was waiting for its owner outside a supermarket and it was raining. The security guard felt sorry for the dog and used an umbrella to keep it dry. Someone took a photo and posted in on social media and the story went viral.

B Tell your story to Student B. Then listen to Student B's story and respond. Use these phrases.

> What happened?   I can hardly believe it.
> Oh no, that's terrible/really funny!   That sounds …

SPEAKING

7 A Think of a current news story (sports news, celebrity gossip, local news, world news, news about a discovery, etc.). Plan to talk about it. Answer the questions. Use the phrases in Ex 4A.

1 What is the story about?
2 Who was involved?
3 When did it happen?
4 Why is it interesting?
5 How did you hear about it?

B Work in groups. Discuss your news stories. Initiate the discussion, then describe and comment on the story using the phrases in Ex 4A.

MEDIATION SKILLS
writing in note form
report a news story

▶ page 150 **MEDIATION BANK**

Unit 4 | Lesson D

4D BBC Entertainment
Fake friends

SPEAKING | a conversation with an old friend
WRITING | a personal email/letter

PREVIEW

1 A Work in pairs. Are you good or bad at keeping secrets for family, friends and colleagues? Think of examples.

B Read the programme information. How do you think Holly might try to create a 'secret life'?

Ordinary Lies

Ordinary Lies is a BBC drama series that follows the lives of an ordinary group of colleagues and friends and the extraordinary secrets they keep. In each episode, we see how quickly small lies can become big secrets, and how there can be shocking consequences when they are revealed. In this episode, Holly feels her life is too boring, so she creates a 'secret life' for herself which she thinks looks more interesting.

VIEW

2 A ▶ Watch the BBC video clip and number the events (a–g) in the order that they happen.

a Holly follows Adam to a supermarket and pretends that she just bumped into him.
b Holly is looking at old photos and feeling sad. **1**
c Holly and Adam catch up and she gets his phone number.
d Holly looks up an old friend, Adam, on social media.
e Holly updates her social media profile with some stolen photos and a new job title.
f Holly goes to the office where Adam works and she waits.
g Holly gets dressed up and puts on some make-up.

B ▶ How do they respond? Choose the correct sentences to complete the conversations. Then watch again to check.

1 Adam: Whoa, this is … crazy!
   Holly: **I know. / Yes, isn't it?**
2 Holly: I thought you were living New Forest way?
   Adam: **That's right, but I moved back a while ago. / Yeah, I moved back a few months ago.**
3 Adam: You look good.
   Holly: **So do you. / Thank you very much.**
4 Adam: So, do you live round here, or … ?
   Holly: **Not really. I live about half an hour away. / Er, not far. I have an apartment.**
5 Adam: Um … It's amazing bumping into you. We should … catch up.
   Holly: **That would be great. / How about Wednesday?**

C Work in groups and discuss the questions.
1 What do you think will happen next? Do you think Adam will find out the truth about Holly? How?
2 Do you think what Holly did was a good or bad idea? Why?
3 Do you think it's ever acceptable for people to post information which is untrue on social media? Why/Why not?

4D

SPEAKING

a conversation with an old friend

3 A 🔊 **4.06** | Listen to two friends having a conversation. Are the statements True (T) or False (F)?

1. Jade and Nikolas haven't seen each other for about five years.
2. Nikolas lives in New Zealand.
3. Nikolas works for a film company.
4. Jade works in a bakery.
5. Their friend Robert is married and has three children.
6. Nikolas has gained his ski instructor qualification.

B 🔊 **4.06** | Listen again and tick the phrases you hear.

> **KEY PHRASES**
>
> How amazing to see you!
> It's really great to see you again.
> This is crazy … . How long is it since we've seen each other?
> I thought you were living in New Zealand/Barcelona/Italy.
> Are you still working for that film company/living in … ?
> Did you ever finish your degree/start your own company?
> (Did) you know he's married now/I passed my exams?
> Wow, that's amazing/brilliant!
> Really?! I can't believe it!

4 A Imagine you bump into a friend you haven't seen for a few years. Prepare to talk to them about your life and what has changed. Think about these things and make some notes.

> experiences   friendships/family   hobbies
> new skills/qualifications   where you live   work

B Work in pairs. Have a conversation with your friend and find out about their life. What has changed? Try to use the Key phrases.

C Work with another partner. Tell them about the conversation you just had.

WRITING

a personal email/letter

5 A Read the email. Is all of the information correct according to the conversation in Ex 3A?

Hi Rob,

How are things? Guess who I bumped into the other day? Nikolas! I was just going for lunch in the café and he saw me walking across the street. It was such a surprise. Anyway, we got chatting and caught up on all our news. Did you know he came back from New Zealand and now he's working for himself as a freelancer? He's still directing films. He's also planning to do his ski instructor exams. He wants to be able to teach during the ski season. It was so nice to talk to him and to catch up. He asked after you and I told him you were married now with two kids. He couldn't believe it! It's amazing how quickly time has gone since we were all working together. We were thinking it would be really nice to try and get together. Perhaps we could arrange a meal sometime? Let me know what you think. It would be great to see you.

Best wishes,

Jade

B Write an email to a friend telling them about the conversation you had in Ex 4B. Tell your friend about the conversation in detail and make some plans to meet.

C Work with your partner from Ex 4B. Read your partner's email. Is all the information about your conversation in Ex 4B correct?

4 REVIEW

GRAMMAR

past plans and intentions

1 A Choose the correct words to complete the sentences about some famous people.

Before they were famous

1 Angela Merkel was **going / intended** to be an academic, and got a PhD in chemistry before getting the job that made her famous.

2 Hugh Jackman thought it **will / would** be a good idea to get a steady job before following his dreams, so he worked as a physical education teacher.

3 Nicole Kidman always intended to **doing / do** the job that made her famous, but did a course in massage therapy first, in order to learn how to massage her mother, who was sick.

4 Mario Vargas Llosa was hoping **to become / become** president of his country but lost in the election. A famous author, he won the Nobel Prize in Literature twenty years later.

5 While Harrison Ford was **planning / planned** to become an actor, he trained as a carpenter. In fact, he was working in film director Francis Ford Coppola's office when George Lucas gave him the role that made him famous.

6 While Beyoncé Knowles always **meant / meaning** to use her musical talent, for a while she swept floors in her mother's hair salon.

B Work in pairs. Which of the people in Ex 1A have you heard of? What else do you know about them?

indirect and negative questions

2 A Read the interview questions with a film director. Correct the mistakes in the questions.

1 Could I to ask you how you became a film director?
2 Aren't you think it's easier these days to make films than it was in the past?
3 How you are able to cope with so many things like actors, finance, equipment and schedule?
4 Can you explain me how you find locations for your films?
5 Isn't it but extremely difficult to get your film into cinemas?
6 Do you know where can I start if I want to be a film-maker?

B Work in pairs. Roleplay an interview. Student A: You are a journalist. Student B: You are a famous film director. Ask and answer the questions in Ex 2A. Then swap roles.

VOCABULARY

3 A Complete the conversation with the words in the box.

clean   deceiving   doubted   enjoyable
extraordinary   intelligent   lived   pretended

A: Did you hear about that guy who [1]............ to be a doctor, a lawyer and an airline pilot, all while he was still a teenager? He [2]............ a lie for years.
B: How is it possible that no one [3]............ his story?
A: He was just really good at [4]............ people. He was obviously very [5]............ , too. The FBI spent years trying to catch him.
B: What an [6]............ story! I've never heard of anything like that before. Did he eventually come [7]............ ?
A: Yes, he was caught eventually. His story was made into a really [8]............ film called *Catch Me If You Can*.

B Work in pairs and discuss. Have you heard of this story or watched the film?

4 A Choose the correct options (A–C) to complete the text.

Facts & fiction: when Hollywood gets it wrong

The [1]............ exists to tell us stories and sell us dreams. But are films supposed to [2]............ the truth? Aren't they a mixture of fact and fiction? Read these examples of Hollywood getting the details wrong and judge for yourself.

A scene from *Apollo 13* is set in April, 1970. Astronaut Jim Lovell's daughter holds The Beatles' album *Let It Be*. It's a good scene, but can anyone explain [3]............ had this album, which didn't come out until August, five months later?

In *Raiders of the Lost Ark*, set in 1936, a map appears onscreen, showing Indiana Jones's journey. We read the name Thailand. You might ask, 'Is this a problem? [4]............ this possible?' The journey certainly was, but Thailand wasn't named 'Thailand' until 1939. It was Siam before that.

Occasionally, the [5]............ makes deliberate mistakes. Sofia Coppola's *Marie Antoinette* is all about the queen of the same name, who was born in 1755. In one scene, there's a pair of Converse trainers. (The shoe company was founded in 1908.) Coppola thought this [6]............ a way to show how young Marie Antoinette was.

1	A film trade	B film industry	C industry film
2	A make	B talk	C tell
3	A how she	B she	C that she
4	A Didn't	B How wasn't	C Wasn't
5	A star	B shoot	C director
6	A can do	B would be	C will be

B 🔊 R4.01 | Listen and check your answers.

consumer 5

VLOGS

Q: When was the last time you had a problem with a product or service?

1. ▶ Watch the video. What problems do people talk about?

2. What problems can you remember having?

GSE LEARNING OBJECTIVES

5A LISTENING | Understand people making complaints: personality adjectives (2)

Pronunciation: word stress in adjectives

Roleplay making complaints: clauses of purpose: *to, so as to, in order to/that, so that*

Write a complaint email

5B READING | Understand an article about marketing tips: advertising; money

Discuss a marketing campaign: comparative and superlative structures

Pronunciation: linking *r* in phrases

5C HOW TO … | summarise information from different sources: describing products

Pronunciation: intonation in summarising phrases

5D BBC STREET INTERVIEWS | Understand people talking about what they do themselves and what they have done

Talk about planning an event: causative *have* and *get*; reflexive pronouns

Write a meeting summary

Unit 5 | Lesson A

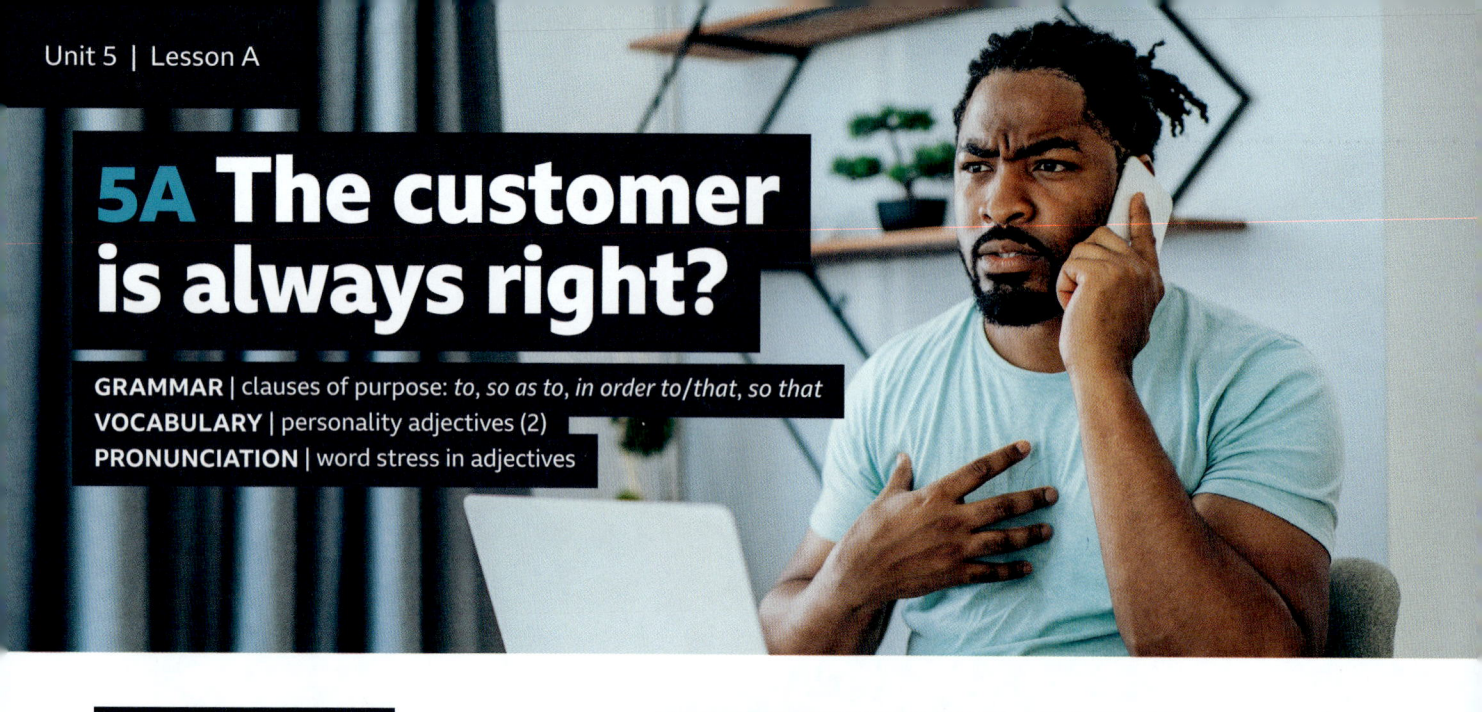

5A The customer is always right?

GRAMMAR | clauses of purpose: *to, so as to, in order to/that, so that*
VOCABULARY | personality adjectives (2)
PRONUNCIATION | word stress in adjectives

VOCABULARY

personality adjectives (2)

1 A Work in pairs. Look at the photo and discuss the questions.
1. Do you ever complain about products or services?
2. Are you usually successful when you complain? Why/Why not, do you think?

B Work in pairs. Do the quiz and discuss your answers. Do you agree with your results in the key?

C Discuss the questions.
1. Is it common to complain about products and services in your country?
2. Can it be useful to show anger when complaining?

D Complete the sentences with the words in the box.

| aggressive | calm | confident | direct |
| patient | pleasant | sensible | shy |

1. I get nervous speaking to strangers. I'm rather ....
2. I tend to lose my temper and argue. I'm quite ....
3. I don't mind waiting a long time. I think I'm ....
4. I never lose my temper or get angry. I always stay ....
5. I always speak my mind. I'm very ....
6. I'm always polite and smile a lot. I try to be ....
7. I don't think I can do it well. I'm not very ....
8. I'd never complain about something which can't be changed. People say I'm really ....

PRONUNCIATION

2 A | **word stress in adjectives** | Work in pairs. Match the adjectives in Ex 1D with the syllable patterns.
1. O calm   2 Oo   3 oO   4 Ooo   5 oOo

B 🔊 5.01 | Listen and check.

C Work in pairs. Take turns to ask questions based on the sentences in Ex 1D. Answer using the correct adjective.

A: Do you tend to lose your temper and argue?
B: Well, I can be quite aggressive sometimes. For example …

Quiz: **What kind of complainer are you?**

Answer the questions to find out …

1 How do you behave when you complain?
   a I tend to lose my temper and argue.
   b I usually start by saying, 'I'm sorry, but'. I'm always polite and smile a lot.
   c I never get angry and I always keep my cool.

2 When you complain, which of these is true for you?
   a I don't waste time and I always speak my mind.
   b I understand that I might have to wait a while for a solution.
   c I know exactly what I want to achieve and I tell the person clearly.

3 Do you try and build a relationship with the person?
   a No. They represent the company.
   b I'd like to, but I get a bit nervous speaking to strangers.
   c I treat them with respect. The problem may not be their fault.

4 Do you ever make threats against the company?
   a Yes, I always tell them I'm going to give them negative feedback on social media.
   b No, I don't think that's effective and it's unfair.
   c I usually say something like, 'I was going to recommend you, but I've changed my mind'.

5 How often do you complain?
   a A lot. Whenever I have any sort of problem.
   b Not very often. I don't think I can do it well.
   c I never complain about things which can't be changed.

56

5A

LISTENING

3 A 🔊 **5.02** | Listen to two customers complaining about a service or product and answer the questions.
1 What does each person complain about?
2 What might happen next?

B Work in pairs. What does the word in bold refer to in each sentence?

Conversation 1
1 He leant back and **it** broke.
2 But **that's** not the point.
3 If **it's** over three years ago, we won't be able to help.
4 I'm sorry, but there's nothing I can do about **it**.
5 **He** should be back in an hour.

Conversation 2
6 He assured me **it** would be here today.
7 **It** says the suitcase was delivered to your address this morning.
8 Is it possible to do **it** now?

C 🔊 **5.02** | Listen again and check your ideas.

D Work in pairs and discuss.
1 In which conversation do you think the complainer was more effective, 1 or 2?
2 What would you do differently from them in either situation?

4 A 🔊 **5.03** | Listen and write the word you hear first. Then listen again and use each extract to work out the meaning of the words you hear first.

B Work in pairs and discuss. What helped you guess the meaning? Tick the strategies you used.
1 It must be a verb/noun/adjective because of its position in the sentence.
2 It must be a verb/noun/adjective because of its ending.
3 I understood the meaning from the situation.
4 The meaning is given in the surrounding sentences.
5 It's made from a word or words I recognise.

C Go to page 141 and check the meanings. Which ones did you guess correctly?

Key

Mostly a) It's good to be firm, but your style could make the other person feel as if they're being attacked and as a result they could get upset, which is likely to be ineffective. Work on staying calm in these situations.

Mostly b) You're sensitive to other people, but perhaps you need to believe in yourself more. Don't give up so easily. Practise complaining firmly but politely.

Mostly c) You're likely to be an effective complainer. You only complain when it's necessary and you treat people with respect whilst at the same time being firm and knowing what you want.

GRAMMAR

clauses of purpose: *to, so as to, in order to/that, so that*

5 A Work in pairs. Find the clauses of purpose in the sentences (1–5).
1 I'm here to make a complaint.
2 We will need the receipt so as to check the date when you bought the chair.
3 What do I have to do in order to get someone to help me?
4 I'll need to take the flight number so that I can check what has happened.
5 I can hold on so as not to waste time.

B Look at the sentences in Ex 5A and answer the questions.
1 How many clauses of purpose include an infinitive with *to*?
2 What structure is used when *to* is NOT used?

C Notice the position of *not* in Ex 5A sentence 5. Make the clauses of purpose in the sentences (1–4) negative.
1 I treat the person with respect so as to upset them.
2 I usually write an email to avoid talking to someone, but because I want a record of the communication.
3 I keep receipts in a file in order to lose them.
4 I breathe deeply so that I'll lose my temper.

D Learn and practise. Go to the Grammar Bank.

⏩ page 118 **GRAMMAR BANK**

6 A Work in pairs and read the sentences (1–6). What do you think is happening?
1 In order ...., I switched it on and off, but …
   A: Maybe someone is checking if a light is working?
   B: Or a phone?
2 At first I didn't take it out of the box in order not .... Then I noticed that …
3 The strings were broken, and we took it back to the shop so that .... At the shop, the manager …
4 It was the worst one I'd ever eaten, but I was pleasant with the waiter so as not .... I was surprised then that he …
5 The reason I asked to speak to the manager was to ...., but the sales assistant didn't want …
6 We took a taxi in order ...., but in fact …

B Complete the sentences in Ex 6A with your own ideas.

In order to check if the light was working, I switched it on and off, but nothing happened.

C Work in pairs and take turns reading out your sentences. Which ones remind you of real-life experiences you have had?

Unit 5 | Lesson A

SPEAKING

7 A Work in pairs. You are going to phone to complain about a product. Complete the phrases (2–3) with adjectives from Ex 1D. Then complete the sentences with your own ideas.
1 To complain effectively, you need to treat people with respect in order to …
2 Remember to be .... and .... so that …
3 It's important not to be too .... or .... so as not to …

B Which of these phrases do you think would be effective in the conversation?
1 I'm phoning to make a complaint about …
2 Look, I know it's not your fault, but this really isn't good enough.
3 I demand to speak to your manager, right now.
4 I'm really not happy with the situation.
5 Do you have any thoughts on what we should do next?

C Work in pairs. You are going to practise making and dealing with customer complaints. Student A: Go to page 141. Student B: Go to page 143.

WRITING

a complaint email

8 A Work in pairs and discuss the questions.
1 Have you ever written an email or letter of complaint?
2 What do you think is important in a complaint email or letter?
3 What sort of problems might happen when you stay in a hotel? List five or more.

B Read the complaint email, then discuss with another student.
1 Does the writer do any of the things you discussed in Ex 7A?
2 Does the writer mention any of the problems you listed in Ex 8A?

To the Manager:

I am writing to complain about my recent stay in your hotel.

I was a guest for two nights last weekend. When I arrived, the receptionist was polite, but I found it extremely annoying that it took over twenty minutes to check in. When I went to our room, I was shocked to discover that the beds weren't made and there was a used towel on the floor of the bathroom. I was given another room, but by this point I was beginning to regret choosing your hotel.

Unfortunately, the problems didn't end there. At night, as I was falling asleep, the people in the next room started playing music. I phoned reception to ask them to ask my 'neighbours' to quieten down, but nothing happened. So I went and knocked on their door, and I am afraid to say that their behaviour was aggressive, almost frightening. A hotel guest should never be put in this situation, and it was the fault of your staff that something wasn't done.

I was reasonable and patient with your staff as well as other guests, but my experience was completely unacceptable. However, I am confident that we can reach a sensible resolution. I feel that a refund of one of my two nights at the hotel would be a fair compensation for my unpleasant experience.

I look forward to hearing your reply.

Regards,

J. Oldman

C Read the email again and find phrases that mean:
1 I'm writing because I'm unhappy about …
   I am writing to complain about …
2 It made me angry that …
3 I was very surprised and upset that …
4 After this happened, I wished I hadn't …
5 That wasn't the last thing that went wrong.
6 I'm sorry to have to say this but …
7 It's wrong for this experience to happen.
8 I was polite with all of your employees.
9 What happened to me was absolutely terrible.
10 I'm sure we can find a solution.

9 Choose the correct words to complete the instructions on how to write emails and letters of complaint. Use the complaint email in Ex 8B to help.

Length
The email should have ¹**a lot of detail** / **only as much detail as is necessary**.

Structure
The email should have three sections.
- Say ²**why you're writing** / **your name and job**.
- Describe ³**your feelings** / **the problem**.
- State what action ⁴**you want** / **you're going to take**.

Style
The style of the email should be ⁵**formal** / **informal**. You:
- should ⁶**use** / **avoid using** contractions in positive sentences,
- ⁷**can often** / **usually can't** use contractions with verbs in the negative,
- should ⁸**use** / **avoid using** the passive, to be less direct.

10 A Work in pairs and discuss the questions.
1 Have you ever had a bad meal or experience in a restaurant? Give details.
2 What things can go wrong when you have a meal at a restaurant? List four or five.
3 What do you do if you have bad service or a bad meal in a restaurant?

B Write a complaint email to the manager of a restaurant where you had a bad meal or bad service. Imagine a situation if you need to. Use your ideas in Ex 10A.

C Swap emails with another student. Read the other student's email and use the information in Ex 9 to check it.

5B Too good to be true

GRAMMAR | comparative and superlative structures
VOCABULARY | advertising; money
PRONUNCIATION | linking *r* in phrases

VOCABULARY

advertising

1 A Work in pairs and discuss the questions (1–3).
 1 What was the last thing you bought?
 2 What kind of things do you enjoy buying?
 3 What kind of things don't you enjoy buying?

B Match the sentences (1–5) with the responses (a–e).
 1 I'm **a bargain hunter**. I'm always looking for **a good deal**.
 2 TV advertisements don't **influence** me. I buy the same brands no matter what.
 3 It's not **worth** buying inexpensive products. You spend less but then the product doesn't last as long.
 4 Look, it says '**limited availability**'!
 5 For a smart **consumer** it's important to find out about a product before they **make a purchase**.

 a Ah, so for you **brand loyalty** is stronger than marketing.
 b I agree, good **quality** usually costs more, and you get what you pay for.
 c Really? Then I'm not one of them. I buy things without finding out anything about them.
 d So you love it when something is **on offer** and the price is low.
 e Well you should buy it now; there might be none left by tomorrow.

C Work in pairs. Look at the words and phrases in bold in Ex 1B. Which do you already know? Which can you understand from the context?

D Match the words and phrases in bold in Ex 1B with the definitions (1–10).
 1 buy something
 2 how good or bad something is
 3 change a person's behaviour
 4 having a lower price for a limited time period
 5 good or useful to do
 6 someone who buys things
 7 when someone buys things from a company because of the name, they have this
 8 someone who looks for low prices
 9 a good price or agreement
 10 only being sold for a short time or in small quantities

2 A How would you describe yourself as a consumer? Make notes using the words and phrases in bold in Ex 1B.

B Work in pairs. Describe yourself as a consumer. Use at least five of the words and phrases from Ex 1B.

3 A Work in pairs. List any nouns you know to talk about money and price in different situations.
 price, bargain

B Learn and practise. Go to the Vocabulary Bank.

▶▶ page 134 **VOCABULARY BANK** money

Unit 5 | Lesson B

READING

4 A Work in pairs. Look at the image in the article and discuss the questions.

1. What do you know about the marketing technique that's shown in the image?
2. How easily do you think you are affected by advertising and marketing?

B Read the article. Which of the three techniques do you think is the most unfair? Which is the cleverest?

C Work in pairs and look at the phrases (a–h). Match each one with the marketing technique (1–3) it is connected to.

1. The decoy effect
2. Hidden fees
3. Scarcity marketing

a additional costs
b miss their chance
c spend a lot of time
d the price of the middle product is closer to the price of the most expensive
e there aren't many more
f three products
g a very low price
h X number of people are currently looking

D Read the article again and check your ideas.

5 A Complete the summaries with the phrases (a–h) in Ex 4C.

The decoy effect: There are usually ¹ _f_ offered, and ² ___ . This influences consumers to buy the most expensive one.

Hidden fees: There's an online advertisement for a product at ³ ___ , one that is much lower than the competition. People ⁴ ___ entering information, and then they find out that there are a number of ⁵ ___ , and the final price is much higher than the one advertised.

Scarcity marketing: The advertisement tells the shopper that ⁶ ___ at the same product at the same time as them or that ⁷ ___ examples of this product available. The shopper feels that if they don't buy now, they may ⁸ ___ .

B Work in pairs and discuss. How much do you think you are influenced by the three techniques in the article? Give examples.

6 🔲 Find a real-life example of one of the marketing techniques from the text. Prepare to tell the class about it and if possible, bring a photo.

Tricks of the trade

Whenever you're shopping, someone out there is trying to convince you to buy something. You walk into a coffee shop for a takeaway coffee, and you're given a choice between three sizes. The medium costs a lot more than the small, but the large is only slightly more expensive than the medium. You really only wanted a medium, but for a few more pennies, why not get the big one? Everybody loves a bargain!

The decoy effect And that's just it. Nearly everybody goes for the large, and all those pennies add up for the seller. You've just experienced the decoy effect, one of many marketing techniques that influence people to spend more than they had intended. The price does not reflect the size of the coffee; instead, it's carefully designed so you feel you're getting a good price by choosing the big one. The medium is the decoy. And even if you know that, you can't resist. It still feels like a good deal.

The hidden fee Among the most annoying marketing techniques is the 'hidden fee', a technique which is often used for online purchases of items like concert tickets. There's a concert you desperately want to see. You find a website with tickets on offer at a much lower price than elsewhere. So you click and start choosing … the date, where to sit, etc. You enter your details and go to the payment page and … What's this? A service fee of €4. OK, they have to make a profit, but then there's an ordering fee of €3. As you go deeper and deeper into the process, there are more extra charges. But you can't turn back now, so you pay, spending fifty percent more than you intended. Marketing companies know this: the more time you spend, the less likely you are to stop. But, you think, at least I've got my tickets!

Scarcity marketing And finally, there's 'scarcity marketing', which exploits the fact that people value things more when they are available in smaller numbers. If you've ever booked a hotel room online, you'll know the phrases 'Only two more rooms at this price' and '14 people are viewing this listing right now!' You need to book now or you'll miss your chance! It's not altogether certain that those numbers – the two more rooms, the 14 people viewing – have any connection with the truth. Still, you'd better make that booking just in case they do.

Consumers are more aware than ever of the different tricks that marketing people use to get them to spend, and spend more. Ironically, that awareness doesn't seem to change our behaviour. Perhaps knowing the tricks makes us feel we are not being fooled – just accepting that it's part of the consumer world!

5B

GRAMMAR

comparative and superlative structures

7A Look at the sentences from the article and find the full comparative or superlative structure.

1 The large is only <u>slightly more expensive than</u> the medium
2 Among the most annoying marketing techniques is the 'hidden fee'.
3 As you go deeper and deeper into the process, there are more extra charges.
4 The more time you spend, the less likely you are to stop.
5 Consumers are more aware than ever of the different tricks that marketers use.

B Look at the sentences (1–5) in Ex 7A and find:

1 two comparatives that use repetition.
2 a comparative that refers to a time period.
3 a word used in a comparative which shows only a small difference.
4 a phrase used in a superlative that means 'one of the'.

C Learn and practise. Go to the Grammar Bank.

▶▶ page 119 **GRAMMAR BANK**

PRONUNCIATION

8A | linking *r* in phrases | Work in pairs and look at the words in bold. Where is *r* pronounced at the end of a word and where is it silent? Why?

1 The best **ever** advert I've seen was one **for** jeans.
2 TV ads **are** becoming **more** and **more** like mini films.
3 Phones **are** getting **cheaper** and **cheaper**.
4 The **more** I buy, the **better** I feel.

B 🔊 **5.04** | Listen and check.

C 🔊 **5.04** | Listen again and say the sentences with the speakers. Focus on the pronunciation of the *r*.

9A Change one or more words in each sentence in Ex 8A to make it true for you.

The best ever advert I've seen was one for a phone.

B Work in pairs. Read out your changed sentences and give an example of what you mean.

SPEAKING

10A Work in pairs and discuss. How could you use the three techniques in the article in Ex 4B to market these products?
- a premium gym membership
- a mobile phone and internet package
- a microwave

B Work in pairs. Look at the notes from a marketing discussion and answer the questions.

1 Which ideas use one of the techniques in the article in Ex 4B?
2 Which two ideas do you think are the most effective? Why?
3 Which tag line* do you like best?

*tag line = a memorable phrase or sentence used in marketing, often at the end of an advert

⟨ **Notes** ...

Target: sell more premium gym memberships

- Free T-shirt and water bottle for new members
- Offer first month free if you apply by midnight tonight, and no charge for cancelling after one month
- Market three levels, e.g. basic, 'be fit', premium; price 'be fit' close to premium
- Bring-a-friend special – 50% discount for 2nd person
- Offer 50% off the personal trainer fees
- Promise a refund if not 100% satisfied

Tag line

- The healthier, the happier
- Best ever offer: first month free
- One of the fastest-growing health clubs in the country

C Work in pairs. Write three ideas and a tag line for the other two products in Ex 10A.

11A You are going to have a discussion to share ideas. Read the Future Skills Box and answer the question.

> **FUTURE SKILLS**
> **Communication**
>
> When people are coming up with ideas, it's important to encourage them in order to help a discussion become more productive. What words could you use in these comments? Can they all be made positive?
>
> I think that's a really .... idea! That's a very .... point.
> What a/an .... idea! Maybe it needs to be a bit more …

B Work in groups. Choose one product in Ex 10A and discuss a marketing campaign. List as many ideas as you can think of.

C Which idea and tag line do you think is the most effective? Does the idea use any particular marketing technique?

D Tell the class about your most effective idea, and explain why you think it is effective.

Unit 5 | Lesson C

5C Which should I buy?

HOW TO ... | summarise information from different sources
VOCABULARY | describing products
PRONUNCIATION | intonation in summarising phrases

VOCABULARY

describing products

1 A Work in pairs and discuss the questions.

1 When you are thinking about buying something, where do you get information about it?
2 Look quickly at the texts in Exs 1B and 2. Where does the different information come from?
3 Have you ever ridden an e-bike? What do you know about them?

B Read the message exchange. What useful information does Sam tell Lynn?

> **Lynn + Sam**
>
> Hi Sam, I'm shopping for an e-bike and you're a bit of an expert. What type should I get? I don't mind paying for something good if it's really worth it. 13:40
>
> Hi Lynn. Big question. There are mountain bikes, cruiser bikes, commuter bikes ... What do you want to use it for? 13:48
>
> Basically for getting to and from work, and for doing shopping. Maybe a bit of exercise, but nothing major. 13:55
>
> OK, so a commuter bike would probably be best for you. 14:01
>
> One question. What if I want to ride in the forest? You know how hilly it is here. Maybe I should get a mountain bike, but I don't want anything too heavy. 14:05
>
> You can't put a rack or a basket on most mountain bikes. They're not good for shopping or carrying a laptop to work and they're often quite heavy. 14:08
>
> OK. But can I ride a commuter bike in the forest? 14:13
>
> Depends. Some models can, like the Dorith and the Wells Rider. I'd recommend one of those, actually. 14:16
>
> What's the difference between those two? 14:22
>
> Good question. Why don't you have a look at some online reviews? 14:25

2 Read the reviews of two e-bikes. How might these help Lynn with her decision?

Review of the Dorith ★★★★ 4 months ago

My overall experience with the Dorith was positive. It was comfortable to ride, though the ride was nothing special. The motor is quiet and the battery range of 80 km is **impressive**. The bike is **solid** and feels very **stable**. At 26 kg it's a bit heavy, but I didn't mind this.

If you're in the market for a **decent** electric bike for commuting and maybe the occasional weekend ride in the hills, but not serious climbing, then the Dorith is a really excellent choice. It's a good all-rounder, very practical, and for £1,899 it's **superb** value.

Review of the Wells Rider ★★★★ 2 days ago

Excellent value, good enough for me!

I purchased the Wells Rider two weeks ago and I've been mostly happy with it. It is especially **suitable** for getting around the city. The small motor means it isn't too heavy, about 22 kg. The only thing I'm disappointed with is the range – the manufacturer promised 60 km on a single charge, and I've lost power after 40 km, which is **acceptable** for me but not what I expected. I've been off-road with the bike and it was a pleasant surprise, it moved really well. For the **reasonable** price of £1,400, I think it's not a bad buy at all!

3 A Match the adjectives in bold in the reviews with the meanings (1–6).

1 good enough for the purpose (2 words) decent
2 very good (2 words)
3 having the right qualities for a particular person or situation
4 fair, not too high (or low) when we talk about price
5 strong, not likely to break easily
6 not falling down easily

B Look at the phrases (a–d) from the reviews. Number them in order from most to least positive.

a not a bad buy
b nothing special
c a pleasant surprise
d an excellent choice 1

C Work in pairs. Talk about things you bought recently. Use words and phrases from Exs 3A and 3B.

62

How to ...
summarise information from different sources

4 A 🔊 **5.05** | Listen to Lynn and her friend discuss the e-bikes. Which one does Lynn decide to buy? Why?

B Work in pairs. Complete each sentence with one word.
1 From .... he says, it depends on what you want to use it for.
2 The only .... is that a mountain bike is no good for carrying things like shopping.
3 According .... Sam, it's quite heavy.
4 Long .... short, it's a better bike.
5 So it's a .... of whether you want to pay more for more range and a better uphill ride?
6 Yes, in the ...., it's a question of how much I want to pay.
7 All .... all, reviewers of both models were happy with their bikes.
8 It all comes .... to the price.
9 Well, just .... something's less expensive, it doesn't mean it's not good.
10 Yes, taking .... into account, I think the Wells Rider is good enough for me.

C 🔊 **5.06** | Listen and check your ideas.

5 A Work in pairs. Put the phrases in bold in Ex 4B into the correct group.

saying where you got the information	From what he says, ...
summing up ideas	Long story short, ...
focusing on a specific point	The only thing is that ...

B Learn and practise. Go to the Grammar Bank.
▶▶ page 120 **GRAMMAR BANK**

PRONUNCIATION

6 A | intonation in summarising phrases | Work in pairs. Look at the phrases in Ex 4B and find the ones that are followed by commas.

B 🔊 **5.07** | Listen to the phrases with commas from Exercise 4B. Does the intonation go up or down at the end of the phrase?

C 🔊 **5.07** | Listen again and say the phrase at the same time as the speaker. Pay attention to intonation.

7 A Think of something that you've recently bought or have read or heard about. Prepare to talk about it using at least four of the phrases in Ex 5A.

B Work with a different partner from Ex 3C and tell them about the item. Pay attention to the intonation of the summarising phrases.

SPEAKING

8 A Work in pairs. What are the features and qualities of a good backpack? Look at the images and discuss.

B Work in pairs. You are going to choose the best backpack for two people. Read the information (a and b) about them. Then go to page 142. Use more detailed information about the backpacks to decide on the best bag for each person.
  a a college student who carries a laptop and some books to and from college every day, and also sometimes takes weekend trips to see friends
  b a businessperson who carries a laptop and documents to and from the office, and also takes short overnight business trips from time to time

MEDIATION SKILLS
selling an idea
explain something clearly to sell an idea to other people

▶▶ page 152 **MEDIATION BANK**

Unit 5 | Lesson D

5D BBC Street Interviews
I do it myself

Dean

GRAMMAR | causative *have* and *get*; reflexive pronouns
SPEAKING | planning an event
WRITING | a meeting summary

Imogen

PREVIEW

1 Work in pairs. Look at the things in the box and answer the questions.

> cook dinner   cut hair   cut the grass
> do the cleaning   do the shopping
> fix things   walk the dog

1 Which things do you do? How often do you do them?
2 Which things does someone else do for you?

Q1: What kind of things do you always do yourself?

Q2: What things do you pay someone to do for you?

VIEW

2 A ▶ Watch the first part of the video. Which speakers are the most similar to you?

B ▶ Watch the first part again. Match the speakers with the reasons that they give for doing things themselves.

1 I can save money.   a Dean
2 I'm the only one who wants to do it.   b Imogen
3 I want to solve my own problems.   c Rory
4 I'm very good at it.   d Jane

3 A Think of a job you can ask other people to do for each item (1–6).

1 garden   2 car   3 hair   4 food   5 windows   6 nails

B ▶ Watch the second part of the video. What do the speakers ask other people to do for the items in Ex 3A?

C ▶ Work in pairs and complete the sentences. Then watch again and check your ideas.

1 He does the best job, so it's .... the money.
2 So, I get my food delivered, I get my hair .... and I get my nails ....
3 We get our windows .... every month.
4 I get a mechanic to .... my car every year.
5 I'd get someone to .... my hair rather than do it myself.

GRAMMAR

causative *have* and *get*; reflexive pronouns

4 A Look at the sentences (a–d) from the video and answer the questions (1–3).

a I actually always **cut my** own **hair**.
b I always **get my hair cut** professionally.
c I always **have my car cleaned**.
d I **get a mechanic to check** my car.

1 Who does the things in sentences a–d: the speaker or someone else?
2 In sentences b and c what grammatical form is *cut* and *cleaned*?
3 In sentence d what verb form is used after *get*?

B Complete the reflexive pronouns. Look at the example below and the last sentence in Ex 3C to help.

I	you	he	she	it	we	you	they
		himself					

C Learn and practise. Go to the Grammar Bank.

▶▶ page 121 **GRAMMAR BANK**

64

5D

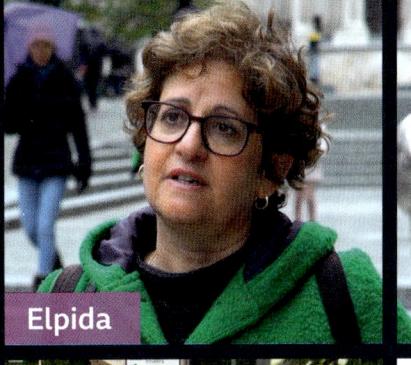

BBC

SPEAKING

planning an event

5 A Work in groups and choose one of the projects below. Make a list of at least eight tasks that need to be done.
- organise a surprise birthday party for a friend
- renovate and decorate a house
- something else

B Work alone. For each task on your list, put S (self) if you want to do it, and P (pay) if you want to get someone else to do it.

C Look at the Key phrases. Which can you use when you discuss your ideas in the group?

> **KEY PHRASES**
> We should do it ourselves.
> It's better if we get someone to do it.
> Does anyone want to suggest anything?
> It's more professional/expensive/personal if …
> Does anyone have any other ideas?
> I'm good at … , so I'd be happy to do it.
> I've done something like this before so I could …
> What do you think?

D Work in your group. Have a meeting and discuss the agenda below. Make notes on your decisions.

Agenda

1. The purpose of the meeting
2. Action points: Who will do each task? When?
3. Overall decisions
4. Questions still to be discussed
5. Date and place of the next meeting

A: I think we should have the room decorated for the party. It's more professional.
B: I think we should decorate it ourselves. It's too expensive if we get someone to do it.

6 A Look at the Key phrases again and find three phrases for asking people their opinion.

B Work with other students. Tell them about your plan, and ask for their opinion and suggestions. Use the Key phrases.

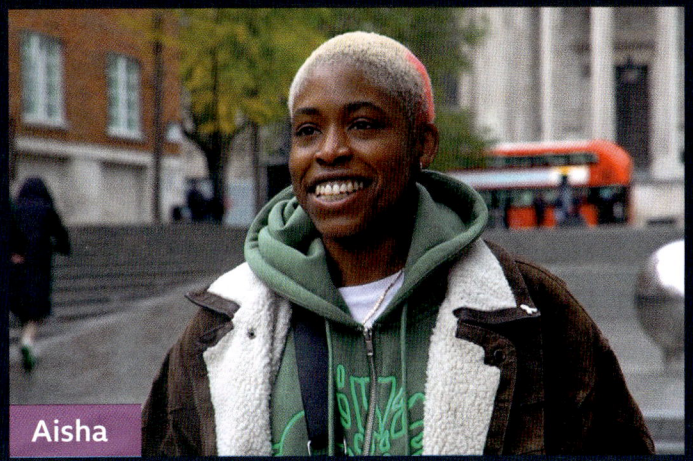

WRITING

a meeting summary

7 A Turn to page 140 and read the summary of a meeting.

B Look at the headings from the meeting summary below. Use these and your notes to answer the questions.

> **Overview**
> **Action points**
> **To be discussed**
> **Next meeting**

1. What information can you put in your 'Overview'?
2. How many points can you put in the 'Action points'?
3. What ideas can you put in the 'To be discussed' section?

C Write a summary of your discussion in Ex 5D. Use the headings in Ex 7B and the model on page 140.

D Read other students' summaries. Whose plans do you think are the most expensive?

65

5 REVIEW

GRAMMAR

clauses of purpose: to, so as to, in order to/that, so that

1 A Complete the text with two words in each gap.

Packing light before your flight

It's important to follow a system when packing for a trip ¹ __so that__ you don't leave anything behind OR carry too much with you.

- Pack the day before leaving ² _____ that there's no panic on departure day.
- Get a friend to help ³ _____ you don't make bad decisions.
- Make a written list so as ⁴ _____ overpack.
- Put all the things you think you need out on your bed in ⁵ _____ see how big a suitcase you need.
- Notice the unnecessary things and remove them so ⁶ _____ to carry more than you need.
- If possible, choose a suitcase with wheels in ⁷ _____ it's easier to move.
- Pack your suitcase, and weigh it ⁸ _____ sure you don't have to pay extra.

If the weight is OK, you're ready to go! Have a great trip!

B Work in pairs and discuss. Which tips are:
- obvious and unnecessary to say?
- useful or not useful to you?

comparative and superlative structures

2 Complete the sentences with comparative or superlative structures using the correct form of the words in brackets.

1 My favourite types of food are among __the unhealthiest__ ones that there are. (unhealthy)
2 When things get difficult, I just try _____ to do my best. (hard)
3 The _____ I get, _____ I become. (old, happy)
4 One of _____ days of my life was this past year. (enjoyable)
5 I think it's great that people nowadays are living _____ than _____ . (long)
6 Winters in my country are now _____ than _____ . (cold)

causative *have* and *get*

3 Work in pairs. Which of you does more of the things in the box themselves? Ask questions to find out.

| buy food | clean your house | cut your hair |
| do the laundry | fix your computer | wash your car |

VOCABULARY

4 A Add vowels to complete the phrases.
1 400 euros is a r_ _s_n_bl_ price for a good mobile phone.
2 I can get a d_c_nt lunch for 8 euros in a restaurant in my hometown.
3 I don't think it's w_rth paying more than 60 euros for a hotel room.
4 50 euros for a good pair of sunglasses is n_t a b_d b_y.
5 Sometimes very c_nf_d_nt people can seem a bit _ggr_ss_v_ .
6 When someone is d_r_ct with me, I feel uncomfortable.
7 The older I get, the less p_t__nt I am.
8 Amazingly few people are truly s_ns_bl_ .

B Work in pairs and discuss the sentences in Ex 4A. Do you agree or disagree with them?

5 A Choose the correct options (A–C) to complete the text.

Shoppers beware!

Every ¹_____ knows about pricing tricks like putting 99 at the end of the price, but what about other things a shop does ²_____ get you to ³_____ a purchase? One example is the location of products. Even if you don't have a particular brand ⁴_____ , you're more likely to buy things because shops put them at eye-level ⁵_____ you see them first. In supermarkets, the essential things (milk, bread, etc.) are at the back of the shop so ⁶_____ make you pass everything else on the way.

And shops also pay attention to your senses to ⁷_____ you. Take music, for example. ⁸_____ the music, ⁹_____ you feel and the more time you spend shopping.

And in the end, shops know that price is king so you'll find products ¹⁰_____ in almost every part of a shop. After all, who can say no to ¹¹_____ ?

Next ⌄

	A	B	C
1	hunter	consumer	buyer
2	in order	so that	to
3	make	do	buy
4	tradition	quality	loyalty
5	in order	so that	to
6	as to	as not to	that not
7	get	influence	interfere
8	The slower	Slower is	To slow
9	calmer do	more solid	the calmer
10	on cheap	on offer	to offer
11	a good deal	a big deal	the good deal

B 🔊 R5.01 | Listen and check your answers.

66

places

6

VLOGS

Q: What's your favourite city?

1 ▶ Watch the video. Note down the speakers' favourite cities. Why do they like them?

2 Work in pairs and answer the question. Give your reasons.

GSE LEARNING OBJECTIVES

6A LISTENING | Understand people talking about great neighbourhoods: areas of a city

Describe your favourite neighbourhood: *so* and *such*

Pronunciation: intonation for emphasis with *so* and *such*

Write instructions for how to get somewhere

6B READING | Understand an article about epic journeys: challenges; idioms

Describe a challenging experience: *be/get used to*

Pronunciation: *be/get used to*

6C HOW TO … | ask for and confirm information: city transport

Pronunciation: fast speech: *just*

6D BBC PROGRAMME | Understand a TV programme about how China has changed

Talk about what a place is famous for

Write a description of a business idea

Unit 6 | Lesson A

6A In the city

GRAMMAR | *so* and *such*
VOCABULARY | areas of a city
PRONUNCIATION | intonation for emphasis with *so* and *such*

Barranco district, Lima

VOCABULARY

areas of a city

1 A Work in pairs. Look at the photos and answer the questions.
  1 Do you think these look like interesting places to visit? Why/Why not?
  2 When you visit a city, what kinds of things do you like to do?

B Read the article. Does it include any of your ideas in Ex 1A?

What makes a great place to visit?

What are the things that make a neighbourhood great and make us want to go back there? Is it the **historic buildings** and impressive architecture? Or, away from the **wealthy areas**, you might want to enjoy attractions such as **colourful murals** and bright street art. Perhaps you want to get away from the **high-rise buildings** and walk through **tree-lined avenues** or sit in an old square with a **relaxed atmosphere** and watch the local people come and go. Or find a spot to enjoy a coffee in a more **run-down part of the city**. There may be washing hanging from the windows and paint peeling from the doors, but that makes you feel closer to the lives of the people who live here. A great neighbourhood might have a **busy street market**. It could be **an ideal spot for** some shopping, with interesting, independent shops. Or maybe it's the social scene that you're looking for; somewhere with a **sense of community** and friendly cafés or restaurants, where you can meet up with people, listen to some music or look at art. Or perhaps you're looking for **lively nightlife**. Whatever it is you enjoy, sometimes a great neighbourhood has these things, and then everyone finds out about it. Soon it turns into a popular **tourist spot**, which can mean it loses its appeal. But that's OK, great neighbourhoods change all the time, so it won't be long before you find a new place to visit.

2 A Match the phrases in bold in the article with these meanings.
  1 wide streets with trees planted along the sides
  2 very old and important buildings
  3 somewhere that a lot of people from outside the city like to visit
  4 very tall buildings
  5 a place which is very good for something
  6 an area in the city which is not in good condition
  7 places where there are a lot of rich people
  8 when a lot of people go out to meet each other in the evening or at night
  9 an outdoor market where there are a lot of people
  10 a feeling that you belong in this place and with these people
  11 large paintings in bright colours on a wall
  12 a feeling that the area is peaceful and calm

B Work in pairs. Think about the place where you live or an area near to where you live. Ask and answer the questions.
  1 What is your favourite part of this area? Why do you like it?
  2 Are there any places in the area you have never visited? Why?
  3 Where would you recommend for a tourist to go first? Why?
  4 If you could choose where to live in this area, where would it be? Why?
  5 Which is your favourite spot for shopping? Why?
  6 Which area is best for going out with friends? Why?

6A

LISTENING

3 A 🔊 **6.01** | Listen to three people talking about the places in the photos. For each speaker, tick the things they mention.

Logan

> tree-lined avenues
> lovely spot for walking
> wealthy neighbourhood
> interesting architecture
> lively nightlife

Cecilia

> fantastic views of the ocean
> colourful murals   lively nightlife
> popular tourist spot   run-down area
> bookshops

Amy

> colourful murals   busy market
> food from all over the world
> bakeries   coffee shops
> live music   sense of community

B 🔊 **6.01** | Listen again. What examples do the speakers give to illustrate the statements?

Rosedale
1 It's a wealthy neighbourhood.
   huge tree-lined avenues, historic century-old houses
2 It has a lot of green spaces.

Barranco
3 It's an artistic neighbourhood.
4 It's a popular area.

Yarraville
5 It's a great place to eat and drink.
6 It has a lot of things to do.

C Work in pairs. Say which neighbourhood you would like to visit. Explain why.

GRAMMAR

so and such

4 A Work in pairs. Look at the sentences (a–h) from the recording and answer the questions (1–2).
   a It's **so beautiful** to walk around.
   b It's **so peaceful that** you hardly realise you're still in the city.
   c The area has become **so popular that** it's quite a tourist spot now.
   d There's **so much** to do in Yarraville.
   e There are **so many** diverse neighbourhoods in Toronto.
   f It has **such a friendly, welcoming atmosphere**.
   g It has **such lively nightlife**, too.
   h It has **such a great sense of community**.
   1 Complete the rules using *so* or *such*.
      We use .... before an adjective (without a noun).
      We use .... before the quantifiers *much* and *many*.
      We use .... before a noun (with or without an adjective).
   2 Tick the options that are possible.
      We can use *so/such* (*a*) + adjective/noun + *that*:
      • to emphasise a point.
      • to talk about the results or consequences of something.
      • to explain the reason for something.

B Learn and practise. Go to the Grammar Bank.

▶ page 122 **GRAMMAR BANK**

PRONUNCIATION

5 A | intonation for emphasis with *so* and *such* | Complete the sentences with *so* or *such*. Which words carry the main stress?
   1 It was .... interesting to learn about the history of the place.
   2 It was .... a lovely place to visit.
   3 The food was .... delicious that we decided to go back the next day.
   4 The neighbourhood had .... a welcoming atmosphere that we didn't want to leave.

B 🔊 **6.02** | Listen and check.

C Work in pairs. Practise conversations about visiting cities. Student A: Go to page 139. Student B: go to page 141.

Yarraville district, Melbourne

Rosedale district, Toronto

69

Unit 6 | Lesson A

SPEAKING

6 A Plan to talk about a favourite neighbourhood either in your city/town or one you have visited. Make notes on these points.
- where it is in the city/town
- how to describe the area
- what it's known for
- things to see and do
- what the atmosphere is like
- the best time to visit

B Read the Future Skills box and do the task.

FUTURE SKILLS
Collaboration

To find out more, we can ask speakers to give more details about what they said. Before you do the activity in Ex 6C, prepare to ask for more details about some of the following: how to get to the area, the best day and time to go there, how much money to bring, what to eat there, and your own ideas.

C Work in groups. Talk about your favourite neighbourhood. Ask for more details about the neighbourhood each speaker describes.

WRITING

instructions for how to get somewhere

7 A Work in pairs and discuss. How do you plan for a trip to a new area? What do you like/dislike about travelling somewhere new?

B Read the email and answer the questions.
1 Why do you think Sara is travelling to Barcelona?
2 Where does Max suggest meeting?
3 Why does he think Sara will like the area?
4 How does he suggest Sara travels to the restaurant?

Hi Sara

I hope everything is OK for your visit to Barcelona this weekend. We're very excited to have you at the conference. We're planning to go out to eat on Friday night in the El Born district and we hope you'll join us. It's a really lively area quite near your hotel, with lots of tapas bars and restaurants to choose from. It's such a lovely place to walk around in the evening and enjoy the atmosphere of Barcelona. I'm sure you'll like it. I know your flight arrives quite late, so I'll book a place and you can meet us there, if that's OK. The restaurant is called El Xampanyet and the address is Carrer de Montcada, 22.

The easiest way to get to there from the airport is to take the airport train. Get off at Passeig de Gracia. Then, from the same platform, take a train to Estació de França. Trains come about every 5 minutes, so you won't have to wait long. The station is just across the road from the El Born area. The restaurant is about a 5-minute walk, 500 m down the road from the Picasso museum.

We'll be there from 9 p.m. Looking forward to seeing you there.

I'll give you my number in case there are any problems. It's +34 7578547623.

Best,

Max

---

8 A Look at the phrases for giving directions. Find similar examples in the email and add them to the correct section.

Suggesting a route
The fastest / best / cheapest / [1] .... way to get to X from Y is to …
It's about a 10-minute drive / [2] ....
The journey takes about 20 minutes.

Detailed instructions
Take the bus / a taxi / [3] .... / [4] ....
Get on / [5] .... at …
Walk down …
Turn right / left …

Describing the exact location
X is just opposite / [6] .... Y.
X is 500 m down the road from Y.
It's on the corner of X and Y.

B Complete the sentences with the words and phrases in the box.

20-minute	best way	get off
on the corner	opposite	
take the bus	walk down	

1 The .... to get to the city centre is to .... from the airport.
2 It's a .... journey and it costs €12.
3 .... at Plaça de Catalunya.
4 .... Passeig de Gràcia and take the first right.
5 The café is .... of Carrer de Casp and Carrer de Bruc.
6 It's just .... the taxi rank.

C Think of good place to meet (for a meal, live music, etc.) in the neighbourhood you described in Ex 6C. Write an email to a friend or colleague telling them where to meet. Explain why you chose this place and give detailed directions to get there.

6B Great journeys

GRAMMAR | be/get used to
VOCABULARY | challenges; idioms
PRONUNCIATION | be/get used to

VOCABULARY

challenges

1 A Work in groups. Discuss the questions.
1. Who in your group has travelled the most and the furthest?
2. Has anyone in your group made a long or difficult journey?
3. What is the best thing about travelling? What is the worst?

B Read the blog post and comments. Which comment do you agree with more? Why?

C Work in pairs. Answer the questions about the words in bold in the blog post.
1. Which two adjectives do we use to describe something difficult?
2. Which two words are verbs? Which means 'get free'?
3. Which two words use prefixes to make them negative? What is the meaning of the positive form?
4. Which three words are nouns? Which is the opposite of 'danger'?

2 A Look at the photo above and the photos on page 73. What do you think are the most challenging things about travelling in these places? Write sentences about each photo using the words in the blog post.

Climbing a mountain covered in snow is **tough**.

B Share your ideas with your partner.

Inside the mind of the adventurer
Lessons from the road

Why do people go on long, difficult journeys? Why climb mountains or cross deserts?

These journeys are **tough** – full of sleepless nights and poor food. Why do people face the **difficulties** and the discomfort? And why **risk** injury or worse? When **conditions** are **challenging** – the rain won't stop and there's no bed to sleep in – surely it's easier to stay at home among **familiar** objects and people. Long journeys are also **unpredictable**: you don't know what will happen next. Is this why people do it: to **escape** the **safety** and boredom of life at home? Some say the journey is more important than the destination, that when we face **unfamiliar** things – languages, people, customs – we learn about ourselves.

Comments

Syz22: Travelling has changed my life. Even if it's not easy at times, it's always so rewarding. Getting to know new cultures allows you to look at the world differently.
Reply Favourite

TomCyp: I don't understand people who put themselves in those situations. I'd much rather stay at home! There's a lot to see and experience where I live. You don't have to travel hundreds of miles to have an adventure.
Reply Favourite

Unit 6 | Lesson B

READING

3 A Work in pairs. Student A: Read Text A on page 73. Student B: Read Text B. As you read, make notes about the following.
1 the achievement
2 difficulties and challenges
3 the positives
4 things learnt

B Tell your partner about your text. Use your notes to help you.

C Discuss the questions.
1 Which of the journeys sounds the most challenging? In what ways?
2 Which of the journeys would you prefer to do? Why?
3 Is there a long or special journey you would like to go on? Tell your partner about it.

4 A Look at the idiom in bold in sentences 1 and 2 from the reading texts. What do you think it means?
1 Local people warned him about how tough it would be, but he had **set his mind on** making his trip and nothing would stop him.
2 Despite all these difficulties, Lyn Man and her husband had **set their minds on** finishing their journey, and so they continued.

B Find the idiom *out of your comfort zone* in your text. Work with other students to guess what it means. Look at the information that comes before and after the idioms to help you.

C Learn and practise. Go to the Vocabulary Bank.

▶ page 135 **VOCABULARY BANK** idioms

GRAMMAR

be/get used to

5 A Read the sentences (1–4). Complete the definitions (a and b) with *be used to* or *get used to*.
1 He **got used to** walking up to 40 km per day.
2 For those who **are used to** all the comforts of home …
3 … **getting used to** living in a tiny space and managing with just four hours sleep a night are huge challenges.
4 After sixteen months … he **was used to** relying on strangers.

a try(ing) to start feeling comfortable in a new situation (a process): ....
b feel comfortable and familiar with a situation because you have done it for a long time (a state): ....

B Which type of word CANNOT follow *be/get used to*?
1 noun   2 *-ing* form   3 infinitive

C Learn and practise. Go to the Grammar Bank.

▶ page 123 **GRAMMAR BANK**

PRONUNCIATION

6 A 🔊 6.03 | *be/get used to* | Listen to the sentences (1–4). How is the *s* in *used to* pronounced?
1 I'm used to travelling alone.
2 We're used to the ocean.
3 I got used to the cold.
4 We're getting used to living on a boat.

B 🔊 6.03 | Listen again and repeat.

C Complete the sentences with your own ideas and read them to a partner. Pay attention to your pronunciation of *used to*.
1 When I … , I had to get used to …
2 After a while, I got used to …
3 I'm now completely used to …

SPEAKING

7 A Think of a challenging experience that you had and prepare to tell other students. Use the ideas in the box or your own ideas. Think about the questions.

> changing school   a journey   a long hike   a mountain climb
> moving to a new town/city   a new job   a new project
> playing a new sport   starting university   a trip abroad

- What was the background (where, when, who was involved)?
- What unpredictable things happened and why was it challenging?
- How did you feel?
- How did you deal with the situation in the end?
- Did you get used to it?
- What things or people helped you?

B Work in groups. Take turns to describe your experiences.

A: Walking across a continent

Motivated by his love of Asia, Rory Stewart walked across huge areas of the continent in the early 2000s. Asked why he was doing it, he replied that there was something magical about leaving a line of footprints behind him across a continent.

He'd always tried to find experiences that were out of his comfort zone, which had prepared him for the hardships of this journey. He got used to walking up to 40 km per day. Local people warned him about how tough it would be, but he had set his mind on making his trip and nothing would stop him. He passed mountains covered in deep snow, slept on villagers' floors and shared their food. Walking through a jungle, he noted the tracks of leopards. In Iran, he wrote about truck stops and chicken farms and in Nepal, the farmers looking after their white oxen. Along the Indian-Nepali border, he followed a line of stones and looked out for signs of ancient history in the land.

He had to get used to the food and eating habits of his hosts. The Kurdish areas of Iran had no vegetables, meat or fruit in winter. He ate bread three times a day, sometimes with goat's cheese if he was lucky. In Pakistan and India he ate bread and lentil curry. In Nepal, meals were at 10 or 11 a.m. and then again in the evening. He got hungry during the day, so he carried snacks with him.

While staying in the homes of villagers, he spent two hours every evening writing in notebooks. He photocopied these pages and posted them to Scotland when he could. In his book about the journey, *The Places in Between*, he describes how people with much less than him welcomed him into their houses. After sixteen months crossing borders between Iran, Pakistan, India and Nepal on foot, he was used to relying on strangers. He learnt that, wherever you go, there are good, kind people.

B: Sailing across an ocean

Sailing across an ocean is extremely challenging. Waves, wind and wild weather make the journey tough and sailors need to be able to operate out of their comfort zone. For those who are used to all the comforts of home, getting used to living in a tiny space and managing with just four hours sleep a night are huge challenges.

Heather Lyn Mann, whose ocean voyage with her husband lasted six years and inspired her book *Ocean of Insight*, describes all the unpredictable things that made life difficult. She experienced injuries, damage to the boat, engines that broke down and the psychological challenge of missing her children. There were also moments of fear, when she believed she might die. Her boat engine overheated dangerously five times. Twice she had to be rescued by bigger boats. On dark nights, when the water is invisible, it felt as if she was travelling blindly through space. Despite all these difficulties, Lyn Man and her husband had set their minds on finishing their journey, and so they continued.

There were positives. Lyn Mann talks about the beauty of the natural world. She describes how sailing on the ocean gave her a chance to learn directly from nature, from the waves, the sun and the moon, and to discover a new way to live. She learnt to see changes in the water, like the different colours that appear as the ocean becomes warmer. She saw all kinds of sea animals, including turtles and whales racing her boat, and gradually got used to living on the water.

At some point in her journey she realised that, in order to sail successfully, she had to forget her human schedule. Everything needed to be based on the weather conditions and the conditions dictated by the ocean. For her, the message was clear: nature is in charge; she was just passing through.

Unit 6 | Lesson C

6C City transport

HOW TO ... | ask for and confirm information
VOCABULARY | city transport
PRONUNCIATION | fast speech: *just*

VOCABULARY

city transport

1 A Work in pairs. Look at the photos and discuss the questions.

1. Have you ever used these types of transport to travel around a city? Which ones?
2. What do you think is the best way to travel around a city? Why?

B Read the article. What problems are mentioned with the different types of transport?

2 A Complete the sentences (1–6) with the words and phrases in bold in the article.

1. I try to avoid travelling around the city during .... when there is so much traffic.
2. I don't like cycling in the city unless there are plenty of .... to use. I find it much safer.
3. For a small .... the train ticket can be sent to your home address.
4. It's important to keep the .... low in the city to avoid accidents.
5. I have a travel pass which gives me .... around the city, so I can go wherever I want.
6. I don't often get a taxi as they are quite expensive, but when I do, I always ....

B Work in groups. Are any of the sentences in Ex 2A true for you? Give examples.

Best ways to get around the city

The best tourist cities have excellent public transport systems: trains, subways, buses, boats and trams that can get you quickly and cheaply to where you want to go. As technology improves, there's an ever-growing menu of options. With the introduction of car-sharing and bike-hire schemes, ideas about what is public and what is private transport are changing. Here are some of our favourites:

E-scooters

Cheaper than taxis, less effort than a bike and more convenient than buses, electric scooters have become popular in many cities. They can be great in cities which are flat and have good **cycle lanes**, like Amsterdam and Copenhagen. They are not popular with everyone, though, and there have been increasing numbers of accidents, especially where riders don't respect the 20 km/hour **speed limits**.

Bike-share

Public bike-sharing systems have been great for cities trying to reduce the amount of traffic on their streets. They've been really successful in cities like London, Dublin and Barcelona. You don't need to **book in advance** and often a small fee will give you **unlimited travel** for a set period of time. But it's important to return within that time or you have to pay an **additional charge**. In China, the schemes were so popular that at one point, Chinese cities had far too many public bicycles. The bike-share companies failed and hundreds of thousands of bikes were abandoned.

Tuk-tuks

Originally from Thailand, tuk-tuks are now popular in cities around the world, from Cambodia to Bangladesh, Guatemala, India and Peru. These small vehicles can be a great way to see a city. Lisbon, Portugal has become the e-tuk capital of the world as their tuk-tuks are electric and pollution-free. One tip for taking a tuk-tuk – try to avoid **rush hour**; otherwise you might find yourself sitting in a traffic jam with car fumes in your face!

How to ...
ask for and confirm information

3 A 🔊 **6.04** | Listen to the conversation. What does Tonya recommend?

a a night trip on the Thames Clipper from Westminster to the South Bank
b a Thames River cruise from London Bridge to Westminster
c a day trip on the Thames Clipper from Westminster to Greenwich

B 🔊 **6.04** | Listen again. Are the statements about the trip Tonya recommends True (T) or False (F)?

1 It is more expensive than some other tours.
2 You don't need to buy a special ticket.
3 There is just one main route and it goes from Westminster to Greenwich.
4 You can see many famous landmarks from the boat.
5 You can buy food and drink on the boat.
6 A guided tour is included with your ticket.

4 A How do the speakers ask for and confirm information? Complete the sentences.

1 So what _____ is the Thames Clipper is cheaper.
2 I didn't _____ what you said about …
3 Sorry, can you just say that last _____ again?
4 So let me just _____ I've got this right.
5 In other _____, we see nearly everything.
6 Have I got this _____? There isn't a guided tour.

B 🔊 **6.05** | Listen and check.

C Look at the phrases in Ex 4A. Which ask for repetition? Which are used to check information?

D Learn and practise. Go to the Grammar Bank.

▶ page 124 **GRAMMAR BANK**

PRONUNCIATION

5 A 🔊 **6.06** | **fast speech: *just*** | Listen to the phrases. Add the word *just* to the sentences.

1 Could you go over those options again, please?
2 So let me check, …
3 Can you say that last bit again, please?

B How is *just* pronounced in fast speech? Why do we sometimes add it to sentences?

C Work in pairs. Add *just* to the sentences (1–4) and practise saying them fast.

1 Could I check something with you?
2 Let me ask you a question …
3 Can you say the last bit again please?
4 Can you go over those options?

SPEAKING

6 A Use the prompts to complete the conversation between a tourist (A) and someone working in a cruise office (B).

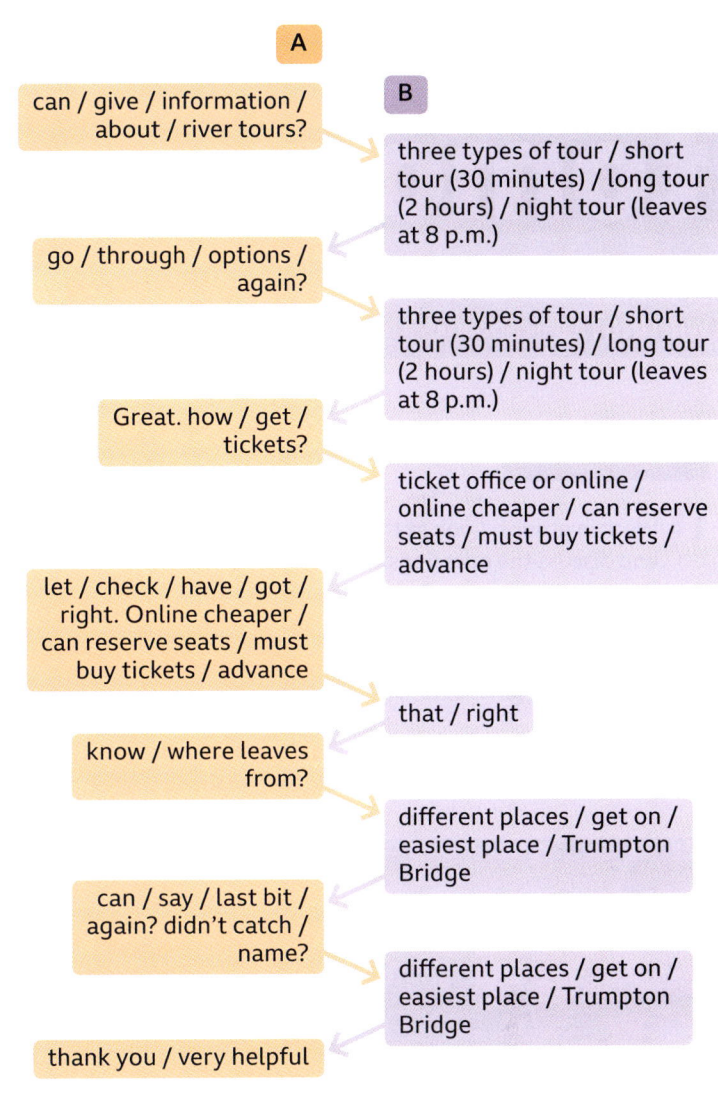

A
- can / give / information / about / river tours?
- go / through / options / again?
- Great. how / get / tickets?
- let / check / have / got / right. Online cheaper / can reserve seats / must buy tickets / advance
- know / where leaves from?
- can / say / last bit / again? didn't catch / name?
- thank you / very helpful

B
- three types of tour / short tour (30 minutes) / long tour (2 hours) / night tour (leaves at 8 p.m.)
- three types of tour / short tour (30 minutes) / long tour (2 hours) / night tour (leaves at 8 p.m.)
- ticket office or online / online cheaper / can reserve seats / must buy tickets / advance
- that / right
- different places / get on / easiest place / Trumpton Bridge
- different places / get on / easiest place / Trumpton Bridge

B Work in pairs and take turns. Roleplay the conversation. Use the flowchart in Ex 6A to help.

7 Work in pairs. Ask for and give information about different types of transport. Student A: Go to page 144. Student B: Go to page 143.

8 🔗 Look up some interesting ways to travel around a city you would like to visit. Can you find information about a specific tour you would recommend? In the next lesson work with a partner and tell them about the trip/tour you chose and why.

MEDIATION SKILLS
collaborating on a task
discuss a proposal

▶ page 153 **MEDIATION BANK**

Unit 6 | Lesson D

6D BBC Documentary
A city of tomorrow

SPEAKING | a discussion about what a place is famous for
WRITING | a description of a business idea

PREVIEW

1 A Work in groups. Look at the photo of Shenzhen, China, and discuss the questions.
1. What can you guess about the city? Think about population, technology, architecture and culture.
2. What might it be like to live there? How might it be different from where you live now?

B Read the programme information. How has Shenzhen changed and what do you think Reggie might do there?

VIEW

2 A ▶ Watch the BBC video clip and answer the questions.
1. Why do you think this episode is called 'City of the Future'?
2. Why did the person Reggie meets go to live in China?
3. What are some of the inventions that Reggie sees?

B ▶ Complete the sentences with the words in the box. Work with a partner and look up any words you don't know. Watch again and check.

| addictive | expats | innovators | metropolis | pace |

1. It's become a teeming .... of over 12 million.
2. Among Shenzhen's population are a growing number of ....
3. It's just the speed of change here. It's actually ....
4. .... from all over come here with their ideas.
5. The .... of change here is undeniable.

C Work in groups and discuss the questions.
1. What might be interesting about Shenzhen as a city, and what might you like/dislike about it?
2. Reggie says not much has changed in his lifetime in the place where he grew up, compared to Shenzhen. What about where you grew up? Have there been many changes in your lifetime?

Reggie in China

Reggie in China is a BBC travel programme. Reggie, a British presenter, visits different parts of China and sees how the country is transforming both itself and the world. In this episode, Reggie goes to Shenzhen. Until the late 1970s, Shenzhen consisted of farmland and fishing villages and had just 30,000 inhabitants. Now it's a centre of new technology and home to 12 million people.

6D

SPEAKING

a discussion about what a place is famous for

3A 🔊 **6.07** | Listen to Lupita talking about Oviedo in Spain. Make notes about the following.

1 architecture   2 food   3 language

B 🔊 **6.07** | Listen again and tick the Key phrases you hear.

> **KEY PHRASES**
>
> These traditions have stayed the same …
> An example of the culture is …
> One of the best-known … is …
> … is world-famous
> … is famous for its …
> So, for example, let's take …
> Another speciality of the region is …
> It's well-known for its …
> When it comes to … , the region even has …

4A Think of a city or town that is famous for something. Prepare to tell other students about it. Use your ideas or the ideas in Ex 3A. Make notes using some of the Key phrases.

B Work in groups. Tell other students about the place you chose.

WRITING

a description of a business idea

BBC

5 You are going to think of a business idea or a new company based in a particular place. Read the example, then complete the table by adding short notes (1–3).

FLD Global is a company based in India that is led by Bishan Pataudi. It invites start-up businesses to develop their new environmental technology in its Bengaluru office. The young innovators who go there include a lot of expats. For example, there are people from Denmark, the US, Ghana and Australia. All the inventions they are working on are connected to the environment. One example is a type of plastic that is made from plants. Another is a jacket with sensors that give you information about pollution levels in the air. One of the main reasons FLD Global is based in Bengaluru is that the city has a strong focus on technology. For instance, India's two biggest IT companies are based there, and it is known as The Silicon Valley of India. FLD Global has a motto: 'Build today to create tomorrow'.

Name of company	FLD Global
Who runs the business	Bishan Pataudi
Who works there	Innovators; a lot of [1]
What field	Environmental technology
Where	Bengaluru, India
Why there	Focus on [2]
Company motto	[3]

6A Read sentences 1 and 2. Which is the main point? What is the purpose of the other sentence?

1 The young innovators who go there include a lot of expats.
2 For example, there are people from Denmark, the US, Ghana and Australia.

B Find other main points and examples in the text. Which words are used to introduce the examples?

C Discuss the questions in pairs.

1 Why do you think it is important to give examples in texts?
2 How do examples help the reader?

7A Think of a place and imagine a business or project you could run there. Use the questions below to help you.

- What does the company do?
- Where is it based?
- What is it called?
- What type of people work there?
- Why is the company based in this particular place? What advantages does this place have?
- What is the company motto?

B Write a description of your ideas, including main points and examples. Use the text in Ex 5 to help you.

C Work in pairs. Read your partner's description. Do you think their business or project will be successful?

77

6 REVIEW

GRAMMAR

so and such

1 A Complete the sentences with *so*, *such* or *such a*.

1 We had .... good time in Turkey that we're planning to go back next year.
2 The food in the new restaurant is .... good that we've been going once a week.
3 The reason I love Mexico is that the people are .... welcoming.
4 We had .... fun on our cycling holiday. It was great.
5 Our Chinese hosts treated us .... well that we became friends.
6 The train is .... great way to travel. It's so easy and relaxing.
7 In Brazil, everyone was .... friendly.
8 Our Italian friends have .... style. They dress really well.

B Make sentences about places, people or travel using *so* and *such*. Compare with other students.

be/get used to

2 A Read the situation and then choose the correct words to complete the advice.

Paul, from Florida, USA, is thinking of moving to the UK. Minty is giving advice.

M: You'll need to ¹**be / get** used to driving on the left.
P: That won't be a problem. I ²**get used / used** to live in Japan. They drive on the left, too.
M: Then there's the British accent. It's probably not too hard to ³**be / get** used to.
P: ⁴**I'm / get** used to it already! Have you forgotten my wife is British?
M: Do you think you'll be able to ⁵**get / be** used to the weather?
P: Oh, ⁶**I'll get / 'm** used to that easily. I love the rain.

B Work in pairs. Think of advice and questions for two of the following situations. Use *be/get used to*.

- someone from another country (you choose which) is coming to live in your country
- a friend is getting a pet (you choose the animal)
- your colleague is starting a hobby that you have done for a long time
- someone is coming to live in your home

Are you used to hot weather? You'll need to get used to our climate.

VOCABULARY

3 A Complete the words by adding the missing letters.

My city has incredible architecture. It's full of ¹h_ _ _ _ric buildings from the seventeenth century. Some are probably ²f_ _ _liar to you. It's illegal to build new ³h_ _ _-rise buildings there, so the city has good views, too.

Where I live is very ⁴r_ _-down with a lot of broken windows and rubbish on the street. It's ⁵t_ _gh to find work there and many people have no job. Also, ⁶s_ _ _ty can be a problem at night as it's quite dangerous.

My town is ⁷ch_ _ _ _ging to get to because it's high in the mountains. But it's an ideal ⁸s_ _t if you want to ⁹e_ _ _pe from a big city.

B Work in pairs. Name as many of the following as you can.
- a historic building near where you live
- an ideal spot to escape from your normal routine
- a place with a lively atmosphere

4 A Choose the correct options (A–C) to complete the text.

Astronaut

They drive the crew to the launch pad. You stand and look up at this spaceship seventeen storeys high, with its huge rocket boosters on each side. You feel fear and excitement. Before, you were ¹........ busy training that you didn't have time to feel scared. You didn't think you were ²........ your life. Now it becomes real.

You take a lift to the launch platform thirty metres in the sky. You go into a white room and put on your equipment. Next, you look into a camera and say goodbye to your family. The other astronauts become your new family. ³........ used to them and their habits; you've been training together for months.

You enter the shuttle. Inside it's tiny. It's one of many things you have to ⁴........ . You are strapped in and you check your equipment one last time.

Space is silent, but the rocket isn't. The engines make ⁵........ a loud noise you can't hear yourself think. Soon you're travelling at 17,500 miles per hour. After eight and a half minutes, you've left Earth's atmosphere. Suddenly, the noise stops. You remove your helmet, let it go and watch it float. You trained for these ⁶........ . Everything is ⁷........ . Yet nothing will ever be the same after you've been in space.

1 A	so	B too	C such
2 A	at risk	B challenging	C risking
3 A	You	B You're	C Getting
4 A	used to	B be familiar	C get used to
5 A	such	B really	C so
6 A	difficulties	B conditions	C risks
7 A	unpredictable	B familiar	C used to

B 🔊 **R6.01** | Listen and check your answers.

78

connect 7

VLOGS

Q: What's your favourite word?

1 ▶ Watch the video. Note down the speakers' favourite words and what they mean.

2 Work in pairs. Do you have a favourite word? What is it? Why do you like it?

GSE LEARNING OBJECTIVES

7A LISTENING | Understand a podcast about misunderstandings: reporting verbs; ways of speaking
Talk about conversations you had recently: reported speech
Pronunciation: stress in reporting verbs
Write a story about an event

7B READING | Understand an article about oversharing online: computer use; internet words
Discuss issues connected to internet privacy: passives
Pronunciation: stress and weak forms in passives

7C HOW TO … | keep a conversation going: adverbs
Pronunciation: intonation in short questions

7D BBC STREET INTERVIEWS | Understand people talking about good and bad communication
Talk about communication: avoiding repetition: *so, to, not, be*
Write an email giving advice about a problem

Unit 7 | Lesson A

7A Mix-up

GRAMMAR | reported speech
VOCABULARY | reporting verbs; ways of speaking
PRONUNCIATION | stress in reporting verbs

LISTENING

1 A Work in pairs and discuss. What possible misunderstanding could come from these sentences?
  1 'I'd like to invite you to the Hilltop Restaurant.'
  2 'Could you close the door?'
  3 'Are you doing anything next Saturday?'
  4 'Are you boring?'

B 🔊 **7.01** | Listen to the podcast and check your ideas in Ex 1A. What was the misunderstanding for each sentence?

2 A Work in pairs. How much do you remember? Choose the best option (a–c) to complete each sentence..
  1 The podcast host believes that miscommunication:
    a is the main cause of problems between people.
    b is rarely related to language.
    c is never caused by just one word.
  2 Luisa's friend:
    a sent Luisa a happy birthday message.
    b doesn't like expensive restaurants.
    c invited Luisa to a party.
  3 Luisa:
    a hadn't been to the restaurant before.
    b thinks the problem wasn't her friend's fault.
    c was annoyed with the other guests.
  4 Rich's manager:
    a made him feel nervous during the conversation.
    b was interested in how he was getting on in the job.
    c was angry with him.
  5 Rich:
    a helped his manager check her computer.
    b got up and locked the door.
    c thought he had followed his manager's instruction.
  6 Endre:
    a was in trouble but wanted to keep it a secret.
    b asked Josh to come early.
    c wanted Josh to meet him at a restaurant.
  7 Moni:
    a was surprised to see Josh.
    b asked what happened to her birthday party.
    c wasn't home.
  8 The Scottish woman:
    a was good friends with Ela.
    b thought Ela was very rude.
    c asked to meet Ela again.
  9 Ela:
    a realised immediately what she had said.
    b thought the Scottish woman's reaction was unfair.
    c continues to feel sorry about what happened.
  10 The podcast host:
    a thinks the Scottish woman was boring.
    b asks Ela to talk about a different experience.
    c wants to hear more stories.

B 🔊 **7.01** | Listen again and check your ideas.

C Work in pairs and discuss the questions.
  1 Which situation do you think was the most embarrassing? Why?
  2 Has anything like these situations ever happened to you or someone you know? What happened?
  3 Are there any words in your language which you make mistakes with? How about in English?

7A

GRAMMAR
reported speech

3 A Complete the reported speech sentences with ONE word.

1 'I'll be there!'
   I messaged her back and replied that I .... be there.
2 'Do you like the job?'
   She wanted to know .... I liked the job.
3 'Have you had any problems with colleagues?'
   She asked whether I .... had any problems with colleagues.
4 'Are you doing anything next Saturday?'
   My friend Endre asked me if I was doing anything the .... Saturday.
5 'I'm giving a surprise party for my wife Moni.'
   He said he .... giving a surprise party for his wife Moni.
6 'Can you come?'
   He asked me if I .... come.
7 'You'll be in trouble if you tell her.'
   Endre told me I .... be in trouble if I told her.
8 'I'll keep it a secret.'
   I promised that .... 'd keep it a secret.

B 🔊 **7.02** | Listen and check.

C Work in pairs. Choose the correct words to complete the rules. In one case both options are correct.

When we change direct speech to reported speech we:
1 often move the verb tenses further **back / forward**.
2 make changes to **personal pronouns / time phrases**.
3 **must / sometimes** use *that* after the reporting verb to report a statement.
4 **must / sometimes** add *if* or *whether* to report a *yes/no* question.
5 use **question / statement** word order to report a question.

4 A 🔊 **7.03** | Work in pairs and listen to the sentences. Take turns to report what the person said. Use *said* or *asked*.

1 He asked me if I was going out that night.

B Learn and practise. Go to the Grammar Bank.

⏩ page 125 **GRAMMAR BANK**

VOCABULARY
reporting verbs

5 A Replace the words in bold with the verbs in the box. Make any other changes needed in the rest of the sentence.

| add   argue   confirm   convince |
| enquire   mention   warn   ~~wonder~~ |

1 She **wanted to know** if I was enjoying the work.
   She wondered if I was enjoying the work.
2 I **replied that I was sure** I'd go.
3 He **told me** that I'd be in trouble.
4 And **she said after that** that she didn't want to see me again.
5 I should have **asked for information about** whether we had to pay for our own meal.
6 I wanted to **give the reason** that it was an ordinary mix-up, but he was too angry.
7 I **said (without giving any details)** that I'd had problems with my computer, but that my colleagues had been great.
8 My mistake **made me feel sure** that I needed to study English more.

B Complete the sentences using your own ideas.

1 If I had one minute to introduce myself, I'd mention that …
2 If a stranger asked me for money, I'd wonder if …
3 I'm fine speaking English on the phone in some situations, for example if I have to enquire whether …
4 When I send out invitations to my party, I expect people to confirm that …
5 If someone said cars should be banned, I'd argue that …
6 When I was young, I was convinced that …
7 If you said that English was a beautiful language, I'd add that …
8 If I saw someone crossing the road without looking around, I'd warn them that …

C Work in pairs and take turns. Student A: Read out one of your sentences. Student B: Ask a question about what Student A says.

A: If I had one minute to introduce myself, I'd mention that I love being outdoors.
B: What do you like doing outdoors?

PRONUNCIATION

6 A | **stress in reporting verbs** | Work in pairs. Put the reporting verbs in the box into two groups according to their stress.

| agree   answer   argue   complain   confirm   convince |
| enquire   explain   mention   promise   reply   wonder |

1 Oo   2 oO

B 🔊 **7.04** | Listen and check.

C Work in pairs. Student A: Point to a word in Ex 6A. Student B: Say it with the correct word stress.

7 A Work in pairs. What words do you know for speaking loudly or quietly?

B Check your ideas in the Vocabulary Bank.

⏩ page 136 **VOCABULARY BANK** ways of speaking

81

Unit 7 | Lesson A

SPEAKING

8 A You are going to tell someone about two conversations you had recently. Student A: Read the conversations on this page. Student B: Read the conversations on page 138. Where do they take place? What is the problem in each one?

Conversation 1

Fernanda:	Are you OK Lisa?
Lisa:	What's the matter with this door? I can't open it. It's completely stuck.
Fernanda:	Let me try. Look. Open. No problem.
Lisa:	But you pulled it open.
Fernanda:	Yes? And?
Lisa:	It says 'push'.
Fernanda:	No, it says 'puxe'. In Portuguese 'puxe' means 'pull'.
Lisa:	How confusing.
Fernanda:	Don't worry. All my friends from the UK make the same mistake.

Conversation 3

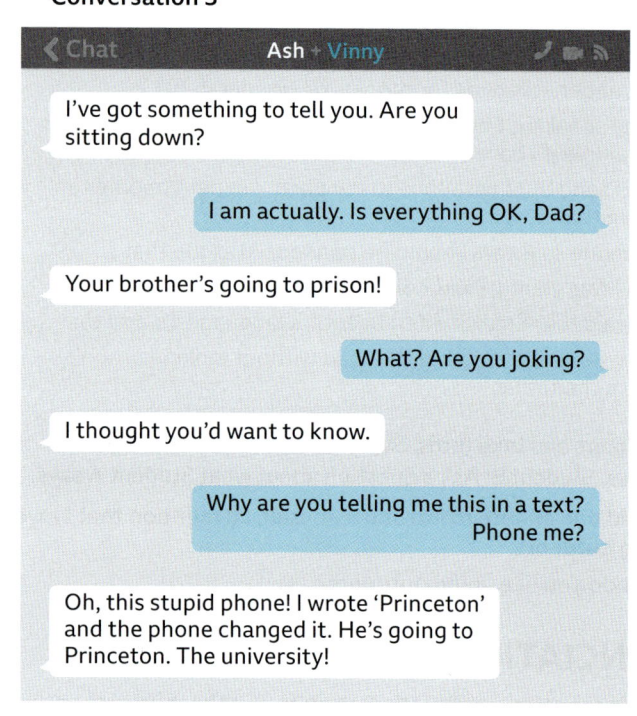

Chat — Ash + Vinny

- I've got something to tell you. Are you sitting down?
- I am actually. Is everything OK, Dad?
- Your brother's going to prison!
- What? Are you joking?
- I thought you'd want to know.
- Why are you telling me this in a text? Phone me?
- Oh, this stupid phone! I wrote 'Princeton' and the phone changed it. He's going to Princeton. The university!

B You are Fernanda in conversation 1 and Vinny in conversation 3. You're going to tell Student B about the conversations. Write six words and phrases for each conversation to help you remember what happened.

Conversation 1: door, stuck, I pulled, says 'push', 'puxe' = pull in Portuguese, confusing

C Work with Student B. Take turns to tell each other what happened in your conversations. Only use *said* once. Try to use at least three verbs other than *said*.

Something funny happened a few days ago. I was …
I had a very funny conversation yesterday.
I was with …
And then he told me …

WRITING

a story about an event

9 A Read the story. What was the misunderstanding?

Wedding guest

A few years ago, I was driving to a wedding somewhere in the countryside in England. I saw a man walking along the road, a well-dressed older man, obviously a wedding guest. I stopped and asked him if he was going to the wedding and he said yes and got in. I tried to make conversation, but he didn't reply. We arrived at the wedding and got out of the car, **at which point** the guy walked quickly back down the driveway to the road. **Things got more bizarre when** the police arrived a few minutes later with the man and enquired whether he was a guest. **It turned out that** he wasn't, and that the whole misunderstanding came from the fact that he was Swedish and spoke almost no English. **Apparently**, he was visiting his son in the village, and he went for a short walk and got lost. **Funny thing is**, the son hadn't noticed that his father was missing.

B Read the story again and answer the questions.
1 How could you divide the story into three paragraphs?
2 What would be the function of each paragraph?
3 How many different reporting verbs are used?
4 Which words and phrases in bold can be replaced with the phrases (a–e)?

a and this was when
b we discovered that
c it's amusing but
d this was strange enough, but then
e it seems that

10 A Choose one of the following situations and write a story. This can be from your life or can be imaginary.
- people failing to meet because of a misunderstanding
- people meeting through a misunderstanding and becoming friends
- a stroke of good fortune because of a misunderstanding
- an invitation for a party or a meal which you completely misunderstood
- a mix-up over times/places or face-to-face/online meetings
- your own idea

B Reread your story and try to use some of the phrases in bold in the story in Ex 9A.

C Read other students' stories. Which one surprised you most?

7B Oversharing

GRAMMAR | passives
VOCABULARY | computer use; internet words
PRONUNCIATION | stress and weak forms in passives

VOCABULARY

computer use

1 A Work in pairs. Think of three actions that you do on your phone or computer. Do you know the English words for the actions?

B Work in pairs and look at the definitions (1–8). What words do you think they describe?

1 unwanted emails and messages, often advertisements, sent to large numbers of people (noun)
2 make a copy of information on your computer, usually so that it's safe (verb)
3 a small window with an advertisement that suddenly appears on a computer screen when you are looking at a website (noun)
4 put a message, photo or document on the internet for others to see (verb)
5 send something you've received to someone else (verb)
6 the name you use to log on to a computer or program (noun)
7 create a link to mention someone else (verb)
8 a short description or set of information about someone (noun)

C Match the definitions in Ex 1B with the words in the box.

| back up   forward   pop-up   post |
| profile   spam   tag   username |

2 A Complete the sentences (1–8) with the correct form of the words in Ex 1C.

1 I think it's fine to .... a photo of someone on social media without their permission. I do it all the time.
2 I .... my files regularly to a hard drive. I don't like keeping them in the cloud.
3 When I see something on the internet that I really like, I .... it to all my friends.
4 I never check my .... folder. It's full of emails with advertisements and other rubbish.
5 I rarely use my real name as my .... I prefer to use a fake name.
6 I never lie when putting personal information in a user .... form on a website.
7 I don't normally read a .... It's most likely an advertisement, so I just close it.
8 It annoys me when someone .... me in a photo on social media, and doesn't even ask my permission.

B Which of the sentences in Ex 2A are true for you?

C Work in pairs and compare your ideas. Do you think people of different ages respond differently to these issues? In what way?

D Learn and practise. Go to the Vocabulary Bank.

▶▶ page 137 **VOCABULARY BANK** internet words

83

Unit 7 | Lesson B

READING

3 A Work in pairs and discuss. What are the dangers of posting photos of yourself and other people online?

B Read the article and choose the best summary (1–3) of the writer's opinion.

1 Children should learn about the risks of posting photos online from an early age.
2 Think twice before you post something, and if in doubt, don't post it.
3 If someone suffers the consequences of an internet post, it's their own fault.

C Read the article again. Are the statements True (T) or False (F)?

1 Rob and Makayla are worried about the same effect of oversharing by parents.
2 The writer agrees that parents should stop sharing photos if their children don't want them to.
3 Employers almost always use social media to investigate applicants for jobs.
4 All employers strongly dislike seeing employees and job applicants in political photos.
5 The bank intern posted a selfie of himself in costume.
6 The writer feels sorry for the bank intern.
7 The health centre worker thought it was fine to go to a theme park with a shoulder injury.
8 The woman from Pennsylvania hadn't given her permission for her photo to be used.

D Read the Future Skills box and do the task.

> **FUTURE SKILLS**
> **Critical thinking**
>
> Newspaper and magazine articles often combine a reporting of facts with the author's point of view. It's important to notice how the author gives their own point of view, so that you can develop your own. Writers often put their opinion at the beginning or end of a paragraph, and sometimes signal an opinion with words like 'perhaps' or 'maybe'. Look in the article and find at least five places where the author gives their point of view. Do you agree with the author?

Share with care

Isabella is five years old. If she's a typical UK child, by now her photo has already been posted 5,000 times online. Tom is eighteen and is applying for his first job. At this very moment, his social media profile is being analysed in detail by his future employer.

These days children are given plenty of information about the dangers of oversharing, and young people often have strong opinions about what their parents share. 'I feel really embarrassed when my mum posts pictures of me,' says eleven-year-old Rob. 'She thinks it's cute when I have chocolate on my face. I don't want my friends to see me in that way.' Makayla (15) agrees that there's a problem: 'I'm worried that it could have a bad effect when I want to get a job. That's why I feel really upset whenever my parents post photos of me.' In France children can take their parents to court for oversharing. No one in the UK has been taken to court yet, but one would hope that that's going to change. Parents need to understand how their kids feel, and why.

Makayla raises a very important point. Many first-time job-seekers do not have a CV to prove they are suitable for a position. So it seems natural that employers search people's social media profiles as part of the application and interview process – and over ninety percent of them do, according to Workopolis.com. A photo of a child accompanying their parents at a political demonstration posted years ago, for example, may affect that child's life, depending on how a future employer views the post.

And once you've got the job, you need to be ultra-careful what you post publicly, as a bank intern in New York found out when he took two days off for a 'family emergency' and ended up getting fired. In the evening he went to a Halloween party dressed up as a fairy. Someone took a photo of him in costume, clearly not dealing with a family emergency, posted it on social media and his manager saw it. That was the end of that internship! Even if he didn't post the photo, it's hard not to blame him.

You can't control how your employer, or anyone, interprets your posting. A health centre worker in Florida in the USA was on leave because of a shoulder injury. One day he went to a theme park and posted photos of himself having a good time there. His actions were considered bad for staff morale and he lost his job. The employee didn't feel there was anything wrong with what he had done. Maybe the key mistake wasn't going to the theme park, but posting the photo.

Even the most innocent postings can be exploited. A woman from Pennsylvania, USA, posted a family photo on her blog – as countless people do every day. When it appeared in a political campaign advertisement in Pennsylvania, she began to look for the photo on the internet and eventually found that it had appeared on over thirty websites around the world, including advertisements for apps, sunscreen, pet tracking devices, holiday cards, cameras and vacations. In the end, there wasn't much she could do about it. Perhaps the only solution is not to post at all.

7B

GRAMMAR

passives

4 A Work in pairs and choose the correct words to complete the sentences.

1 By now her photo **has already posted / has already been posted** 5,000 times online.
2 At this very moment, his social media profile **is analysing / is being analysed** in detail by his future employer.
3 These days children **give / are given** plenty of information about the dangers of oversharing.
4 No one in the UK **has been taken / was taken** to court yet.
5 He took two days off for a 'family emergency' and ended up **get fired / getting fired**.

B Check your answers in the article.

C Work in pairs. Look at the sentences in Ex 4A and answer the questions.

1 How do we form the passive? Find two ways.
2 Is the main focus on the person who does the action or the person/thing affected by the action?
3 In how many sentences is the 'doer' unknown or obvious?

D Learn and practise. Go to the Grammar Bank.

▶▶ page 126 **GRAMMAR BANK**

PRONUNCIATION

5 A 🔊 7.05 | **stress and weak forms in passives** | Listen and write the sentences.

B Work in pairs. Find the stressed part of the verb phrases. How do you pronounce the auxiliary verbs *been* and *was*?

C 🔊 7.05 | Listen again and say the sentences at the same time as the speaker.

6 A Make the sentences in Ex 5A true for you.

B Work in pairs and discuss your sentences.

SPEAKING

7 A Work in pairs. Read this extract from an article about online privacy and discuss the questions.

> … in many countries consent is required to both take and share a photo of someone in a public place, although this rule is being broken all the time. By 2021, France already had even stricter rules on sharing photos taken in a private place. If you shared a person's words or image without their consent, you could be fined 45,000 euros and jailed for a year. For minors, parents could give consent, but it had to be both parents.

1 Do you think the rules are reasonable or too strict?
2 Do you think any of them should be adopted by other countries?
3 What other laws do you think should be made to protect people in connection with online sharing?

B Work in pairs. Match the phrases (1–6) with their uses (a–c). Add any other phrases you use.

1 That's a good point, but …
2 Another thing is …
3 Actually, …
4 Don't you think that … ?
5 And the key thing is …
6 Isn't it true that … ?

a strengthening or adding to your own ideas
b disagreeing with the other person
c getting the other person to agree with you

8 A Work in pairs. Read the statements (a–d) about internet use and privacy and answer the questions. Use the phrases in Ex 7B.

1 What problems are there in each area?
2 How might you solve those problems?

Privacy policy

a A child has no way of giving or refusing permission to post and share photos of themself. Many children have said they want to stop these postings.
b Many websites ask users to confirm their age so that they don't open adult websites. Is it enough?
c False user profiles are being created all the time. As a result, we don't know who actually wrote a lot of the content that we read.
d Photos from social media are often downloaded and used on stock photo websites. There's no clear system for stopping people from using your photos without permission.

B Work in groups. Discuss the statements in Ex 8A. For each one, identify any problems and agree on one possible solution.

C Compare your ideas with another group.

Unit 7 | Lesson C

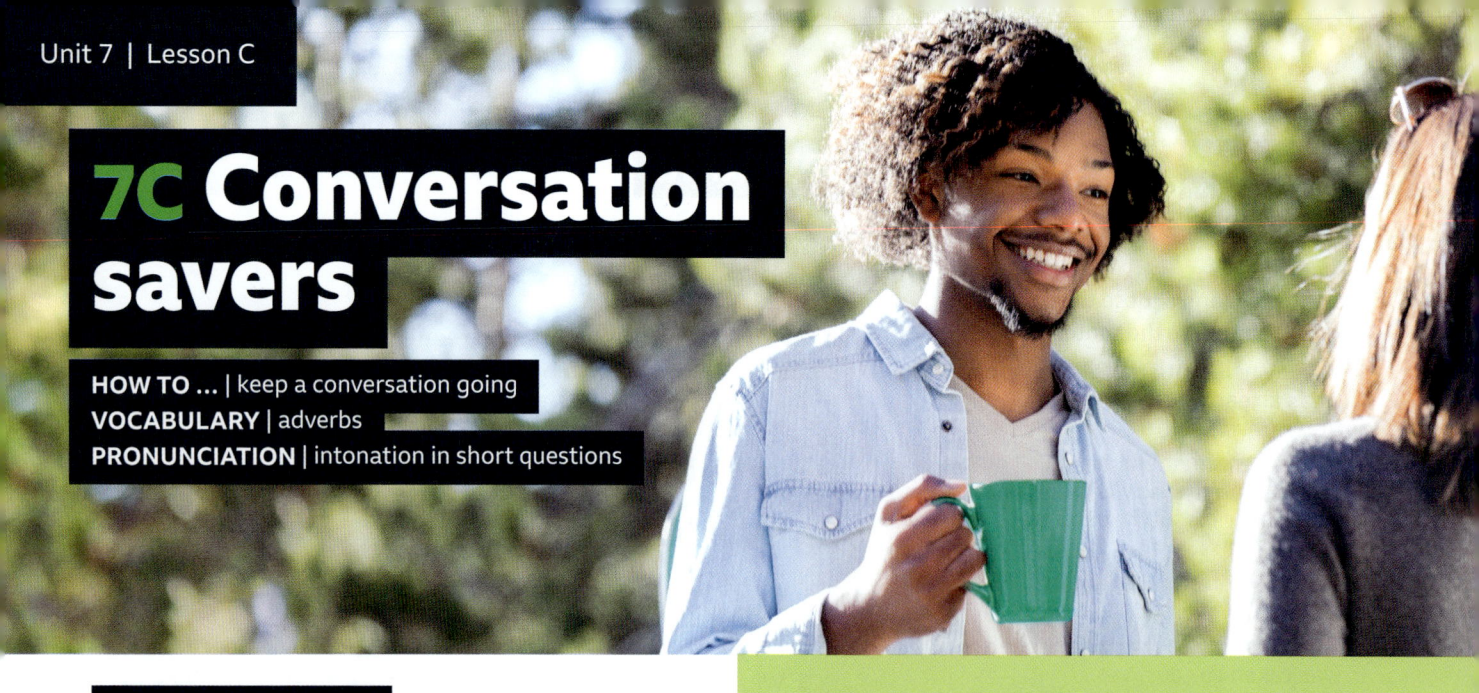

7C Conversation savers

HOW TO ... | keep a conversation going
VOCABULARY | adverbs
PRONUNCIATION | intonation in short questions

VOCABULARY

adverbs

1 A Work in pairs and discuss the questions.
  1. Do you enjoy parties and gatherings where you don't know many people? Why/Why not?
  2. What sort of things do you usually talk about with people you don't know?
  3. What do you do to keep the conversation going?

B Work in pairs. Look at the headings in the article. What do you think each one is suggesting?

C Read the article. Which ideas do you think are useful? Which don't you agree with?

2 A Find six adverbs ending in -*ly* in the text and match them with the meanings (1–5). One of the meanings matches two adverbs.
  1. completely *perfectly*, ...
  2. very very ....
  3. more than usual ....
  4. more than a little, less than very ....
  5. a little/a bit (often before negative ideas) ....

B Work in pairs. In each sentence find one adverb that does NOT fit with the adjective that follows.
  1. I'm **extremely / fairly / slightly** good at handling a conversation with a stranger.
  2. It's **totally / particularly / perfectly** normal to feel awkward sometimes.
  3. I think most people are **fairly / totally / extremely** interesting.
  4. Good use of body language can be **slightly / particularly / extremely** powerful.
  5. I find it **perfectly / particularly / slightly** strange when people don't ask me questions.
  6. If they ask me a personal question, that's **fairly / totally / perfectly** fine.

C Work in pairs and discuss. Which sentences in Ex 2B are true for you?

The art of conversation

You're at a party and someone you don't know comes up to you and starts chatting. Things are going fairly well and then ... the conversation just dies. You panic as you try to think of something to say, but by then ... the person has walked away.

Does that sound familiar? It should, because it's a perfectly normal experience, shared by most of us. The good news is that there are some tricks and techniques that can help you become an expert and deal with that uncomfortable silence. The first one is ...

... don't stick with small talk.

It's normal and comfortable for a conversation to start with a basic get-to-know-you exchange, but be careful in case you get stuck on small talk. Small talk ISN'T conversation. If you notice you're stuck, then it's time to ...

... ask, don't tell (and no *yes/no* questions!).

Ask questions, and not just any questions. Avoid *yes/no* questions and questions you don't care about the answer to. Listen out for a detail that's particularly interesting or something you don't understand; that's the 'hook'. Now it's time to ...

... ask a POWER question.

These are short, simple but extremely powerful questions. Once you've found a 'hook', use a POWER question to energise the conversation. *What do you mean by that? Why's that?* They show that you really ARE interested. And all the time, remember to ...

... listen with your whole body.

Face the other person, don't turn to the side as if you're watching for someone more interesting. Make eye contact, but not too much (that would be slightly strange!). Don't let your eyes move around the room – the person you're talking to will think that you've lost interest. And if the other person is doing this, you should ...

... know when to give up.

Not everyone wants to be your friend, or even have a conversation with you. That's totally fine. If the energy really isn't there, move on – before the other person does.

How to ...
keep a conversation going

3 A 🔊 **7.06** | Listen to the conversation and look at the headings in the article in Ex 1C. What does the man do wrong?

B 🔊 **7.07** | Listen to the next conversation. What do Paul and Denise do right, according to the article?

C Work in pairs. Complete the phrases with one or two words.

Denise: I'm Denise. Nice to meet you.
Paul: And you. ¹_____ you know Celia?
Denise: We went to college together.

Denise: Yes, we both did food technology.
Paul: Oh. ²How did you _____ into that?

Denise: Well, obviously you learn a lot about cooking, but it covers all sorts of other things.
Paul: ³Such _____ ?

Paul: ⁴That sounds _____ . ⁵What do _____ by 'researching new flavours'?
Denise: Well, I once developed a banana-flavoured crisp.
Paul: ⁶_____ terrible. What was it ⁷_____ ?

Paul: I was a waiter there, but I left.
Denise: Really? ⁸Why's _____ ?
Paul: I liked the people I was working with, but I didn't like some of the customers.
Denise: ⁹_____ come?

Paul: They were always complaining.
Denise: How did that ¹⁰_____ you feel?

D 🔊 **7.08** | Listen and check.

4 A Work in pairs. Match the phrases (1–10) in Ex 3C with their uses (a–d).
 a starting new topics
 b commenting to show interest
 c short follow-up questions (two or three words)
 d other follow-up questions

B Look at audioscript 7.07 on page 167. Find more examples of the uses (1–4) in Ex 4A.

C Learn and practise. Go to the Grammar Bank.

⏩ page 127 **GRAMMAR BANK**

PRONUNCIATION

5 A 🔊 **7.09** | intonation in short questions | Listen to the questions. Does the intonation go up or down?
 1 Such as?   2 Why's that?

B Work in pairs and look at the questions (1–4). For each one, decide if the intonation goes up or down.
 1 Because?   3 How come?
 2 What's it like?   4 For instance?

C 🔊 **7.10** | Listen and check.

D Work in pairs and have a conversation. Use the sentence beginnings below and ask follow-up questions from Exs 5A and 5B. Then continue the conversation.
 1 This weekend I want to …
 2 I've just bought …
 3 I'd like to change a few things about …
 4 I refuse to lend anyone …
 5 I recently met …
 6 I need to throw out a lot of …

SPEAKING

6 A Look at the list of conversation topics and choose six that you would be happy to have a two-minute conversation about.
- job/work
- travel/holidays
- social media
- pets
- free time activities
- films
- food
- books
- shopping
- news
- music
- friends

B Work in pairs and decide on:
 1 four topics you would both be happy to talk about.
 2 an opening question or comment for each of the topics.
 3 an unusual question for each topic.
 4 an adverb and adjective pair you could use to talk about each topic.

I'm particularly interested in …
I'm slightly bored/tired of …
That's extremely surprising, because …

C Work with a new partner. Find a topic that both of you chose, and have a conversation about it. You have two minutes. Use the phrases in Ex 3C to help keep the conversation going.

D Work with a new partner. Find a different topic that both of you chose. Talk about it for two minutes.

MEDIATION SKILLS
describing diagrams
explain a chatbot flowchart

⏩ page 154 **MEDIATION BANK**

Unit 7 | Lesson D

7D BBC Street Interviews
A good communicator

Zoe   Joshua

GRAMMAR | avoiding repetition: *so, to, not, be*
SPEAKING | a discussion about communication
WRITING | an email giving advice about a problem

Janine

PREVIEW

1 Work in pairs and discuss the questions.
  1 How easy or difficult do you find it to communicate in these situations?

  > face to face   making a complaint
  > speaking to an audience
  > video meetings

  2 How do the following affect your communication?
  - speaking in another language
  - how you feel (stressed/happy, etc.)
  - talking to people you don't know

Q1: Are you a good communicator?
Q2: In what situations do you have difficulty communicating?

VIEW

2A ▶ Watch the first part of the video. How many speakers say they are good communicators, but not in all situations?

B ▶ Watch again and choose one or both people.
  1 **Zoe** / **Joshua** says it depends on what's happening.
  2 **Janine** / **Monica** says there can be problems with the language.
  3 **Pear** / **Lily** says it depends on the method of communication.
  4 **Yiannis** / **Raihan** talks about speaking in front of a lot of people.

3A ▶ Watch the second part of the video. Tick the topics (1–5) each time a speaker mentions them.
  1 arguments
  2 speaking to a lot of people
  3 speaking via the internet
  4 their mood or feelings
  5 talking to particular people

B ▶ Watch again and complete the sentences.
  1 It's easier to work .... to face with people. I think it's more creative.
  2 But yeah, practice makes ....
  3 I'm not thinking about how I'm coming .... to other people.
  4 When you're under .... , choosing the right words can be difficult.
  5 I can't find the .... to explain why I'm angry.

C Work in pairs. Which of the statements in Ex 3B do you agree with?

GRAMMAR

avoiding repetition: *so, to, not, be*

4A Work in pairs and complete the sentences with the words in the box.

  > hope   like   so

  1 A: Are you a good communicator?
     B: I hope .... / Yes, I think so.
  2 A: Do you want to be a better communicator?
     B: I'd .... to be.
  3 A: Do you think it's impossible to improve?
     B: I .... not.

B Learn and practise. Go to the Grammar Bank.

▶▶ page 128 **GRAMMAR BANK**

88

7D

BBC

SPEAKING

a discussion about communication

5 A Look at the situations (a–e) and number them in order from 1 (most difficult for you) to 5 (easiest for you).
  a giving a speech to a large group
  b giving your opinion in a class or a meeting
  c sending a voicemail message in English
  d talking on the phone in English
  e telling a friend that they have upset you

B Work in pairs and discuss your answers to Ex 5A.

C Work in pairs. Look at the Key phrases. Which of the short answers could you use with which questions?

D Work with a new partner. Discuss the situations you each find difficult in Ex 5A, and how to improve them. Use the Key phrases to help.

KEY PHRASES

Questions
Which situation do you find the most difficult?
Do you think you're good at communicating when giving a speech/sending a message, etc.?
Do you think you're a friendly/communicative/positive person?
Would you like to get better at talking on the phone in English?
Do you avoid talking to people sometimes?

Short answers
I (don't) think so.	I'm going to try (to).
I hope so.	I guess so.
I'd like to.	I suppose so.
I want to.	I try not to.

WRITING

an email giving advice about a problem

6 A Read the email giving advice. Which of Anya's ideas would work best for you? Do you have any other ideas that could help?

Hi Alessandro,

Nice to hear from you. I don't think it's at all unusual that you're worried about giving a speech at Leonardo's wedding. I've thought a bit about how I became more confident in public speaking and perhaps one or two of these ideas could help you.

When you're writing the speech, make it personal, for example by including lots of stories. People love stories and they can make people laugh, and that will help you relax. Then, in order to sound confident and natural, practise, practise, practise. And make sure you practise out loud, then you'll be able to sound more natural on the day.

Before your speech, you could do some relaxation exercises, such as slow breathing and simple stretching. This always helps to calm me down and to control my voice.

Also, if you're generally feeling nervous about standing in front of people, then to build your confidence you could take a class, like a singing or dancing class. I had some singing lessons once to help me project my voice better and it really worked.

So anyway, I hope these ideas help. Remember everyone there wants you to succeed and I'm sure you'll be brilliant.

Anya xxx

B Work in pairs. Choose a situation in Ex 5A that is challenging for each of you. List ideas for making both situations less difficult. Use your ideas from Ex 5D.

C Write an email to your partner giving them advice on their situation. Use your ideas from Ex 6B.

D Work in pairs. Read your partner's email. Did they include all of the ideas you listed in Ex 6B?

7 REVIEW

GRAMMAR
reported speech

1 A Read the reported conversation. Rewrite sentences 1–10 using direct speech to give the original conversation.

The strangest conversation I ever had? It was back in college, and my roommate was talking in his sleep – at 4 a.m. ¹He asked me if I'd got up early that morning. ²I told him I hadn't, and that it wasn't really morning yet. ³He asked if I was planning to do anything that evening. ⁴I told him that I hadn't planned anything special. ⁵He asked me whether we could meet for dinner the next day. ⁶I told him that I was happy to, and I added that we had dinner together every day anyway. ⁷He asked me if I'd ever tried Thai food. ⁸I said I hadn't, but I'd like to. Then ⁹he said that he'd contact me the next day. ¹⁰I said he should go back to sleep. So strange – I wonder who he thought I was.

1 A: Did you get up early this morning?
2 B: No, I …

B Work in pairs. Ask each other the direct questions in Ex 1A. Make notes of your partner's answers.

C Work with a new partner. Tell them about your conversation in Ex 1B. Pay attention to the time references.

I asked him if he had got up early today and he said …

passives

2 A Put the words in the correct order to make questions.

1 you / lost / a / get / ever / you / when / Did / child / were ?
2 that / a / been / hated / ever / you / really / Have / given / you / present ?
3 get / do / what / do / in / you / traffic, / stuck / you / When ?
4 ever / a / been / you / give / to / speech / Have / asked ?
5 Whose / influenced / are / you / by / opinion / most ?
6 asked / question / today / the / yet / you / a / teacher / Have / been / by ?

B Work in pairs and discuss the questions.

avoiding repetition: *so, to, not, be*

3 A Complete the conversations. Write one word in each gap.

1 A: **Do you think you**'ve passed the exam?
   B: I hope _____ .
2 A: **Can you help me with this** puzzle?
   B: I'll try _____ .
3 A: **Do we have** homework?
   B: I don't think _____ .
4 A: **This isn't the best time to** chat.
   B: I suppose _____ .

B Make sentences starting with the phrases in bold in Ex 3A.

A: Do you think you'll go to the party tonight?

C Work in pairs. Student A: Say one of your sentences. Student B: Use a short answer to reply.

VOCABULARY

4 A Complete the words to make sentences.

1 It's p_____ normal to talk to y_____ , but maybe it's better to w_____ if other people are around.
2 It's s_____ uncomfortable for me when someone y_____ at their partner in public.
3 It's e_____ important to s_____ up when you feel something is unfair.
4 It's totally impossible to c_____ me to change my mind about most things.
5 It's fairly annoying to discover an important email in your s_____ folder instead of the i_____ .

B Work in pairs and discuss the sentences in Ex 4A. Which do you agree with?

5 A Choose the correct options (A–C) to complete the text.

Imperfect inventions

They say that necessity is the mother of invention – if there's a need, then the solution ¹_____ . But there seem to be some needs for which the perfect solution ²_____ developed yet. Here are some of your ideas.

Earplugs that work
More and more people live in noisy environments, and many said they ³_____ waiting for years for the perfect ear plug. 'I'm often ⁴_____ up by the neighbours, and nothing I've tried has worked.'

No-jam printer
Many of you asked if ⁵_____ possible to invent a printer that never jammed. 'It's ⁶_____ annoying when I'm in a hurry and I get a ⁷_____ saying the printer's jammed.'

Scratch-proof sunglasses
What can make you angrier than when you drop your expensive sunglasses and they ⁸_____ damaged? 'When I spend a lot of money on sunglasses, I expect no scratches – zero.'

Self-labelling computer filing system
'It shouldn't be too hard – the program could scan the documents in a ⁹_____ and choose a label that fits.'

	A	B	C
1	will be found	will find	is found
2	has been	hasn't been	isn't
3	are	were	had been
4	awake	woke	woken
5	it was	was it	was
6	perfectly	particularly	being
7	tag	post	pop-up
8	have	get	got
9	folder	username	profile

B 🔊 R7.01 | Listen and check your answers.

wisdom 8

VLOGS

Q: What's the best piece of advice you've ever been given?

1 ▶ Watch the video. Do you agree with any of the advice?

2 Work in pairs. What's the best piece of advice you've ever been given?

GSE LEARNING OBJECTIVES

8A READING | Read advice from people of different ages: phrases of advice

Describe a situation and give advice: third conditional and *should have*

Pronunciation: contractions in complex sentences

8B LISTENING | Understand an account of the origins of one man's curiosity: learning; phrasal verbs

Discuss the qualities of a mentor: *would*

Pronunciation: contracted *would*

Write a short biography

8C HOW TO ... | give a presentation: presenting

Pronunciation: stressing words in key phrases

8D BBC PROGRAMME | Understand a TV programme about entrepreneurs pitching ideas

Talk about pitching a business idea

Write an email giving work-related news

Unit 8 | Lesson A

8A Wise words

GRAMMAR | third conditional and *should have*
VOCABULARY | phrases of advice
PRONUNCIATION | contractions in complex sentences

VOCABULARY

phrases of advice

1 A Work in pairs. Read the definition of a motto. Can you think of any mottos in your language?

motto (noun): a short sentence or phrase that expresses someone's beliefs or ideas, e.g. about life, e.g. *Hope for the best and prepare for the worst.*

B Read the mottos (1–8) and match them with the ideas (a–h).
1 Learn something about everything and everything about something.
2 Take risks. If you win, you'll be happy; if you lose, you'll be wise.
3 Listen a hundred times, ponder a thousand times, speak once.
4 The journey is more important than the destination.
5 If you want something you've never had, you have to do something you've never done.
6 Live each day as if it were your last.
7 The best time to plant a tree was twenty years ago. The second best time is now.
8 Laughter is the best medicine.

a **Be careful not to** always take the safest option.
b **Stop worrying about** where you'll be in the future and enjoy the present.
c **Take time to** think before you give your opinions.
d **Make the most of** your time on Earth.
e **Don't be afraid to** do something new.
f **Don't take** life **too** seriously.
g **Be ready to** act even if it seems too late.
h **Pay attention to** the world around you and try to understand it.

C Look at the phrases in bold in Ex 1B. Which is/are:
1 warnings saying what you shouldn't do? (four phrases)
2 about not responding too quickly?
3 about focusing?
4 about being prepared to do something?
5 about using an opportunity as much as you can?

2 A Work in pairs and discuss the questions.
1 Which of the mottos in Ex 1B have you heard before in English or in your own language?
2 Where do you see these kinds of mottos? How do you feel about them?
3 Are there any you disagree with?

B Choose five of the phrases in bold from Ex 1B. Complete them with your own ideas. Then compare with a partner.

Don't be afraid to meet new people; you might make a friend for life.

Stop worrying about things you can't control.

READING

3 A Discuss in pairs. Whose advice do you listen to? In what situations?

B Read the text. Which advice do you like the best?

C Read the Future Skills box and answer the questions.

> **FUTURE SKILLS**
> **Critical thinking**
>
> When we read, we sometimes have to 'read between the lines'. This means we try to guess things that might not be said, e.g. the writer's personal history, ideas, character and attitudes. This is part of critical thinking.
>
> Read what John says about his schooldays again. Do you think John did well in his school exams? What information in the text gives you the answer?

D Work in pairs. Choose the correct option (a–c). Which words in the text give you the answers?

1. What do you think Indira does?
   a She studies fashion at a local university.
   b She works in an organisation.
   c She looks after a young child at home.
2. What sort of child do you think Alexandra was?
   a She was similar to her parents.
   b She was friendly and her friends thought she was funny.
   c She had strong opinions.
3. What type of person do you think Lisbeth is?
   a She is probably creative.
   b She might be shy and quite serious.
   c She is probably careful and not very friendly.
4. What is Lee's attitude to the past?
   a He thinks his mistakes cost him a lot of money.
   b He believes it's important to spend time thinking about the past and decisions you made when you were younger.
   c He doesn't worry about the mistakes he made.

4 Work in pairs and discuss. Do you think our views on our past opinions and actions change as we get older? In what ways?

Advice across the ages

What is the best way to live our lives? What can we learn from other generations? *123 Magazine* spoke to people ranging in age from 19 to 100 and asked for life advice. Here are some of their answers.

John, age 19

Make the most of your schooldays. They're a lot easier than working. You're with your friends all day and the worst thing you have to do is a few exams every year. If I'd realised this, I would have had more fun at school instead of complaining all the time. Also, I should have studied more. The exams weren't that difficult, but when you aren't prepared, everything is difficult. So, overall, my advice to anyone who's still at school is to enjoy yourself. Those days will be gone before you know it.

Indira, age 28

If I had to give one piece of advice, it would be to spend less time worrying about stuff. When I was younger, I worried about everything – my appearance, what people thought of me and whether all my plans would work out. I shouldn't have paid so much attention to those things. Now I think I'm more relaxed, especially when tasks aren't urgent. At least that's what my colleagues tell me. My best friend always says, 'Everything will be OK in the end and if it's not OK, it's not the end.' So that's my advice: stop worrying so much.

Alexandra, age 40

Don't take yourself too seriously. No one else will. And you don't have to win every argument. If I'd known that when I was younger, I'd have lost more arguments and kept more friends. Enjoy your youth. Believe me, when you're young is the best time to make mistakes. You still have time to recover. And listen to your parents. You may sometimes do the opposite of what they say, but at least be polite enough to listen.

Lisbeth, age 65

Take time to enjoy the little things. Imagine you're a child again, when going to the supermarket was an adventure and trees were for climbing. Be grateful and don't compare your life to other people's because you don't know what they're going through. Make things. Any things. Make meals, make a mess, make art. Just bring things into the world and see what happens. Be good to others. If you're not sure what to do or how to treat someone, always take the more generous option. You'll never regret it.

Lee, age 100

Forgive yourself and everyone else. We all get things wrong. I spent twenty years in the wrong job in the wrong industry in the wrong town. Now I just laugh about it. I moved on and life got better. Don't waste your energy with what-ifs: 'I should have done this and I shouldn't have done that.' Forget it. It's too late. Pay attention to the here and now. Finally, spend all your money – or your kids will do it for you!

Unit 8 | Lesson A

GRAMMAR

third conditional and *should have*

5 A Read the sentences (1–4) and find the verb forms.

1 If I'd realised this, I would have had more fun at school.
2 If I'd known that when I was younger, I would have lost more arguments and kept more friends.
3 I should have studied more.
4 I shouldn't have done that.

B Work in pairs and answer the questions (a–e) about Ex 5A.

a Are the sentences about the past or present?
b Are the speakers happy with what happened in the past or do they wish things had been different?
c Which verb tense comes after *if* in sentences 1 and 2?
d Which verb form comes after *would have* in sentences 1 and 2?
e Which verb form comes after *should(n't) have* for talking about past regrets/wishes?

C Learn and practise. Go to the Grammar Bank.

▶▶ page 129 **GRAMMAR BANK**

PRONUNCIATION

6 A 🔊 8.01 | contractions in complex sentences |
Read the sentences (1–4). How do we pronounce the parts in bold in fluent speech? Listen and check.

1 I **should have been** nicer.
2 You **shouldn't have** paid any attention to him.
3 If I'd known, I **would have** done things differently.
4 If we'd known, we **wouldn't have been** so worried.

B 🔊 8.01 | Listen again and repeat the sentences.

C Complete the sentences (1–4) in any way you choose. Then read them to a partner.

1 Last night, I should have …
2 When I was younger, I shouldn't have …
3 If I'd woken up earlier, I would have …
4 If I'd known then what I know now, I wouldn't have …

SPEAKING

7 A You are going to describe a situation, then give advice. Read the example. Do you agree with the advice?

Situation

When I was seventeen, I had a chance to go to Australia to do an English course with my school. The course was in Melbourne, a wonderful city with a lot of interesting things to see and do. I would have been away for one month of intensive study. I thought about it for a little bit, but I decided to stay at home and get a summer job. At the time, I really wanted to make some money. That July, several of my friends went to Melbourne. When they got back, they told me they'd had a great time. They'd loved the city and they'd made lots of new friends. It was then that I realised I'd made the wrong decision. I should have gone to Australia. I've never had the opportunity again. If I'd thought more carefully, I would have gone because I would have improved my English and seen a new country.

Advice

So, my advice to anyone in that situation would be to make the most of your opportunities. Take time to think about decisions. I made my decision too quickly because I wanted to work that summer. Be ready to do something different, maybe something that wasn't in your original plan.

B Prepare to describe a situation and give advice.

1 Choose a situation in your past. What would have been useful to know? Should you have done anything differently? Use the ideas in the box or think of your own.

> dealing with a problem   planning a trip
> your first job   your time at school or university

2 Make notes on the situation and the advice you would give someone in a similar situation.

C Work in groups. Describe the situation and give your advice. Then listen to other students and think of how you can respond. Do you agree with their advice? Why/Why not? What alternatives can you think of?

I agree! If you'd done that, it would have been better.

Maybe. But if you'd moved, you wouldn't have met Sophie.

I'm not sure you should have done that. It's difficult to say.

8B Life lessons

GRAMMAR | would
VOCABULARY | learning; phrasal verbs
PRONUNCIATION | contracted would

VOCABULARY

learning

1 A Work in pairs. Ask and answer the questions.
  1 Do you have any particular interests which you have had since you were a child?
  2 How did you learn about them?
  3 Have your interests changed over the years? Can you give examples?

B Read the article about how three people became interested in their subject. According to the article, who:
  1 enjoyed learning about new technology?
  2 studied in order to share their knowledge and ideas with younger people?
  3 had a mentor who influenced them?

2 A Complete the sentences (1–8) with the words and phrases in bold in the article.
  1 I started learning Japanese. At first, I _____ but then I found it too difficult.
  2 Playing the piano has been my _____ . I've played for as long as I can remember.
  3 When I have no ideas, I look at other people's work to _____ me.
  4 My grandmother always _____ me to study hard at school. She said 'Education is wealth'.
  5 I enjoy baking and I'm trying to _____ the art of baking perfect bread.
  6 A holiday in Athens _____ in archaeology, and he went on to study it at university.
  7 In my work, I am _____ wanting to help people more than earning lots of money.
  8 At school I usually worked hard and _____ good grades.

B Work in pairs. Change two or three of the sentences in Ex 2A so that they are true for you or people you know. Tell your partner.

C Look at the phrasal verbs highlighted in the text. Do you know what they mean? Learn and practise. Go to the Vocabulary Bank.

▶▶ page 137 **VOCABULARY BANK** phrasal verbs

How it all started

How David Attenborough learnt about the natural world

Despite living in a city, David Attenborough spent his childhood collecting fossils, stones and natural specimens. His **lifelong passion** for the natural world developed early and by the age of seven, he had a large collection of bird eggs and fossils. He was **encouraged** by the young archaeologist Jacquetta Hawkes, who admired his 'museum'. He later attended a lecture by famous naturalist Grey Owl in 1936 which **deepened his interest** in Natural Sciences, which he studied at Cambridge University.

How Gitanjali Rao became a world-famous scientist and inventor when she was a young child

Gitanjali Rao is a scientist and inventor who was named *Time* magazine's first 'kid of the year'. Gitanjali was just four years old when she first discovered her love of science. She worked hard to **master** the skills and techniques needed to develop her ideas and at thirteen, she **achieved** the title of 'America's top young scientist' for her invention of a water-testing kit. She is fascinated by new technologies, and as well as the water-testing kit, she has developed an app which can detect cyberbullying. Now she hopes to **inspire** others to dream up ideas to 'solve the world's problems'.

Why Priscilla Sitienei says it's never too late to learn

Priscilla Sitienei was a midwife in rural Kenya. She grew up without free primary school education and had never learnt to read or write. As she got older she had a powerful longing to write down her experiences and knowledge in order to pass them down to the next generation. **Motivated by** this desire, she started attending lessons at the local school, together with her six great-great grandchildren. She was ninety at the time. Known as 'Gogo' to her teachers and classmates, Priscilla **made good progress** in school and enjoyed telling stories to inspire and motivate the younger children.

Unit 8 | Lesson B

LISTENING

3 A Read the information about the BBC Radio programme. Who was Hans Rosling?

> **How I Learned to Understand the World** BBC
>
> *How I Learned to Understand the World* is Hans Rosling's own story of how he grew from a young scientist into a famous doctor, academic and public speaker. He was passionate about how poverty affects health in countries around the world and how science can help us to improve global health.

B 8.02 | Listen to the programme and answer the questions.

1 What did Hans learn from his father?
2 How did this inspire him?

C 8.02 | Work in pairs. Choose the best option (a or b) to complete the statements (1–7). Then listen again and check.

1 Hans Rosling's father worked in:
   a a café.
   b a factory.
2 When he came home in the evening, he:
   a smelt of coffee.
   b drank a lot of coffee.
3 Hans would wait for his father to return from work and ask him:
   a the same question every evening.
   b lots of questions about the coffee beans.
4 His father would bring home coins:
   a when he travelled to Brazil.
   b he found inside the coffee sacks.
5 His father would show Hans an atlas and:
   a tell him a story about where the object came from.
   b test his knowledge of geography.
6 Hans began to understand about the differences between:
   a how Swedish and Brazilian people enjoyed drinking coffee.
   b the lives of coffee pickers in Brazil and the people who enjoyed drinking coffee in Sweden.
7 Hans thinks that his 'powerful longing to understand the world' began with his father:
   a teaching him the details of the coffee process.
   b telling him stories related to different countries in the atlas.

D Work in pairs and discuss the questions.

1 Why do you think Hans's father told Hans these stories?
2 What are the best ways to encourage young children to be interested in the world?

GRAMMAR

would

4 A 8.03 | Listen and complete the sentences.

1 I watched out for him cycling along the street and .... the same question every time: 'Did you find anything today?'
2 Pappa .... these things home and tell me a story about every one of them.
3 He .... me sit on his lap, open up the world atlas in front of us and tell the story: 'It's a large country and very hot.'
4 'This coin turned up inside a sack from Santos', he .... pointing at the Brazilian port city.
5 He .... the working men and women …

B Work in pairs. Choose the correct words and answer the question.

1 In the sentences in Ex 4A the contraction *'d* is short for **had** / **would**.
2 We can use *would* to talk about **a past habit or routine** / **something we plan to do in the future**.
3 What other structure can we use to talk about a past habit or routine?

C Learn and practise. Go to the Grammar Bank.

▶▶ page 130 **GRAMMAR BANK**

PRONUNCIATION

5 A 8.04 | contracted *would* | Listen and choose the words you hear.

1 **I** / **I'd** wait for him every evening.
2 **He'd** / **He'll** always answer my questions.
3 **He explained** / **He'd explain** where Santos was on the map.
4 **He'd** / **He'll** point to the Brazilian city.

B Work in pairs. Think about three things that you and your family or friends would do when you were younger that are happy memories. Tell your partner. Remember to use contractions.

> When we were younger, my sister and I would always play games together. We'd spend a lot of time in our bedroom inventing new games. We'd play for hours and hours.

6 A Think of some people who you learnt from in your early life (parents, grandparents, teachers, mentors, friends, etc.). Prepare to talk about what you learnt and what these people would do to teach you.

> Something my taekwondo teacher taught me was that even when something seems impossible, you can usually achieve it if you break it down into small steps. She would always encourage us to work hard to master each new skill before moving onto the next.

B Work in groups. Take turns to tell your stories.

SPEAKING

7 A Work alone. What qualities do you think are important in a mentor? Add to the ideas below.
- desire to help others
- understanding everyone is different

B Read the Future Skills box and do the task.

> **FUTURE SKILLS**
> **Collaboration**
>
> When discussing ideas in a group, it's important to respond to other people's suggestions, as well as put forward your own ideas. You can use phrases like: 'That's a good point' and 'I'm not sure about that idea.'
>
> Can you think of any other useful phrases for responding to ideas and suggestions?

C Work in groups and discuss. What do you think is the most important quality in a mentor? Give examples from your own experience to justify your ideas and respond to other people's suggestions.

D Compare your ideas with other groups. What do you think of their ideas? Do you have similar suggestions?

8 Look up a video of Hans Rosling talking about statistics. Try *The Joy of Stats* or *How not to be ignorant about the world*. Did you enjoy the video? Why/Why not? Did you learn anything? Tell your class about any surprising information you learnt.

WRITING

a short biography

9 A Read a short biography about a childhood hero. Why does the writer admire this person?

B A short biography might include some or all of the following details. What do we learn about these details in the text about Olga Mumford?
1. date and place of birth (and death)
2. other important places in their life
3. education and jobs
4. achievements
5. important moments in their life
6. family/relationships
7. character

10 A Put the linkers in bold in the text under the correct heading.

Showing results	Showing reasons
Consequently … ; So …	For this reason …
1 ……………	3 ……………
2 ……………	4 ……………

B Choose the correct words to complete the sentences.
1. My father was a successful businessman and **because** / **as** of this I have always been very ambitious.
2. Both my parents were teachers and as a **consequently** / **result** of this I decided to work in education.
3. He was an incredible musician and **so** / **as** I was inspired to be like him.
4. She loved writing and **consequently** / **because** she decided to become a writer.

C Choose a person you have admired for a long time. Make notes using the categories in Ex 9B.

D Use your notes to write a short biography and explain why you admire this person and how they have influenced you.

My childhood hero

Olga Mumford was an artist and school teacher. She was born in Hungary in 1947 and lived there until she was thirty years old. She was working as an artist and a teacher when she met my grandfather, who had travelled to Hungary from Canada on business. They fell in love and married soon afterwards, and **as a result of this**, Olga left Hungary and moved to Canada. She stayed there and worked as a successful artist, exhibiting regularly in art galleries in and around Vancouver, until she died in 2016.

Olga was my grandmother and my childhood hero. When we visited her she would always take us into her studio and tell us stories about her paintings. I remember being fascinated by the beautiful pictures and the stories behind them. She would give us big sheets of paper and huge paint brushes and encourage us to make a big colourful mess. We would have such fun splashing paint everywhere and **as a consequence** my mother would always get angry, because we would end up with our faces, hands and clothes all covered in paint. But those times were special.

I admired my grandmother because she was always laughing and enjoying herself. She loved spending time with all her grandchildren and always had chocolates hidden in her pockets. She was a very independent woman who always enjoyed life, so she was always smiling. She also loved her work and enjoyed teaching other artists. She is my childhood hero **as** she always inspired me. It is **because of** her that I decided to study design at art school.

Unit 8 | Lesson C

8C One thing I know …

HOW TO … | give a presentation
VOCABULARY | presenting
PRONUNCIATION | stressing words in key phrases

VOCABULARY

presenting

1 Work in pairs. Discuss the questions.
1. Do you have to give presentations for work or your studies? If so, on what subjects?
2. Describe a time when you had to speak in public (a project in school, a presentation at work, a wedding, teaching a class, etc.).
3. What do you think makes a good or bad presentation? Can you think of any examples that you have seen?

2A Read the text and answer the questions.
1. According to the author, what was unusual about this presentation?
2. Why was it so popular?
3. Have you seen it? Would you like to?

B Work in pairs. Discuss the meanings of the words in bold in the text. Use a dictionary if necessary.

C Choose the correct words to complete the sentences.
1. A good **talk / field / delivery** always has a clear message.
2. It's important to present lots of **fields / outlines / facts and figures** to show the audience that you are an expert in your **point / field / outline**.
3. If the **talk / subject matter / delivery** of a presentation is bad, e.g. the presenter doesn't speak clearly or engage the audience, sometimes the key points are lost.
4. It's not essential to use **slides / subject matter / presenters** to illustrate your points, but it helps audiences who like to see information written down or shown in images or diagrams.
5. You should always write a good **outline / delivery / key point** so that you have a clear beginning, middle and end.
6. You should give examples to **engage / illustrate / argument** your key points.
7. Jokes can help to **illustrate / talk / engage** an audience, but make sure they're funny or they'll have the opposite effect!

D Work in pairs. Which of the statements in Ex 2C do you agree with? Why?

The most popular presentation ever?

This presentation broke lots of 'rules'. It didn't use any **slides**. There was no clear **outline**, although the **presenter** did name his **key points** in the first few minutes. He knew his **subject matter** well and was clearly an expert in his **field**, but he didn't provide lots of **facts and figures**.

It was his **delivery** that was unforgettable. The speaker, Ken Robinson, told jokes to **engage** his audience and stories to **illustrate** his points. And what were those points? His main **argument** was that schools need to help students to discover and develop their creativity. Robinson's **talk**, *Do Schools Kill Creativity?*, has been watched online over 85 million times and translated into over sixty languages. It inspires educators and others all over the world.

How to ...
give a presentation

3 A 🔊 **8.05** | Listen to the presentation and complete the notes.

> ## Five things you need to know to give a great presentation
>
> ① People learn best in _____ -minute chunks. Keep your presentation short.
> ② Make sure _____ information is easy to read and helps people _____ what is being said.
> ③ Think about _____ to deliver your presentation.
> ④ Include a call to _____. Tell people what you want them to do.
> ⑤ Be _____ about your subject – people will copy your emotions.

B Work in pairs. Do you think this was a good presentation? Why/Why not?

C 🔊 **8.05** | What does the presenter say? Choose the words the speaker uses (both options are possible). Then listen again and check.

1 Today I'm going to **talk** / **speak** about …
2 So, to begin with, can I just get **an idea of how many** … ? / **a show of hands** … ?
3 This brings me to my **first** / **last** point.
4 Next, my second **slide** / **point**, …
5 Moving on **to talk about** / **to the next point**, …
6 Turning **now** / **back** to …
7 As a **final** / **last** point, …
8 Just to **recap** / **summarise**.
9 Does anyone have any comments or **questions** / **suggestions**?
10 That's a very **good** / **interesting** question. I'm not sure I can answer that now.

4 A Work in pairs. Look at the phrases in Ex 3C. Which phrases are used for:
1 starting the presentation?
2 going through the main points?
3 finishing?
4 dealing with difficult questions?

B Learn and practise. Go to the Grammar Bank.

⏩ page 131 **GRAMMAR BANK**

PRONUNCIATION

5 A 🔊 **8.06** | **stressing words in key phrases** | Listen to the phrases. Which word(s) are stressed?

1 To begin with, …
2 The first point …
3 Moving on to …
4 As a final point, …
5 To sum up, …
6 Just to recap, …

B 🔊 **8.06** | Listen again and repeat the phrases.

SPEAKING

6 A Prepare to give a five-minute presentation to other students. Choose a topic that interests you. Use the ideas in the box or your own ideas.

| a hobby   favourite art, book or music |
| a place   a sport   work/studies |

B Answer the following questions. Use the bullet points for ideas.

1 How will you engage your audience at the beginning?
   • by telling a joke or story
   • by including some facts and figures
2 What are your key points? In what order will you talk about them?
3 How will you prepare your outline?
   • in note form
   • in a list
   • in a diagram
4 How will you deliver and illustrate your message?
   • by telling a story
   • by making a slideshow presentation
   • by showing pictures
5 How will you conclude your talk?
   • with a summary
   • with a call to action
   • by inviting the audience to ask questions

C Practise your presentation, then deliver it to other students.
   • Try to use the advice you heard in Ex 3A.
   • When you listen to the other presentations, think of at least one question and ask it at the end.

D Read the Future Skills box and do the tasks.

> ### FUTURE SKILLS
> **Communication**
>
> When giving feedback, start by saying something positive. Never give only negative feedback because this can cause bad feelings. Instead, talk about things you liked and things the speaker can improve.
>
> For each presentation, think about one thing you liked and one thing the presenter could improve. Give your feedback.

> ### MEDIATION SKILLS
> **asking someone to elaborate on what they said**
>
> ask follow-up questions after a presentation
>
> ⏩ page 156 **MEDIATION BANK**

Speak anywhere Go to the interactive speaking practice

Unit 8 | Lesson D

8D BBC Entertainment
Dragons' Den

SPEAKING | pitch a business idea
WRITING | an email giving work-related news

PREVIEW

1 A Read the programme information. Match the words in bold with the meanings (1–5).

1 the equal parts that a company's value is divided into. People can buy and sell these parts.
2 people who put their own money into a business or product and hope to receive more money in return
3 people who organise and run their own business
4 a description of a business idea, aimed to get people interested in buying or supporting it
5 say that you will pay a certain amount

B Read the programme information again and answer the questions.

1 What might be difficult about pitching a business idea to wealthy investors on *Dragon's Den*?
2 Do you have a programme like this in your country? If so, is it popular?

VIEW

2 A ▶ Watch the BBC video clip and answer the questions.

1 What kind of products does Jacob Thundil's business produce?
2 Is Jacob's pitch successful? What happens in the end?

B Are the following statements True (T) or False (F)?

1 Jacob grew up in Kerala, which in Sanskrit means 'land of coconuts'.   T
2 The market for coconut oil and coconut water in the US is worth around $50 million.
3 Jacob's business had a turnover of £1 million for three years.
4 Jacob would like to offer an investor 5% of his business in return for £75,000.
5 Jacob is responsible for sales, marketing and purchasing, and Manisha deals with operations (logistics, deliveries, etc.).
6 Deborah offers the team all of the money for 30% of the business.

C ▶ Watch again and check.

D Work in groups. Discuss the questions.

1 Do you think Jacob made the right decision? Why/Why not?
2 Have you ever had to give a presentation or a pitch like this? If so, what was it for? How did it go? If not, how would you feel about it?
3 What advice would you give to someone who has to make this kind of pitch for their business?

Dragons' Den

Dragons' Den is a BBC business programme. In each episode, **entrepreneurs** have three minutes to describe their business idea to five wealthy **investors**. After the entrepreneur's **pitch**, the investors ask questions. If an investor likes the idea, they **make an offer** to invest their money. In return, the investor will get **shares** of the business.

100

SPEAKING

pitch a business idea

3 A ◆ 8.07 | Listen to a couple pitching their business and answer the questions.
1. What type of service do they offer?
2. How much money are they asking for, and for what percentage share of the business?
3. What questions does the investor ask?

B ◆ 8.07 | Listen again and tick the phrases you hear.

> **KEY PHRASES**
> We run a business called …
> Examples include …
> What's special about [our business] is that we …
> We offer …
> Our [holidays/products] offer …
> The market for … is worth …
> We'd like to expand our business to cover …
> Our long-term plan is to …
> We're asking for [X] euros for a(n) [X] per cent share of the business.

4 A Work in pairs. You are going to pitch a business idea. Choose a product or service from the box or think of your own.

> a food product   a clothes range
> a company that organises creative activities
> an invention (e.g. a new gadget/app)
> a home delivery service   an educational tool

B Plan your pitch. Go to page 144.

WRITING BBC

an email giving work-related news

5 A Read the email. What news does it describe?

Subject: Two new cafés
From: brennanmg@cafebotas.com
To: all

Dear All,

We are delighted to provide an update on some exciting news. As you know, we recently talked to a number of investors about opening two new cafés. I'm pleased to announce that the food investor VJ Picaldi made an offer which we have accepted. This allows us to start searching for two new locations and hiring more staff.

We will organise a meeting next week to present the plans for the new cafés, and discuss all the tasks that will need to be done. We'll also take a close look at the schedules and try to get an opening date for both cafés in the diary. We look forward to seeing you all there.

Please let me know if you have any questions or concerns at this stage.

Marilyn Brennan

CEO, Café Botas

B Which pieces of advice (1–5) does the email follow?
1. have a clear and accurate heading
2. use a positive tone
3. explain a new development or situation
4. describe any follow-up actions, e.g. meetings
5. include an opportunity for a response

C Plan an email to colleagues describing the outcome of the pitch you made in Ex 4B. Explain what happened and describe any follow-up actions, e.g. meetings. Use the advice in Ex 5B to help you.

D Now write your email. When you are finished, compare your email with your partner in Ex 4B. Which information did they include from Ex 5B?

8 REVIEW

GRAMMAR

third conditional and *should have*

1 A Use the prompts to make sentences.
1. If / know / the job / be / this difficult / I / not offer / help
2. I failed my exams. I should / study harder
3. If study / harder / at school, / I / might / go / university
4. If / have / more confidence, / I / change jobs / earlier
5. I / not oversleep / this morning / if / I / go / to / bed earlier / last night
6. I / should not / drink / so much coffee / last night. I couldn't sleep.
7. There was a lot of traffic so we were late. If / not be / so much traffic, / we / arrive / on time.
8. I sent the application form in but it was too late. I / should / send it in / sooner.
9. He would / be / on time / for the interview / if / he / left / the house / at 8 a.m.
10. If / she / go to / university, / she / might / become / a teacher.
11. If / they / give / us / the correct directions, / we / not / get lost.
12. I would / go / on the course / if I / know / about it.

B Think of three things you have done in the last ten years. Discuss the questions with a partner.
- How would things have been different if you hadn't done them?
- Should you have done anything differently?
- Why/Why not?

2 Choose the correct words.
1. I hate living in this old house. I **would be / would have been** happier if we **had bought / buying** a modern apartment.
2. If I **had met / met** Sandra before I'm sure I **would have recognised / recognised** her face.
3. They should **offering / have offered** her the job – she was definitely the best candidate.
4. If they hadn't **leave / left** their passports at home, they **would be / were** in Indonesia now.
5. I **shouldn't have / should have** taken on so much work – I'll never be able to finish everything on time!
6. If she **should have trained / had trained** harder she **would win / would have won** the race.

would

3 A Replace the past simple verb in bold with *would* where possible. Where it is not possible, use *used to*.
1. My best friend **lived** in Vienna when she was younger.
2. I **spent** most weekends with my grandparents when I was a child.
3. I **didn't think** money was important, but I changed my mind when I wanted to buy an apartment.
4. Every summer holiday I **worked** in a café to earn some money.
5. After class I **played** football in the park with my friends.
6. My parents always **made** a special cake for my birthday.
7. Stefan **was** a bank manager, but he gave it up and decided to go into acting instead.
8. When we went on a long car journey, my sister and I **sang** all our favourite songs.
9. I was so untidy when I lived at home. I always **left** my clothes all over the floor!
10. I **played** the guitar, but I gave it up because I didn't have time.

B Change four of the sentences in Ex 3A so they are true for you. Compare your sentences with a partner. Find three things that you would both do as children, but you don't do now.

VOCABULARY

4 A Complete the sentences with the words in the box.

| afraid | attention | deepened | encouraged |
| most | passion | seriously | time | worrying |

1. You should stop _____ so much and try not to take everything so _____ .
2. I watched an amazing documentary which _____ my interest in the world of plants and insects.
3. I'm learning jujitsu – I'm never _____ to try something new.
4. Let's go out. We need to make the _____ of our time here.
5. My grandmother always _____ me to dance. She was a ballerina when she was younger.
6. You should take some _____ to think about your options before you make a decision.
7. He never seems to pay _____ to what's going on around him.
8. Literature has been my lifelong _____ . I can't read enough.

B Work in pairs. Change some of the sentences in Ex 4A so that they are true for you. Do you have anything in common?

102

5

A Choose the correct words to complete the sentences.

1 I am not very motivated **on** / **for** / **by** money, but it's really important that I enjoy my work.
2 I can't wait to try **in** / **out** / **on** this new idea!
3 I might have reached a different decision if I'd had more time to think things **out** / **around** / **through**.
4 I just can't figure **on** / **out** / **in** how this is supposed to work!
5 We'll arrange another meeting to follow **up** / **down** / **out** on this idea.
6 It will be lovely to get together **in** / **with** / **on** a few other musicians.
7 Whenever you have a good idea, you must write it **on** / **down** / **in** so you don't forget it.
8 If the goal feels too difficult, you need to break it **up** / **down** / **through** into small steps and do one thing at a time.

B Choose three phrasal verbs from Ex 5A. Write three sentences about your life using the phrasal verbs. Compare your sentences with a partner.

6

A Complete the text with the words in the box.

> delivery   engage   expert
> field   figures   illustrate
> outline   points   presenter
> slides   subject   talk

My presentation was a complete disaster! First of all, the ¹_____ before me spoke for much too long, so my ²_____ started late and I didn't have time to set up properly. Then, I couldn't get my laptop to work, so I couldn't show the ³_____. I'd prepared to ⁴_____ my points. Luckily, I'd made some notes with a(n) ⁵_____ of what I wanted to say, but I forgot some of the key ⁶_____ and I got several of the facts and ⁷_____ wrong, too! I felt nervous, so my ⁸_____ wasn't very confident and I didn't manage to ⁹_____ the audience, even though I am a(n) ¹⁰_____ in this ¹¹_____. It looked like I just didn't know my ¹²_____ matter.

B Work in pairs. Tell your partner about a time when you gave or listened to a presentation. What was it like?

7

A Choose the correct options (A–C) to complete the text.

Inventing a better world

Ann Makosinski grew up in Canada, but she didn't have a lot of toys as a child. Her first toy was a box of electronic parts. Later her parents bought her a hot glue gun. Should her parents ¹_____ her more toys? She doesn't think so. Having these 'toys' ²_____ her to collect things around the house and piece them together to make new 'inventions'. These inventions rarely worked, but she was never ³_____ to do something new. She had discovered her love for dreaming ⁴_____ new ideas and inventing things, and this became her lifelong ⁵_____. ⁶_____ by the story of a friend in the Philippines who had failed her school exams because she had no electricity, Ann ⁷_____ to work on inventing a light source that didn't need batteries. At fifteen, she won the Google Science Fair with a torch powered using only the heat in your hand. Two years later, she invented her eDrink coffee mug which uses the heat from a drink to charge your phone. Ann ⁸_____ the world around her, so she is always ⁹_____ and never runs out of ideas. It's possible that if she'd ¹⁰_____ more toys as a child, she ¹¹_____ so creative in her free time, and she might never have become an inventor. She also didn't own a mobile phone when she was a teenager, but she doesn't think her parents ¹²_____ her have one. She enjoyed being different to the other kids and it gave her a chance to ¹³_____ her interest in her inventions.

	A	B	C
1	has bought	bought	have bought
2	encouraged	discovered	mastered
3	discovered	afraid	encouraged
4	up	on	in
5	passion	skill	progress
6	Motivated	Discovered	Longing
7	stopped worrying about	made the most	took time
8	is careful not to take	takes seriously	pays attention to
9	inspired	encouraged	worried
10	have	having	had
11	should have been	wouldn't have been	would have been
12	let	should had let	should have let
13	invent	deepen	master

B 🔊 **R8.01** | Listen and check your answers.

103

GRAMMAR BANK

1A narrative tenses

REFERENCE ◀◀ page 9

When we tell a story, we often use a variety of tenses. These are called 'narrative tenses' and they include the past simple, the past continuous and the past perfect. It is important to use the correct tense as this gives us information about the sequence of events and the most important details of the story.

It **was** a cold, wet day and the wind **was blowing**. Josh **was walking** down the road when suddenly, he **heard** a terrible crash. He **turned** around and **saw** that a woman **had crashed** her moped. Luckily, the woman **was** fine, but the moped **had been** badly **damaged**.

Past simple

We use the past simple to talk about the main events of a story and other completed actions.
Suddenly, he **heard** a terrible crash.
She **woke up** early and **decided** to go out for a walk.

```
        she decided
she woke    to go out
up early    for a walk
   X          X
past        now       future
```

Past continuous

We use the past continuous:
- to give background information to a story.
- to refer to temporary or changing past states and situations.

The sun **was shining**. The wind **was blowing**. (background information)
He **was living** in Brazil. (at the time of the story, temporary)
We **were travelling** around Australia. (temporary)

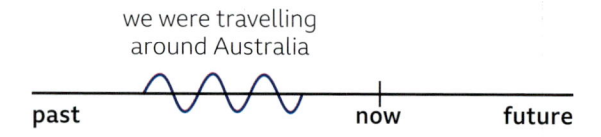

```
    we were travelling
     around Australia
       ∿∿∿∿∿
past        now       future
```

Past perfect

We use the past perfect to talk about an action which happened before the main events.
When I **got** to the top floor office I realised I **had left** my phone in the car.
When we **arrived** at the station, the train **had** already **left**.

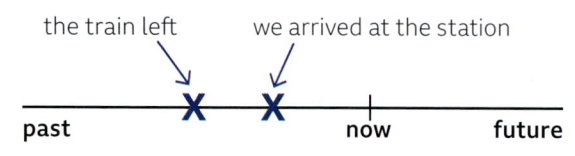

```
the train left    we arrived at the station
      ↓                    ↓
      X                    X
past              now              future
```

The past perfect links a past point (*we arrived at the station*) to a point further back in time (*the train had left*).

PRACTICE

1 Choose the correct words to complete the sentences.

1. I **was jogging / jogged** along the beach when suddenly, I **realised / had realised** I didn't have my wedding ring. I **was dropping / had dropped** it on the beach somewhere.
2. I **was looking / looked** for my ring when an old lady **came / had come** up to me. She **was finding / had found** my ring on her morning walk.
3. My granddad **was fishing / fished** when he **was catching / caught** an old wallet with his fishing rod. He was amazed to see it was his own wallet, which he **was losing / had lost** in the same lake twenty years earlier!
4. I **was studying / had studied** at university in California when my sister suddenly **decided / was deciding** to come and visit me from Hong Kong. I was so surprised because she **hadn't said / wasn't saying** anything about her plans.

2 Complete the stories with the words and phrases in the boxes.

| arrived | gave | had just returned | hadn't seen |
| opened | was carrying | were staying |

This old leather suitcase is very special to me. It belonged to my father and it's a bit damaged now. I remember when I was a child, my mother and I ¹_____ at my grandmother's house. I ²_____ my father for a long time. When he ³_____ at the house, he ⁴_____ this old suitcase, and it had all these labels on it from around the world. He ⁵_____ from a trip across Asia. When he saw me, he sat down and ⁶_____ the suitcase. He pulled out a beautiful doll and ⁷_____ it to me. It's one of my earliest memories, and I've always kept the doll and the suitcase.

bought	crashed	drove	had always loved
had completely broken	realised	was going
was laughing	were staying

When I was six years old, my parents ⁸_____ me a large, red, toy car for my birthday. I ⁹_____ cars and I was so excited to try out my new present. We ¹⁰_____ at my grandparent's house for the summer holidays and I asked if I could try the new car outside. I ¹¹_____ it down the hill outside their house. I remember I ¹²_____ and the car ¹³_____ faster and faster down the hill. Suddenly, I ¹⁴_____ that I didn't know how to stop. I ¹⁵_____ into the tree at the bottom of the hill. Luckily, I wasn't hurt, but when I got out of the car I realised I ¹⁶_____ the new car.

3 Complete the stories with the correct form of the verbs in brackets.

One morning I ¹_____ (look) for my car keys and I couldn't find them anywhere. Eventually, I ²_____ (find) them in my son's bedroom. He ³_____ (hide) them because he didn't want me to go to work.

When I ⁴_____ (study) at high school, my friends ⁵_____ (spend) a lot of their time skateboarding. I ⁶_____ (not try) it before and I ⁷_____ (think) it looked fun. I ⁸_____ (buy) myself a really cool skateboard and I was so excited to use it. Unfortunately, the first time I went out, I ⁹_____ (fall) and broke my arm. I ¹⁰_____ (not realise) how difficult it was! My skateboard stayed in my room after that.

GRAMMAR BANK

1B verb patterns

REFERENCE ⏪ page 12

Sometimes we put two verbs together.
They hope to learn Spanish.
I like playing ball games.

When the first verb takes a preposition (except *to*), the second verb is usually in the *-ing* form.
You should **think about doing** that course.
I finally **succeeded in finding** a job.
We **believe in telling** the truth.
You should **concentrate on passing** your exams.
I **dream about playing** for that team.
She **apologised for getting** angry.
He **struggles with working** at night.
I **care about saving** the environment.

When a phrasal verb is followed by a verb, the second verb is usually in the *-ing* form.
We **carried on driving** for another hour.
I **look forward to reading** your new book!
She **gave up studying** at night.
We **put off making** that decision.

Some phrasal verbs can be followed by an infinitive or an *-ing* form, but with a change in meaning.
Compare the two sentences.
She **went on dancing** even after her accident.
She **went on to be** a great dancer.
Go on + *-ing* means 'continue'.
Go on + *to* infinitive means 'end up'.
He **grew up watching** his father play football.
He **grew up to be** a great footballer.
Grow up + *-ing* means 'do something while changing from being a child to an adult'.
Grow up + *to* infinitive describes what a person becomes as an adult.

Some verbs (without prepositions) can be followed by a *to* infinitive or an *-ing* form, but with a change in meaning.
I **stopped to talk** to Felipe.
I **stopped listening** to rock music years ago.
Stop + *to* infinitive means 'paused an action in order to do a different action'.
Stop + *-ing* means 'change a habit or finish a repeated/extended action'.
I must **remember to set** the alarm.
I **remember playing** with those toys when I was five or six.
Remember + *to* infinitive means you have a responsibility which you must not forget.
Remember + *-ing* means you have a memory of something that happened in the past.

PRACTICE

1 Complete the sentences with the correct form of the verb in brackets.
1 She's never cared about .... (have) lots of possessions.
2 After university, Ahmed went on .... (become) a TV presenter.
3 I gave up .... (collect) treasure years ago.
4 That house we rented turned out .... (be) ideal for my family.
5 Yoko apologised for .... (arrive) late.
6 I'm looking forward to .... (start) my dream job.

2 Match each pair of sentence beginnings with the endings (a–b).
1 Kim went on to play
2 Kim went on playing
a his guitar even after a string broke.
b the guitar at several famous venues in London and Paris.

3 Pete remembers calling
4 Pete remembers to call
a his grandmother every day to check she's OK.
b me, but he's forgotten what we talked about.

5 She stopped drinking
6 She stopped to drink
a soda because it's unhealthy.
b water halfway through the run.

3 Choose the correct options (A–C) to complete the text.

Three signs you have too much stuff

1 You buy things not realising you already have them
Problem: You'd always dreamed about ¹............ that book or dress or vase. You order it online, open the package and realise you already own it.
Solution: Stop ²............ attention to advertisements and new trends. Concentrate on ³............ the things you already have.

2 There's nowhere to sit down or eat
Problem: You have chairs, a table and a sofa, but they are full of stuff. 'I can't carry on ⁴............ like this,' you say. But you do.
Solution: Before you go to bed, remember ⁵............ everything in its place, so every surface has some space on it.

3 You can never find what you're looking for
Problem: This happens with clothes. You have piles of them, but can't find what you want. Eventually you give up ⁶............ and just buy something new.
Solution: Go through your clothes. Throw away anything you haven't worn for over 18 months. It might turn out ⁷............ the most important thing you do in the house.

	A	B	C
1	owning	own	to own
2	paying	to pay	pay
3	to appreciate	appreciate	appreciating
4	live	living	to live
5	to put	put	putting
6	to look	looking	look
7	being	be	to be

105

GRAMMAR BANK

1C How to … leave phone messages

REFERENCE ◀◀ page 15

Direct requests

We can make a direct request by using *Can you/Could you … ?* or *Will you/Would you … , please?*

Can/Could you call me back?
Will/Would you (look for it/pick some up), **please**?

Indirect requests

We can soften a request to make it sound less direct by using phrases like:

Do you think you could/you'll be able to … ?
I wonder if you could/would …
I wonder if you'd mind … + *-ing*
Do you think you could have a look for it for me?
I wonder if you'd help me set the alarm.
I wonder if you'd mind helping me lock up.

Notice with indirect requests, the word order is the same as for affirmative statements.

Do you think you could NOT ~~Do you think could you~~

Leaving a phone message

We use particular phrases when speaking on the phone or leaving a phone message. For example, we say:

It's Max speaking./It's Max here./This is Max speaking/calling about … NOT ~~I'm Max.~~

things you'll hear on a recorded message

You've reached (Riccardo's) **mobile**.
Please leave a message and **we'll get back to you**.
Thank you for calling (Dr Singh's office). **Our (office) hours are** (8 a.m. to 6 p.m.).
I **can't take your call right now, but if you leave a message** with your name and number, I'll get back to you as soon as I can.

starting a message

It's (John) here.
This is (Marcelo Fagundes). I'm calling about …
I'm calling to (ask for/request) …
I was ringing to (see if/find out if) …

making a polite request

Can you/Could you (call me back/check) … ?
Will you/Would you (look for it/explain …), please?
Do you think you could (have a look at it for me)?
I wonder if you would mind (having a look/helping me) … ?

giving detailed information

You'll need to (open the … /speak to …).
It's the (one) that's (sitting on the desk).
You'll find it (on the table next to the …).
The event starts at … , (so you have to be there at …).

asking for further phone actions

Can you call me back?
You can reach me on (this number/0775867435).

PRACTICE

1 Match 1–6 with a–f to make phone messages.

1 Hi you've reached Miguel's number. I can't take your call right now, but
2 Thank you for calling ElectroStars Ltd. Our hours
3 Hi, it's Ivan here.
4 Hi, this is Pete Sciberras. I'm calling about
5 Can you call
6 You can

a me back on this number?
b I'm calling about tomorrow night.
c are 9 a.m. to 5 p.m. Monday to Friday.
d reach me on 0886537564. Thanks.
e please leave a message and I'll get back to you.
f my appointment on Monday.

2 Choose the correct words to complete the requests.

1 Hi Sara. Could you please **arrange** / **arranging** for the plumber to come and fix the kitchen sink?
2 **Would you** / **You would** be able to help me tidy up the sitting room?
3 Do you think **could you** / **you could** be here by 7?
4 I wonder if you would be able to **look** / **looking** after Sammy for me?
5 **Would** / **Could** we try to finish the meeting on time?
6 I wonder if you would mind **go** / **going** to the shop to pick up some sandwiches.
7 **Will you** / **Do you think you will** please hang up your clothes before you leave?
8 I wonder if you would mind **to stay** / **staying** behind to help me clear up afterwards?

3 Complete the phone messages with the words in the boxes.

| can | here | message | reached | think | this | to |

A: Hello. You have ¹_____ Denbells Alarm Systems. Please leave a ²_____ .
B: Hello, ³_____ is Monika Ingham ⁴_____ . I'm calling ⁵_____ ask for your help. My alarm system is faulty and the alarm keeps going off. Do you ⁶_____ you could send somebody round to look at it for me? ⁷_____ you call me back on 03544 82212? Thanks.

| could | get | it's | ringing | take | wonder | you'll |

A: Hi this is Sally. I'm sorry I can't ⁸_____ your call right now, but please leave a message and I'll ⁹_____ back to you as soon as I can.
B: Hi Sally, ¹⁰_____ Gabriel here. I was ¹¹_____ to see if you could do me a favour. I left my bicycle downstairs and I think I forgot to lock it. I ¹²_____ if you could go and check it for me? ¹³_____ find the lock in the kitchen, near the door. ¹⁴_____ you let me know when you get this message?

GRAMMAR BANK

1D except for, apart from, (not) even

REFERENCE ⏪ page 16

except for

We use *except for* + noun to say that something is not included.
The school teaches most ball sports **except for** golf.

We use *except for* to introduce the one person/thing that means a statement isn't 100 percent true.
All the children are here **except for** Leila. (Leila is the only child who isn't here.)
I like vegetables, **except for** onions. (Onions are the only vegetables I don't like.)

When *except for* follows a noun, we can omit *for* with no change in meaning.
She loves ball games **except (for)** golf.
They speak all the Latin-based languages **except (for)** Romanian.

When we use *except* as a conjunction that joins two clauses, it cannot be followed by *for*. The meaning is the same as *except for*.
My dogs are similar **except** ~~for~~ the oldest one is bigger.
The books look good **except** ~~for~~ the covers are slightly damaged.

apart from

Apart from + noun means the same as *except for*.
We're open every day **apart from** Sunday.
Apart from Kenzo, the whole family came to the wedding.
I like all types of films **apart from** documentaries.
Apart from the sound of the clocks, the house was silent.

even

We use *even* to emphasise that something is surprising or unusual.
John doesn't usually watch TV, but **even** he liked that programme!
I'll help you with the project. I'll **even** stay with you after work to finish it.

not even

We use *not even* to emphasise a surprising negative point.
Not even Jo, whose English is very good, could understand what he was saying.
She'd changed so much I did**n't even** recognise her!

PRACTICE

1 Are the meanings of sentences a and b the same (S) or different (D)?
  1 a I enjoy reading all types of books apart from romance novels.
    b I enjoy reading all types of books except for romance novels.
  2 a Not even Juan likes that film.
    b Even Juan likes that film.
  3 a She eats everything except for seafood.
    b She eats everything except seafood.

2 Correct the mistakes in the conversations. One conversation is correct.
  1 A: I could live without gadgets, for my phone.
    B: Me too! I really need it.
  2 A: The Tora Grande Hotel is completely empty, isn't it?
    B: Yes, apart two Spanish tourists.
  3 A: Dad said the dog refused to eat yesterday.
    B: That's right. He even want a bone, which is his favourite food.
  4 A: She was so kind when you needed help.
    B: Yes, she even offered to pay my rent.
  5 A: From History, what other school subjects do you like?
    B: I quite like Maths.

3 Choose the correct options (A–C) to complete the text.

The Social Media-Free Teen

For seventeen-year-old Soumaya Hart, it was a special moment on a boat that did it. She was with a group of ten friends on the trip of a lifetime off the coast of Sicily. 'It was the most beautiful place I'd ever seen. [1]_____ Rome could compare with this. I looked at my friends. [2]_____ one person, they were all checking their phones. They'd posted photos on social media and were counting their "likes". They weren't [3]_____ looking at the view.'

At that moment, Soumaya decided to stop using social media. 'Apart [4]_____ calling my family, I don't use my phone. I've seen what it does to people my age. We don't appreciate the things that are important. Half the time we don't [5]_____ see them.'

Everyone in Soumaya's family [6]_____ her grandmother was on social media. What did they think of her decision?

'At first, they thought it was strange. [7]_____ my dad, who's hopeless with technology, is on social media. But after a while, they saw I was spending my time doing really interesting things like volunteer work and sports. [8]_____ from my younger brother, who still thinks I'm strange, the family realises it works for me.'

1	A Except	B Apart	C Not even
2	A Except for	B Even	C Apart
3	A apart	B for	C even
4	A for	B from	C even
5	A even	B except	C apart
6	A apart	B except	C for
7	A Apart	B Except	C Even
8	A Except	B Apart	C Even

GRAMMAR BANK

2A present perfect continuous

REFERENCE ◀◀ page 22

We use the present perfect continuous to talk about actions and situations which started in the past, but are not finished. They continue until now.

I've been studying Mandarin **since last year.** (I'm still studying Mandarin.)
He's been living in the UK **for ten years.** (He still lives in the UK.)

We use the past simple when the action or situation is finished.

I studied Mandarin last year. (I'm not studying it now.)
He lived in the UK for ten years. (He's not living there now.)

We form the present perfect continuous with *have/has + been + -ing* form.

+	I've / She's	been	reading a book.
−	They haven't / He hasn't	been	listening to me.
?	Have you / Has she	been	working here for a long time?

We use the present perfect continuous with *for* or *since* to talk about the length or duration of an activity, or when it started.
We use *since* to refer to a point in time.

They've been living in New Zealand **since** 2020.
She's been waiting for you **since** 2 p.m.

We use *for* to talk about a period of time.

We've been working together **for** over twenty years.

We use *How long ... ?* to ask about the length of time.

A: **How long have** you **been playing** the drums?
B: **I've been playing since** I was six years old.

We use the present perfect continuous with *recently/lately* to talk about actions and situations that are relevant now.

I haven't been sleeping very well **recently**. (I look tired.)
She's been working very hard **lately**. (She deserves a promotion.)

We often use the present perfect simple or the present perfect continuous (with little change in meaning) especially for verbs such as *live, work, teach, study*.

I've lived here for years.
I've been living here for years.

We do NOT use the present perfect continuous with state verbs (e.g. *love, hate, like, have, enjoy, know, understand, believe*, etc.). With these verbs we use the present perfect simple.

I've known him for ages. NOT ~~I've been knowing him for ages.~~
I've had this car for three years. NOT ~~I've been having this car for three years.~~

PRACTICE

1 Complete the sentences with the present perfect continuous form of the verbs in the box.

| do   get up   live   rain   run   study   try   watch |

1 A: How long _____ he _____ in Berlin?
   B: About two years. He's just bought an apartment.
2 I haven't been outside yet – it _____ all day!
3 _____ you _____ that new crime series? It's brilliant!
4 They _____ together at the same university for the last two years.
5 She's exhausted. Lately, she _____ very early for work.
6 A: You look really fit!
   B: Thank you. I _____ five kilometres every morning since the beginning of the year.
7 I didn't know you sang in a band! How long _____ that?
8 A: I thought you'd stopped drinking coffee.
   B: I _____ to give up, but I just can't resist.

2 Choose the correct words to complete the text.

¹**I work / I've been working** in a small tech company for about five years. My business partner, Salman, and I ²**have been knowing / have known** each other since we were children and we're best friends. We ³**have been starting / started** the company when we were university students. Our main product is digital games, although ⁴**we develop / we've been developing** educational tools for about a year, too. Recently, ⁵**we get / we've been getting** a lot of attention from the media, which is great. The only problem is that we work far too much. This ⁶**began / has been beginning** in the early years of the company. When we were just starting, we ⁷**have been having / had** to work long hours because it's a very competitive industry. But in the last two years, ⁸**we work / we've been working** very long days and it's become too much. We're trying to change our working habits!

3 Look at the a and b sentences. Tick the ones that are possible. Sometimes both are possible.

1 a She's always liked music since she was very young.
   b She's always been liking music since she was very young.
2 a How long have you lived in Turkey?
   b How long have you been living in Turkey?
3 a I've known my friend Waleed Bakri for sixteen years.
   b I've been knowing my friend Waleed Bakri for sixteen years.
4 a What have you done this morning?
   b What have you been doing this morning?
5 a They haven't worked here for long.
   b They haven't been working here for long.
6 a I've understood everything so far.
   b I've been understanding everything so far.

GRAMMAR BANK

2B relative clauses

REFERENCE ◀◀ page 24

We use defining relative clauses to give essential information about a person, a thing, a place, a time or a possessive.

We use relative pronouns *who*, *which*, *where*, *when*, *whose* to introduce the relative clause.

A specialist is someone **who knows a lot about a subject**.

Do you remember the time **when we went on holiday together**?

Once there was a girl **whose name was Lilibet**.

In defining relative clauses we can use *that* to replace *who*, *which* or *when*.

Swimming is something **that always makes me feel better**.

We can leave out *who*, *which* and *that* when the relative clause already has a subject.

Rob Jenkins was a teacher **(who) I knew** at college.

I is the subject of the verb *knew*. *Who* is the object of the verb, so can be left out.

Rob Jenkins was a teacher **who taught** me maths.

Who is the subject of the verb *taught*, so we must keep *who*.

We can replace a defining relative clause with verb + -ing.

The winner is the person **ending up** with the most points. = The winner is the person **who ends up** with the most points.

We can replace a defining relative clause with *to* + infinitive. We often use *to* + infinitive with *the first*, *the last*, *the only* and superlative adjectives.

Who was the last person **to see John**? = Who was the last person **who saw John**?

PRACTICE

1 A Join the sentences with defining relative clauses. Use the relative pronouns in the box.

| when   where   which (x2)   who (x2)   whose (x2) |

1 That's the town. I grew up there.
2 Have you got the book? I lent it to you last month.
3 Is this the actor? You were talking about him yesterday.
4 Monday is the day. I start my new job then.
5 Patrizia is the Italian girl. Her painting won a prize.
6 The film was fantastic. We saw it yesterday.
7 Students usually do well. They do lots of practice.
8 The man is a good friend of ours. His mother lives next door.

B In which sentences can you use *that* instead of another relative pronoun?

C In which sentences can you leave out the relative pronoun?

2 Choose the correct words to complete the text. In some cases both options are possible.

Watch your behaviour

Some of the patterns of behaviour ¹**scientists / which** have found over the last hundred years are interesting. In one famous experiment, scientists asked people to hold a warm cup of coffee ²**which belonged / belonging** to someone before they were introduced to that person. They found that people ³**who / that** had been holding a warm drink often had a more positive view of the people ⁴**they / that** met soon after. The reason is that the part of the brain ⁵**judges / which judges** the warmth of something is next to the part ⁶**measures / that measures** a person's personality – how friendly they are as a person.

One of the most interesting studies ⁷**to show / that showed** people's behaviour was a visual test. Students had to identify a line ⁸**that / who** was the same length as a target line. Students who worked alone were very accurate, but students ⁹**who / that** worked with other people often got the answer wrong. The students ¹⁰**taking / took** part didn't know that other people in the experiment were actors ¹¹**who's / whose** answers were incorrect. It was an important experiment and it wasn't the last one ¹²**to find / found** how easy it is to get people to change their behaviour when they are in a group.

GRAMMAR BANK

2C How to … talk about things that annoy you

REFERENCE ◀◀ page 27

We use these phrases to talk about things that annoy us.

I can't stand it.
I can't bear it.
It really annoys me.
It gets on my nerves.
It bugs me.
It drives me crazy/nuts/mad.
Don't get me started on (people who never say thank you).

Notice *It bugs me* and *It drives me nuts* are informal.

With all the phrases above we can continue with *when* and a clause.

I can't bear it	**when** that happens.
It gets on my nerves	**when** people drop litter.
It drives me nuts	**when** people don't answer my messages.

We can also use a relative clause or *-ing*.
Children that misbehave in restaurants really bug me.
I can't stand people **shortening** my name.

We can use other short phrases to agree or disagree.
Yes, so annoying.
I don't mind that.
That doesn't bother me.

Verbs in the continuous form

We can use the present and past continuous with *always, constantly, continually, forever* to describe a habit which we find annoying.
You're always losing your phone!
My dad's forever complaining about noise.
Our car was continually breaking down.

We also sometimes use this structure to show a positive emotion.
Children at this age are so cute. They're constantly laughing!

PRACTICE

1 Complete the conversations with the words in the box. There are three extra words in each box.

Conversation 1: TV

| annoyed | annoying | bugs | constantly |
| drives | sometimes | when | why |

A: I can't bear it [1]......... Karly's looking at her phone and keeps asking me what's happening.
B: Yes, Milo does that too. It [2]......... me nuts.
A: And she's [3]......... taking control of the remote and changing channels without asking.
B: You know what [4]......... me about TV? When you can hardly hear the TV show but then the adverts are really loud.
A: So [5]......... ! And you have to keep changing the volume on the remote.

Conversation 2: Work

| make | on | putting | reading |
| stand | started | talking | under |

A: The job's OK, but there are some things about my workplace that I really can't [6]......... .
B: For example?
A: Well, I'm in an open-plan office and it really gets [7]......... my nerves when people use their phone right next to me.
B: Yes, or people [8]......... their phone on speaker so you can hear the whole conversation.
A: And don't get me [9]......... on people [10]......... *my* phone or computer over my shoulder.

Conversation 3: Cars

| always | drive | is | it | so | who | they | travelling |

A: That car just turned left without giving a signal. I can't stand [11]......... when people do that.
B: Yes, [12]......... annoying and dangerous! Why do people think it's OK to do that? And then there are the people [13]......... never turn off their indicators.
A: Maybe they just forget. But you know what I can't stand? People [14]......... at half the speed limit in the fast lane.
B: I agree. I have a friend who [15]......... forever doing that.

2 Correct two mistakes in each conversation.

1 A: It gets my nerves when people play loud music out of their apartment windows.
B: Yes, and in my block the guy next door is continually sing along with his favourite songs.

2 A: This light above my desk is drives me mad. It's constantly buzzing.
B: It bother me. I guess I've stopped noticing.

3 A: Oh no! I've lost one of my earrings. I'm usually doing that.
B: Yes, so annoyed! I always buy two pairs of earrings so that I have a spare pair.

4 A: I really hate this zip in my bag. It's for getting stuck.
B: Yes I have a bag like that. And don't make me started on zips which come undone above and below the zipper.

GRAMMAR BANK

3A conditional structures: *unless, even if, in case (of)*

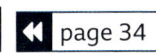

REFERENCE ◀◀ page 34

unless

We use *unless* to mean *if not*.

Unless you hurry up, we're going to leave without you.
(If you don't hurry up, we're going to leave without you.)

Please don't park here unless you're a member of staff.
(Please don't park here if you're not a member of staff.)

When the *unless* clause is first in a sentence, we use a comma at the end of the clause.

Unless she speaks slowly, I can't understand Liz.

When the *unless* clause is second, we don't usually use a comma before it.

I can't understand Liz unless she speaks slowly.

even if

We use *even if* for emphasis, to say that something will not change a situation.

Even if the company pays me twice as much, I'm going to leave.

I'll never speak to her again even if she says sorry.

When the main clause and the *even if* clauses are long, we use a comma to divide them.

in case

We use *in case* to talk about being prepared for the possibility that something might happen.

Take your umbrella in case it rains.

We often use it with *just*.

I'll make some sandwiches just in case we get hungry later.

The *in case* clause is usually second in a sentence. We don't use commas before or after the clause.

in case of

We use *in case of* + noun in formal situations to mean 'if something happens'. It is often about a bad or dangerous situation.

In case of fire, break the glass.

In case of bad weather, the ceremony will be held indoors.

We often use it in formal written information.

The *in case of* clause usually comes first in a sentence.

We use *unless, even if* and *in case* + present tenses to speak about the present or the future.

I can't help you unless you tell me the problem. NOT *unless you'll tell me the problem.*

We can also use *unless, even if* and *in case* + past tenses when we are speaking more hypothetically.

Even if I won a million euros, I wouldn't change my job.

PRACTICE

1 A Choose the correct words to complete the sentences. In two cases both are possible.

1 You'll be in trouble **unless** / **if** you don't stop making all that noise.
2 I'm not going to the party **in case** / **even if** Denise asks me.
3 Careful! You'll hurt yourself **unless** / **in case** you get down from there.
4 **In case of** / **In case** a heart attack, follow these instructions.
5 **Even if** / **Unless** it's really cold, I'm not going to wear a coat.
6 Shall I bring some spare socks **in case** / **if** we get wet?
7 I can't help you **in case** / **unless** you tell me what is wrong.
8 I wouldn't lend Kirk any money **even if** / **in case** he promised to give it back.
9 **In case of** / **In case** I forget later, here's my phone number.
10 Nothing will change **unless** / **even if** the government changes its mind.
11 We won't get a seat **even if** / **if** we get to the festival late.
12 **In case of** / **If** a power cut, use the stairs.

B In the two cases where both are possible, how is the meaning different?

2 Rewrite the sentences using the word in brackets.

1 You need to read Max a story or he won't go to sleep.
  Max won't go to sleep .... a story. (unless)
2 It might rain, but we're definitely going to have a picnic.
  .... have a picnic. (Even if)
3 Always check things you've bought online. They might be damaged.
  Always check .... damaged. (in case)
4 Sometimes I'm in a really bad mood, but I always try to smile.
  I always try .... mood. (even if)
5 Carol needs to stick to her plan or she'll probably fail.
  .... she'll probably fail. (Unless)
6 If there's an emergency, push the red button.
  .... button. (In case of)
7 I need to leave now or I might miss the last train.
  I need to leave now .... train. (in case)
8 I might have to tell Sigrid, but I really don't want to.
  I really don't want .... have to. (unless)
9 There's a possibility that I'll have problems with my phone so I'll bring my laptop.
  I'll bring my laptop .... phone. (in case of)
10 Don't stand near the edge. You might fall.
  Don't .... fall. (in case)

GRAMMAR BANK

3B necessity, obligation and permission

REFERENCE ⏪ page 36

Necessity and obligation

Many phrases can express both necessity and obligation, depending on the context.

I need to take some time off. (It's important that I take time off. It's a necessity.)

I need to finish this report by tomorrow. (Someone, for example my manager, expects me to finish the report. It's an obligation.)

We use *be necessary to*, *be essential to* and *needs to be done* when the focus is on the action.

We use *be necessary to* + infinitive to say that you must do or be something.

It's necessary to have a driving licence. ([You] must have a driving licence.)

We use *be essential to* + infinitive to say that something is necessary and important.

It's essential to take her to hospital immediately. ([We] must take her to hospital immediately. It's very important.)

We can also use *need to* + *be* + past participle to say something is an obligation or a necessity.

This job **needs to be** done by tomorrow morning.

We use *have got to* and *be supposed to* when the focus is on the **person**.

We use *have got to* + infinitive for obligation and necessity. It means *must* or *have to*.

It is a little more informal than *must* or *have to*.

I've got to get home by ten.

In informal spoken English this is often pronounced *gotta*.

She's gotta think about it.

We use *be supposed to* + infinitive for something which is an obligation, but which we don't always do.

I'm supposed to wear a hat when I deliver food, but I don't.

Robbie**'s not supposed** to call customers by their first names, but he often does.

Permission

We use *be (not) allowed to* + infinitive to say that something is OK, you can do it, or it's not OK, you can't do it.

Our children **are allowed to play** computer games for two hours at the weekends.

I'm not allowed to go to bed after midnight.

We can also use *be (not) permitted to* to mean the same thing. It is more formal than *be allowed*.

Office workers here **are permitted to** wear casual clothes on Fridays.

Drivers **are not permitted to drive** more than eight hours without a break.

Other forms of the phrases

We can use most of these phrases in the future and past as well as with modal verbs (*might*, *could*, etc.).

It will be necessary to take your passport with you.

In my first job **it wasn't essential** to speak English.

The apartment **might need to be** painted.

We can use *be supposed to* in the past.

We **were supposed to** go straight home, but we didn't.

We often use *had to* for the past of *have got to*.

This morning I **had to** get up at 4.30 to catch the early train.

PRACTICE

1 Correct the mistakes in the sentences. One sentence is correct.
1 Is essential to print your name after your signature.
2 The video doesn't need to be finish until next Wednesday.
3 Don't do that! You aren't supposed jumping the queue!
4 I got to make a real effort to stop eating chocolate.
5 Is it necessary wear a uniform in your job?
6 Are we allowed to take photos here?

2 Complete the text with the words and phrases in the box.

| are not | don't need | essential | got to |
| is necessary | is supposed | not to | permitted |

Proposed rules for our new neighbourhood social media group

- It is ¹_____ to introduce yourself when you join this group.
- People are not ²_____ to add other people to the group without contacting the administrator.
- You ³_____ permitted to change the group photo unless you are an administrator.
- This ⁴_____ to be a friendly group, so always be polite to each other.
- Even if you are in a bad mood, it's essential ⁵_____ lose your temper.
- Take responsibility! If you see a message which could upset people, you've ⁶_____ say something.
- Don't feel it ⁷_____ to reply to each message. It isn't!
- Emojis are fine, but they ⁸_____ to be sent with every message!

3 Use the prompts to make sentences and questions.
1 At your first school, / you / allowed / wear / own clothes / or / have / wear / a uniform?
2 If you / selling / something / on our site, / essential / be / honest about / its condition.
3 What time / we / supposed / arrive / at the party / this evening / and / we / got / wear / anything special?
4 When / this report / need / be / finish / by?

GRAMMAR BANK

3C How to … take part in an interview

REFERENCE ⏪ page 39

typical interviewer questions

Tell me a bit/something about yourself/your current job/your last job.

Why do you want/Why are you interested in this job/position?

What will/would you bring to the company?

What questions do you have for me about the job/position?

How long have you been working/did you work at … ?

Why have you decided/did you decide to leave your current/last job?

phrases to check

We use these phrases to check we understand the question and how we need to answer:

Where should I start?

How do you mean?

Can I use an example from university?

Are you asking what criticisms they might have?

What do you mean by 'researching new flavours'?

interviewee's answers

I've done some research about the company.

One of my main strengths is that I …

I think I have a lot to offer.

I think people/my colleagues would say (that) I …

I've always loved/worked …

It's important for me to …

PRACTICE

1 Put the words in the correct order to make sentences.

1 strengths / I / that / am / very / is / of / my / One / main / flexible .
2 mean / you / How / do ?
3 have / me / to / challenges / important / It's / for / new .
4 me / bit / a / current / Tell / about / position / your .
5 highly / say / I'm / that / people / would / think / I / professional .
6 the / company / you / will / to / What / bring ?
7 Where / I / start / should ?
8 in / you / this / are / Why / job / interested ?

2 Complete the conversation with the words in the box. You do not need three of the words.

| a | about | be | been | done | is | it |
| me | say | ~~take~~ | tell | to | would | |

A: Good morning. I'm Danica Harding. Please *take* a seat.
B: Hello. Nice to meet you.
A: So, I have your CV, but can you tell _____ something about your recent experience?
B: Yes, over the last few months I've _____ working as a manager at the local railway station.
A: So this would be quite a change for you. Why have you decided _____ leave your current job?
B: Well, I've loved working for the railways, but _____ is important for me to find a new challenge.
A: And why a hotel? What _____ you bring to the company?
B: Well, I think I have _____ lot to offer.
A: For example?
B: One of my main strengths _____ that I'm very good at handling unexpected problems.
A: Yes, I can imagine, with the trains!
B: And colleagues would _____ that I'm flexible and willing to help out with anything that needs to be done.

(twenty minutes later)

A: So, Vineeta, do you have any questions for me _____ the company or the position?
B: Well, I've _____ some research about the company and I have a few questions about your management training programme.
A: Please go ahead.

3 Complete the conversations with phrases to check. Sometimes more than one answer is possible.

1 A: So, what work have you done in this area in the past?
   B: Where _____ ?
2 A: What can you bring to the company?
   B: _____ what skills do I have?
3 A: Tell me about a time when you had to give someone negative feedback.
   B: Can I _____ sport?
4 A: We start early here. Would that be an issue for you?
   B: _____ if I'm reliable?

113

GRAMMAR BANK

3D expressing preferences

REFERENCE ⏪ page 40

would rather

We use *would rather* + infinitive + *than* to talk about:

- our general preferences.
  Zayan **would rather cook** with electricity **than** with gas.
- specific situations.
  I'd rather pay by phone if that's all right.
- hypothetical situations.
  I'd rather be happy **than** (be) rich.
  Would you **rather** spend a night in an aquarium or a library?

To make the negative, we use *would/'d rather* + *not* + infinitive.

I'd rather not answer that question.

We use *would much/far rather* to show a strong preference.

We**'d much rather** go skiing than surfing.
I**'d far rather** cycle to work than go by underground.

prefer, would prefer

We use *prefer* + noun/*-ing* form + *to* to talk about:

- our general preferences.
  I **prefer cats to** dogs.
  In general he **prefers working** alone **to** working with other people.

We use *would prefer* + *to* + infinitive to talk about:

- specific situations.
  I'd prefer to get a takeaway tonight.
- hypothetical situations.
  Would you **prefer to live** in the Arctic or the Sahara Desert?

To make the negative, we use *would/'d prefer not* + *to* + infinitive.

I'd prefer not to meet today. Tomorrow is better.

We use *much prefer* and *definitely prefer* to show a strong preference.

I **much prefer** playing tennis to watching it on TV.
I **definitely prefer** cats to dogs.
I'd much/definitely prefer to go by train.

We can also use *would go for* to mean *would choose/prefer*.

Which would you rather be, a teacher or a doctor?
I'd go for a teacher.

PRACTICE

1 Choose the correct words to complete the sentences.

A: In general, ¹**would** / **do** you prefer going on holiday in the summer or winter?
B: Definitely summer. I prefer hot weather ²**to** / **than** cold weather.
A: And ³**do** / **would** you rather stay in a hotel or an apartment?
B: I'd ⁴**more** / **much** rather rent an apartment.
A: Why's that?
B: I think apartments are better value and I prefer ⁵**cook** / **cooking** to ⁶**eat** / **eating** out.

A: Would you prefer ⁷**have** / **to have** ordinary milk, oat milk or soya milk?
B: I ⁸**wouldn't rather** / **'d rather not** have any milk thanks. I prefer my coffee black.
A: And would you rather ⁹**sit** / **to sit** inside or outside?
B: We'd prefer ¹⁰**being** / **to be** outside. Is there a free table?
A: Where would you rather ¹¹**sit** / **sitting**? There's a table in the sun and one in the shade.
B: I'd ¹²**far rather** / **rather far** sit in the sun, if that's OK, Jan.

2 Use the prompts to complete the answers.

1 A: How about a drink?
  B: I / rather / have / something / eat.
2 A: Shall we stop now?
  B: I / prefer / carry on / until / we / finish.
3 A: Do you have anything to say?
  B: I / rather / not / make / comment / this moment.
4 A: Which car shall we buy?
  B: I / go / first / one / we / saw.
5 A: So, Italy or Spain?
  B: Where / you / rather / go?
6 A: When can you give us your answer?
  B: I / prefer / wait / few / days.

3 Rewrite the sentences so they mean the same. Use the words in brackets. For some questions you will need to change the form of the word in brackets.

1 I don't want to talk about it right now. (prefer)
2 Would you like to stay in or go out on Saturday? (rather)
3 Hu Min likes walking more than running. (prefer)
4 We'd rather not miss our deadline. (prefer)
5 I'd prefer to avoid an argument with the manager. (rather)
6 Kanye doesn't like football as much as rugby. (prefer)
7 Most people like being early more than being late. (prefer)
8 We don't feel like queueing. (rather)
9 Do you want to go on your own to see Luke? (prefer)
10 Do they like going sightseeing more than relaxing on the beach? (rather)
11 They definitely enjoyed living in the country more. (prefer)
12 Sven likes being a student less than being a teacher (rather)

GRAMMAR BANK

4A past plans and intentions

REFERENCE ◀◀ page 45

We use *was/were going to* to talk about a planned action in the past that didn't happen.

I was going to call you, but I was too busy.
They were going to visit the museum, but it was closed.

The negative is *wasn't/weren't going to*.

We can also use *planned to* and *hoped to* as alternatives. These have a similar meaning to *was going to*. We can use these in the past simple or past continuous.

I planned to visit last week, but I couldn't in the end.
I was planning to take you to the new café, but we didn't have time.
I hoped to finish my project yesterday, but something went wrong.
I was hoping to meet your father, but he wasn't there.

The negative of *planned to* is *wasn't planning to*.

I wasn't planning to go anywhere this summer. (But maybe this changed.)

We can use other verbs in the past continuous to describe past intentions:

I was expecting to go to Turkey that year.
They were waiting to finish university before they got married.

We can also use *meant to* to talk about a planned action in the past that didn't happen. We use it more in the simple than the continuous.

I meant to introduce you to Xavier, but he left early.
We meant to invite you, but we couldn't find your phone number.

The negative is *didn't mean to*. We usually use this to describe when someone does something by accident.

Sorry – I crashed the car! **I didn't mean** to!
She **didn't mean to** cause trouble. She was trying to help.

We use *intend to* to show a planned action in the past. This sounds more formal than *meant to*, *hoped to*, etc. We use it more in the simple than the continuous.

The **doctor intended to** see me last week, but he had to cancel.

We often use *intend* to focus on the reasons for an action.

He bought the ring because he **intended** to ask her to marry him.

The negative is *didn't intend*.

She **didn't intend** to do it. It was an accident.

We use *thought it would be* to talk about the reason for a planned action in the past.

I brought you because I thought it would be nice if you met my parents.

PRACTICE

1 Choose the correct options (a–c) to complete the sentences.

1 They didn't .... live a lie for so long.
 a meant to b mean to c mean
2 He thought .... possible to deceive everyone with his scheme.
 a there would be b it will be c it would be
3 He .... to become rich and famous, but it all went wrong.
 a was planning b plans c was planned
4 They .... pretend to be other people.
 a were going b were to be c were going to
5 I .... meet my deadline, but I couldn't cope.
 a was expecting to b was expected c am expecting to
6 The manager .... offer me a permanent contract.
 a was intend to b intended c intended to
7 We were .... get stuck in traffic again.
 a hoping that not to b hoping not to c not hoping
8 She .... to be rude.
 a intend not b wasn't intended c didn't intend

2 Complete the sentences using *was/were going to* and the verbs in the box.

arrive make send tell visit walk watch wear

1 We .... a film about a hoax at the cinema, but there were no tickets left.
2 .... the truth about their scheme or carry on living a lie?
3 They .... up a ridiculous excuse, but in the end they came clean.
4 I .... my jeans, but my friend told me to dress formally.
5 .... or take a taxi home? I can give you a lift.
6 My mother .... me this weekend, but she was too busy to come.
7 I .... you the information by text, but it seems you already have it.
8 .... at the airport today? I think they'll be stuck. The airport's closed because of the bad weather!

3 Match the sentence beginnings (1–10) with the endings (a–j).

1 Sorry. I didn't mean to
2 We were going to
3 I was going to go
4 We thought it
5 I meant to call
6 She planned
7 They weren't
8 What did you intend
9 What were you planning to
10 Who were you going

a to do after graduating?
b to university, but I changed my mind.
c expecting to wait six hours at the airport.
d would be a good idea to buy tickets in advance.
e to do your project with before it got cancelled?
f do this afternoon?
g you before I left, but I didn't have time.
h visit my friend, but she's ill.
i to become a doctor.
j break your watch. It was an accident!

115

GRAMMAR BANK

4B indirect and negative questions

REFERENCE (page 47)

Direct questions

To make direct questions we usually use the word order: (question word) + auxiliary verb + subject + main verb (infinitive).

question word	auxiliary verb	subject	main verb (infinitive) + phrase
What	do	you	know about the situation in … ?
Where	does	he	work?
Where	should	we	put these bags?

Indirect questions

We use indirect questions to sound more polite (and less direct). After the opening phrase (*Could you tell me … ? Can I ask you … ? Do you know … ?*) we use the affirmative form.

Direct: **Where do I have to go?**

Indirect: **Could you tell me where I have to go?**
NOT ~~Could you tell me where do I have to go?~~

Negative questions

We can also use negative questions to sound polite. For negative questions we use the negative form instead of the affirmative form.

Wouldn't you like a drink/something to eat?
Don't you want to take your coat off?

Instead of:

Would you like a drink/something to eat?
Do you want to take your coat off?

We use negative questions when we want to check or confirm information (we think we know the answer). We can also use negative questions to show surprise.

Didn't she win an award? (I think she won an award, so I'm checking the information/confirming my belief.)
Isn't it time to go? (I think it's time to go, and I'm surprised that you are not ready yet.)
Did you see that documentary? (genuine question – I don't know the answer.)
Didn't you see that documentary? (I expected the answer to be *yes*, and by using a negative question I show my surprise that I now think you didn't.)

We can use negative questions to try to persuade people that our idea is the best.

Don't you think that we should take a taxi? (I think we should take a taxi.)
Wouldn't you say that this film is more interesting? (I think this film is more interesting.)

Negative questions can be confusing to answer. To help with this, we can answer a negative question with a short sentence instead of *yes/no*.

A: Wouldn't you like a drink?
B: Thank you, that would be lovely.

PRACTICE

1 Choose the correct options (a–c) to complete the questions.
  1 Do you know who .... ?
    a is the film-maker b the film-maker is c was the film-maker
  2 .... a documentary recently about the Arctic?
    a Didn't he make b Didn't he made c Did he made
  3 .... that we should do something about the problem?
    a You don't think b You would think c Don't you think
  4 Can you tell me where .... a taxi rank?
    a can I find b I can find c find
  5 Do you know how expensive .... ?
    a is it b is this c this is
  6 .... watch it on Netflix recently?
    a We didn't b Didn't we c We did

2 Rewrite the direct questions as indirect questions.
  1 What time does it start? Can you tell me .... ?
  2 Do you think it will make a difference? Don't .... ?
  3 Would you say that this is his best film? Wouldn't .... ?
  4 Have you ever seen one of these before? Can I ask if .... ?
  5 What's the problem? Do you know .... ?
  6 What do you think of the idea? Could you tell me .... ?

3 Choose the correct alternatives to complete the interview.

A: Could you tell us what ¹**you thought / do you think** of the documentary *I am Belmaya*?
B: Yes, of course. I thought it was brilliant, really powerful. It's a wonderful documentary about a young Nepali woman who dreams of being a film-maker.
A: ²**It didn't / Didn't it** just win an award?
B: That's right. It won several media awards.
A: ³**Can I ask you / Can I tell you** what the story is about?
B: It's the extraordinary story of a young Nepali woman, Belmaya, who wants to become a film-maker. However, living in poverty, she has a lot of struggles to overcome in order to achieve her dreams.
A: Do you know how ⁴**she fell in love / did she fall in love** with film-making?
B: Yes, she took a photography workshop when she was a young girl.
A: ⁵**Wasn't / Didn't** she an orphan?
B: Yes, she lost her parents and didn't get a very good education. Her camera was taken away from her and she lived in difficult circumstances.
A: Later, ⁶**didn't / wasn't** she have a husband who also discouraged her from being a film-maker?
B: That's right. But she was very determined and eventually succeeded. Now her film is winning awards.
A: ⁷**Do you would / Wouldn't you** agree that we are seeing more and more documentaries like this being made by women?
B: Absolutely. Films like *He named me Malala*, *I am Greta* and now *I am Belmaya* all show us how powerful young women in all parts of the world are taking control of their futures. It's inspirational.

GRAMMAR BANK

4C How to … talk about the news

REFERENCE ⏪ page 51

We can use the following phrases to help us talk about a news story.

initiating a discussion about a news story

Have you heard about/seen … ?
Did you hear the news about … ?
Are you following the news/story about … ?

describing/summarising the news story

So, basically, what happened was …
I can't remember the details, but, basically, …
It seems/appears …
Apparently, …

commenting on the story

It's all over the news.
I saw it on the news/on TV.
It's on all the news channels.
It's received a lot of coverage.

responding to a news story

Really? I had no idea.
I can hardly believe it.
Oh no! That's (terrible/awful/unbelievable/really funny/sad, etc.).
That's a relief.
That sounds scary.

PRACTICE

1 Choose the correct words to complete the conversations.

A: Did you hear the [1]**new** / **news** about the woman whose taxi driver drove her into a canal?
B: No, what [2]**happens** / **happened**?
A: I saw it on the [3]**news** / **coverage**. So, [4]**awfully** / **basically**, what happened was she was in a taxi and the driver was following his sat-nav because he didn't know where to go. Luckily, he was driving really slowly, at about five miles an hour. And [5]**apparently** / **seems**, he drove into the canal.
B: Oh no! That sounds [6]**scary** / **sad**. Were they OK?
A: Yes, they both escaped unhurt.
B: That's a [7]**relief** / **shame**.
A: But [8]**it** / **that** seems that the taxi driver still tried to make her pay £30 for the journey.
B: [9]**Terrible** / **Really**? That's ridiculous.

A: Are you [10]**following** / **hearing** the news story about the couple who accidentally vandalised a $400,000 painting in South Korea?
B: No. What happened?
A: It's on all the news [11]**coverage** / **channels**. Apparently, they saw the huge canvas covered with big swirls of paint and there were some pots of paint and brushes on the floor in front of the painting.
B: Really? What happened?
A: Well, I can't remember all the [12]**details** / **news**, but [13]**it seem** / **basically**, they thought that it was a 'participatory painting' where anybody can add some paint. So they picked up the brushes and started painting.
B: [14]**Really** / **Apparently**? How funny.
A: I know. Basically, it [15]**appears** / **seem** that the paint and the brushes were part of the original painting, and had been used by graffiti artist JonOne when he created the painting in front of a live audience.
B: Oh no. I can hardly [16]**believe** / **read** it.

2 Correct two mistakes in each conversation.

1 A: Have you listened the news about the student protest?
  B: Yes, it's received a lot of cover.
2 A: Do you follow the story about the woman who disappeared?
  B: Yes, it's all on the news.
3 A: So, basic, what happened was a cat got stuck on the roof of the office and firefighters had to rescue it.
  B: Oh no! That's awfully!
4 A: I can't remember the detailed, but police have arrested lots of the protesters.
  B: I know, I saw it on the new.
5 A: Apparent, the singer Katie has quit the band.
  B: It's really? I had no idea.
6 A: It seem that a tiger escaped from the zoo and it has been seen walking around the streets.
  B: That sound scary.

GRAMMAR BANK

5A clauses of purpose: *to, so as to, in order to/that, so that*

REFERENCE — page 57

Clauses of purpose with *to* infinitive

We use clauses of purpose to talk about our reason for doing something.

(I'm organising a party) (to celebrate my birthday.)
　　the action　　　　　　　the purpose

We use *to* + infinitive and *in order to* + infinitive to introduce purpose clauses.

I'm going downstairs **to lock up**.
I often turn off my phone **in order to avoid** distractions.

We can also use *so as to* + infinitive. We often use this for more formal situations.

The police put up barriers **so as to stop** people entering the building.

Notice The subject of the main clause and the clause of purpose is always the same.

(**She** is studying English) (**in order to get** a better job).
She is studying and *she* wants to get a better job.

Clauses of purpose with *that*

We can use *so that* + subject + verb or *in order that* + subject + verb to talk about purpose.

We use these when the subject of the two clauses is the same or different.

I'd like to move closer to the stage **so that I can hear** better.
The school is changing the exam date **in order that** students have more time to prepare.

Remember: when the subject of the two clauses is different, we use *so that* or *in order that* but NOT *in order to*, *to* or *so as to*.

I'm going to send you all the information **so that you** can make a decision. NOT ~~... in order to make a decision~~

Clauses of purpose in the negative

We put *not* before *to* in negative clauses of purpose: *in order not to, so as not to*.

He set his alarm for 7 a.m. **in order not to oversleep**.
I check my 'to do' list every day **so as not to forget** anything.

We can use *not to*, but it is not common except as a contrast.

I eat a lot of vegetables, **not to** lose weight **but to** improve my health.

We use a normal negative after *so that* and *in order that*.

Let's check this very carefully **so that we don't make** a mistake.
The company gave us our money back **in order that we wouldn't post** a negative review.

Clause order

The clauses of purpose usually come after the main clause, but they can come first.
When they come first, they are followed by a comma.

In order to buy a car, I had to save up for a year.
So that the team could take a break, all matches in August were cancelled.

PRACTICE

1 Choose the correct words and phrases to complete the sentences.

1 Valeria had to stand on a chair **to** / ~~so that she~~ reach the shelf.
2 In order **to** / ~~that~~ save money, we're giving up buying coffee from coffee shops.
3 I put the cake in the oven on a low heat in order **not to** / ~~that it wouldn't~~ burn.
4 You have to stick at things **in order to** / ~~so as~~ achieve your goals.
5 Haruto will do almost anything ~~avoiding~~ / **to avoid** an argument.
6 Dilara moved to Istanbul **so that** / ~~in order~~ Emre could see her more often.
7 Repeat the vocabulary to yourselves in order ~~to not~~ / **not to** forget it.
8 It is essential to practise regularly ~~not so as to~~ / **so as not to** fall behind.

2 Complete the email with one word in each gap.

Hi Mel,
Great to hear all your news! You asked about Ladislav's wedding last week. Well, we had a great time. We'd bought our rail tickets six months in advance in ¹ *order* to get the lowest price and to be sure of getting a ticket on the train.
We took the night train in order ² *to* Krystina (my new sister-in-law) could pick us up from Krakow station early the next morning. We also wanted to have a day in the city ³ *so* that Milan could visit an old friend. I managed to find some lovely plates and also bought a doll, ⁴ *not* to give as a present but ⁵ *to* keep for myself. In order ⁶ *not* to be late for the wedding the next day, we had an early night. We had breakfast at eight in the morning so that there was ⁷ *not* any chance of missing our taxi. And yes, the wedding was fabulous! Photos attached.
Love Katarina xxx

3 Rewrite the sentences using the words in brackets.

1 I need better light so that I can take a good photo. (to)
　I need better light to take a good photo.
2 Could you contact the marketing department to arrange a meeting? (in order)
3 I always use this app in order not to get stuck in a traffic jam. (so that)
4 Let's open the window so that we can let in some fresh air. (to)
5 We often have to work late so that we don't fall behind schedule. (so as)
6 I always take a hat with me so that ~~I don't~~ get cold. (in order)

118

GRAMMAR BANK

5B comparative and superlative structures

REFERENCE ◀◀ page 61

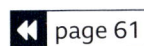

Comparatives

We use comparative adjectives to compare nouns, and comparative adverbs to compare most verbs.
My new company is **busier** than my old one.
Could you speak **more quietly**, please?

We use a comparative adjective with verbs of the senses and feelings (e.g. *look, taste, smell, feel, sound, seem*).
It **seems quieter** here than I remember.

We often use *(not) as* + adjective/adverb + *as*
My chair is**n't as comfortable as** yours.
I do**n't** speak Spanish **as well as** you do.

We use quantifiers (*a bit, a little, slightly, much, a lot*) with adjectives and adverbs to talk about how much difference there is.
This desk is **slightly more expensive** than that one, but it's **much better**.
Dimitris is writing **a lot more confidently** now than he used to.

Superlatives

We use superlative adjectives and adverbs to compare something with the rest of the group.
This is **the least expensive** way to send the package.
Mateo and Luciana have travelled **the furthest** to get here today.

We use quantifiers (*much, by far*) with superlative adjectives and adverbs to talk about how much difference there is.
Hyun Woo is **by far the most talented** young actor I've ever seen.
She talked **much more clearly** than I'd expected.

Emphasising

We can repeat a comparative adjective or adverb to emphasise change.
The situation is **more and more dangerous** every day.
As we left the city, Bianca drove **faster and faster**.

We use *than ever* with comparative adjectives and adverbs for emphasis.
The new series is **better than ever**.
Hillary is working **harder than ever**.

It means the same as *than before*, but gives more emphasis. We can also use *ever* or *ever before*.
We've had more forest fires this year **than before/ever/ever before**.

We also use *ever* with superlative adjectives. We don't use *before* with superlatives.
We've built a lot of hotels, but this is the **tallest ever**.

Other structures with comparatives and superlatives

We use parallel phrases with *the* + comparative adjective/adverb, *the* + comparative adjective/adverb.
The bigger the car, **the more expensive** it is, usually.
The more you practise, **the better** you'll become.
Notice The comparative begins each clause.
NOT ~~you practise the more, you'll get the better.~~

We often use *one of, some of, among* with superlative adjectives.
This model is **among our most expensive** cars.

PRACTICE

1 Correct the sentences. Add a comparative or superlative form of the word in brackets. Some adjectives need to be changed to adverbs.

            shyer
1 Rihanna is much ∧ than her sister. (shy)
2 I've been going to the gym every day and I feel a lot than I used to. (fit)
3 Samuel is always losing his temper. He needs to become. (patient)
4 We're going to be late. Can you drive? (fast)
5 Mohammed is great! He's student I've ever taught. (enthusiastic)
6 The price of petrol is slightly than it was last week. (cheap)
7 The government will need to take the housing problem. (serious)
8 In my opinion, this is Petrov's novel so far. (successful)

2 Correct the mistakes in the sentences. One sentence is correct.

1 Self-driven cars are becoming more more reliable.
2 Natalie is one most intelligent people in the company.
3 The customer service department wasn't helpful as I would expect.
4 The calmer you are, the effective your complaint will be.
5 My new computer is far the most powerful I've ever had.
6 The more dramatic the opening of the film, the better.
7 The new James Bond film is the exciting than ever.

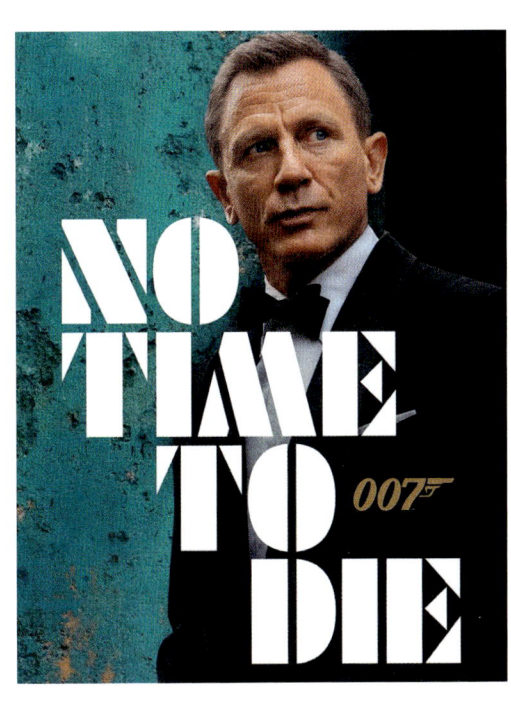

119

GRAMMAR BANK

5C How to … summarise information from different sources

REFERENCE ◀◀ page 63

We use these phrases to summarise information from information that we read or hear.

saying where we got an idea from

From what X say(s), …
From what everyone says, it's a very reliable company.

According to X, …
According to the reviews, the film is the best ever in the series.
Notice that we use a comma after these phrases.

summing up ideas

Long story short, …
Long story short, no-one seems to agree which is better value for money.

It's a matter/question of (whether / how much / when, etc.) …
So, **it's a matter of whether** I want to wait a long time.

All in all, …
All in all, there seem to be a lot of problems with that model.

Taking everything into account / If we take everything into account, …
Taking everything into account, I've decided to stick with my current broadband supplier.

In the end, …
In the end, I decided not to buy a new phone.

Notice We use a comma after these phrases.

focusing on a specific point

Just because something is (+ adjective), it doesn't mean (that) it is (+ adjective).
Well, **just because something's expensive, it doesn't mean it's better**.

It all comes down to (the price / the colour / whether / how much, etc. …)
It all comes down to the colour.

Notice After question words we use normal sentence order, not a question form.
It all comes down to when **it would arrive**. NOT ~~It all comes down to when would it arrive.~~
It's a question of **how much it costs**. NOT ~~It's a question of how much does it cost.~~

focusing on a specific problem

The (only) thing is (that) …
The thing is the watch isn't waterproof.
The only thing is that Piotr advised me not to choose a hybrid.

PRACTICE

1 Choose the correct words to complete the conversations. In two cases, both are possible.

Conversation 1

A: Have you decided on a hotel?
B: Well, taking ¹**all / everything** into account, I think the Sunshine is better.
A: Why's that?
B: From ²**what do / what** the reviews say, it's quiet, the pool is beautiful and the food's great, too.
A: What about the price?
B: It's a lot more reasonable than the other hotel. But ³**simple / just** because something's cheaper, it doesn't ⁴**mean that / mean** it's worse.
A: That's true. And ⁵**in the end, / it all comes down** you have to make a choice and see what it's like.
B: Yeah, basically.

Conversation 2

A: How was the trip?
B: Well, ⁶**all in all / long short story**, it was fine. ⁷**Only a thing / The only thing** is that there wasn't a sauna.
A: Seriously? Is that a real problem?
B: ⁸**According to / From what says** the hotel brochure, there was a sauna. But there wasn't.
A: So did you complain?
B: Well, I don't like to do that. ⁹**It's a matter / It's question** of how much time and energy I want to spend. ¹⁰**Long story short / In end**, everything else was fine. We enjoyed it.
A: ¹¹**It all comes down to that / It's a matter of that**, doesn't it? How much you enjoyed it.
B: Yes, and ¹²**if you take / taking** everything into account – the food, the atmosphere, the rooms – it really was OK.

2 Use the prompts to complete the conversation.

A: Shall / have / dinner / somewhere new tonight?
B: How about the Stagecoach Inn? According / the reviews, / food / be / superb.
A: But just / the reviews / be / positive, / it / not / mean / the restaurant / be / good.
B: you / heard / something / negative?
A: One / my colleagues / eat / there last week. From / she / say, / I / be / not so sure about it.
B: Why, / what / she / say?
A: Basically, / food / be / excellent. / only / thing / be / that / service / bit slow.
B: So, / be / question / whether / we / be / prepared / wait for a good meal.
A: All / all, / I / rather / stay / at home / and order / a takeaway.
B: Let / do / that.

GRAMMAR BANK

5D causative *have* and *get*; reflexive pronouns

REFERENCE ⏪ page 64

Causative *have*

We form the causative *have* with *have* + object + past participle.

I have my hair cut every six weeks.

Use the causative *have*:

- to say when you arrange for someone else to do something for you. You usually pay them for the service.
  We're having our apartment painted at the moment. (Someone else is painting our apartment, not us.)
  When **did you have your bike repaired?** (Someone else repaired the bike, not you.)

Be careful with the word order. The causative *have* is different from:

- the present perfect.
  I have cut my hair. Do you like it? (I have done it (recently) myself.)
  I have my hair cut every month. (Someone else does it every month.)
- the past perfect.
  He **had repaired his** bike so it was safe to ride. (He did it himself.)
  He **had his bike repaired** yesterday. (Someone else repaired it.)

Causative *get*

We use *get* + object + past participle:

- often in speaking more informally.
  You need to **get your eyesight checked**.
- to emphasise that it is difficult to have something done.
  I got my computer fixed, but it took a week to find someone.

We can also use *get* + *somebody* + *to* infinitive:

- when we ask somebody to do something and they do it.
  I got a friend to take me to the airport.
  I got my hairdresser to cut it shorter than usual.
- we use this both for unpaid or paid work.
  We need to **get someone to fix** this gate.

Reflexive pronouns

We can use reflexive pronouns to emphasise that we have done something alone with no help.

Do you like this necklace? I made it **myself**.
Did you organise the wedding **yourselves**?

The reflexive pronouns are:

subject pronoun	reflexive pronoun
I, you	myself, yourself
he, she, it	himself, herself, itself
we, you, they	ourselves, yourselves, themselves

PRACTICE

1 Put the words in the correct order to make sentences. Use the causative *have* or *get*.

1 month / I / once / hair / cut / a / get / my .
2 repaired / do / your / Where / have / car / you ?
3 to / the / fixed / heating / We / winter / before / need / get .
4 on / new / house / the / put / having / a / We're / roof .
5 furniture / have / delivered / should / the / You .
6 having / her / Zara / photo / taken / hates .
7 you / tested / ever / had / Have / ears / your ?
8 get / needs / before / suit / his / dry-cleaned / tomorrow / to / Nicolás .

2 Complete the sentences with one word. Use the past participle or a reflexive pronoun.

1 Who painted their house?
  a They painted it ....
  b They got it .... by a local firm.
2 Your window needs to be fixed.
  a I'm fixing it .... next Tuesday.
  b I'm having it .... next Tuesday.
3 Your apartment looks really clean!
  a We've just cleaned it ....
  b We've just had it ....
4 Where did you get your nails done?
  a I did them ....
  b I got them .... at the nail counter in the shopping centre.
5 I've got a problem with my car. Is that new garage any good?
  a No, you should try and repair it ....
  b Yes, you should get it .... there.
6 Who's making Anya's wedding dress?
  a She's making it ....
  b She's having it .... in town

3 Correct the mistakes in the sentences. Two sentences are correct.

1 Sharon got myself to clean her car.
2 I'm going get a colleague to phone Head Office for me.
3 Could you get your lawyer to check this?
4 We'll get Mike make copies of the report.
5 You need to get to one of your parents to sign this.
6 You should have get a professional jeweller to fix your ring.
7 I'll get someone to come up and check your shower.
8 I can never get Patrizia tidy her room.

GRAMMAR BANK

6A so and such

REFERENCE → page 69

So and **such** have similar meanings. We can use *so* + *adjective/adverb* to show emphasis or strong feelings about something. Without *so* the sentence would still be complete.

That part of the city is beautiful. → That part of the city is **so beautiful**!

She played the guitar brilliantly. → She played the guitar **so brilliantly**!

We can also use *so* + *adjective/adverb* + *that* clause to describe something that leads to a result. In this use, without *so*, the sentence would not be complete.

It was **so cold that** we needed coats. NOT It was cold that we needed coats.

The restaurant was **so busy that** we couldn't get a table. NOT The restaurant was busy that we couldn't get a table.

We can use *such* + *a/an* (+ adjective) + singular noun to show emphasis or strong feelings about something. An adjective often comes before the noun. Without *such*, the sentence would still be complete.

We had **such a nice day** walking around the city.
The hotel was **such a long way** from the station.
It's **such a wealthy area**.
The house was **such a mess**!

We can use *such* + uncountable or plural nouns.

It's **such bad weather**.
The café serves **such good coffee**.
They're **such friendly people**.
We had **such fun**.

We can also use *such* + *(a/an)* + adjective + noun + *that* clause to describe something that leads to a result. In this use, without *such*, the sentence would not be complete.

They had **such a good time that** they went back the next day. NOT They had a good time that they went back the next day.

It was **such a boring job that** she decided to change companies. NOT It was a boring job that she decided to change companies.

I had **such heavy bags that** I couldn't walk very far. NOT I had heavy bags that I couldn't walk very far.

He gave us **such good advice that** we had no problems at all. NOT He gave us good advice that we had no problems at all.

In spoken and informal language we sometimes omit *that* from *so/such* sentences with a clause.

I was **so tired (that)** I fell asleep.
It was **such a boring film (that)** we left before the end.

PRACTICE

1 Match the sentence beginnings (1–8) with the endings (a–h). Add *so/such* to the sentences for emphasis.

1 It's an exciting
2 I'm hungry
3 It was a terrible waste
4 The food in the restaurant
5 The views were
6 He's a heavy sleeper
7 It's a peaceful place
8 It's important that

a that I have to eat soon.
b was delicious.
c that he never wakes up on time.
d of time.
e city to visit.
f you remember to take this with you.
g beautiful to look at.
h to go for a walk.

2 Rewrite the sentences using the prompts in brackets.

1 The music was too loud for us to chat. (so / couldn't)
   The music was ⎯⎯⎯
2 The hotel was a long way from the station, so we got a bus. (such / decided)
   The hotel was ⎯⎯⎯
3 The book was brilliant. I read it twice. (such / that)
   It was ⎯⎯⎯
4 The nightlife was very lively. We couldn't get to sleep. (so / that)
   The nightlife was ⎯⎯⎯
5 The market had a lot of different food from around the world. I couldn't decide what to eat. (such / that)
   The market had ⎯⎯⎯
6 The area by the river was very calm and peaceful. It didn't feel like you were in a city. (so / that)
   The area by the river ⎯⎯⎯
7 The murals are very colourful. I couldn't stop taking photos. (so / that)
   The murals are ⎯⎯⎯
8 I took too many photos. I'll have to delete some of them. (so many / that)
   I took ⎯⎯⎯

3 Correct the mistakes in the sentences.

1 He was angry so that he couldn't think properly.
2 It was such good idea to visit the museum early in the morning.
3 We waited so a long time for our meal to arrive.
4 It was such generous offer that we couldn't refuse.
5 They were such surprised to see us.
6 The neighbourhood had so a friendly atmosphere.
7 She was so that excited about visiting Rome she forgot to call home.
8 It was such lively area that at night we didn't get much sleep.

GRAMMAR BANK

6B be/get used to

REFERENCE ◀◀ page 72

We use *be used to* + noun/*-ing* to talk about something you are accustomed to doing. It is usual for you to do this.

I'm a pilot, so **I'm used to** flying.
The weather is hot, but we live in southern Spain, so we**'re used to** it.
The negative is *be not used to*.
I'm not used to working at weekends.

We use *get used to* + noun/*-ing* to talk about something you become accustomed to. It is no longer unusual or strange.

At first I didn't like the food, but I soon **got used to it**.
I don't think I'll ever **get used to** their accent. It's difficult to understand.
The negative is *not get used to*.
We **never got used to** the pollution in the city.
Notice *be/get used to* are different from *used to*.

We use *used to* + infinitive to talk about a habit or state in the past, which is usually something you don't do now or is no longer the case.
We **used to live** on a boat. Now we live in a house.
I **didn't use to like** climbing. Now I love it.

PRACTICE

1 Choose the correct words to complete the conversations.

1 A: You lived on a boat for years, didn't you?
   B: Yes, it was hard to **get / be** used to staying in a house.
2 A: I don't think the climbers are ready to go up the mountain.
   B: I agree with you. They're still **used / getting used** to the altitude.
3 A: You said that now you're back in England, you never go to cities.
   B: That's right. After spending so much time in the desert, I **get / 'm** used to silence.
4 A: How was the experience of living in Siberia?
   B: It was tough. We **weren't / don't get** used to living in such a cold climate.
5 A: Do the children find anything difficult about living in a new country?
   B: The food here is very different, but they'll **get / be** used to it.
6 A: Will it be challenging for you to do this trip alone?
   B: I'm not worried about spending months on my own. I **used / 'm used** to being alone.
7 A: What was the toughest thing for her when she moved to the UK from the US?
   B: She had to **be / get** used to driving on the left.
8 A: I like going on long walks.
   B: Me too! When I was younger I **was used / used** to hike every day.
9 A: Was it difficult for Jimmy in Switzerland?
   B: Living in a mountain village was challenging, but eventually he **wasn't / got** used to it.
10 A: Working under a manager is hard for her.
   B: I know. She **isn't / doesn't get** used to being told what to do.

2 Complete the text with one word in each gap.

Road trip

When I was a child, my parents used ¹_____ take me on long car rides. I loved these journeys. I got ²_____ to sitting in enclosed spaces and staring out of the window for hours on end. When I turned twenty, I went on a road trip across Europe. Travelling alone was challenging at first, but I soon ³_____ used to it. Another thing I had to get ⁴_____ to was not being able to speak the languages of the countries I visited. I ⁵_____ used to having difficulties communicating, and it felt strange. What I loved was exploring unfamiliar places and waking up alone in a different hotel room every night. I also had no problem ⁶_____ used to the food everywhere I went.

3 Read the situations and complete the sentences with *be/get used to*. Write three words in each gap.

1 Your friend has just moved to a place where it rains all the time.
   She'll need to **get used to** the rain.
2 A friend moved to a small town. He'd lived in a big city all his life.
   He wasn't _____ in a small town.
3 Your new home is different to your old one, but you're starting to feel more comfortable.
   I'm _____ it.
4 You ate a huge plate of pasta. Now you're too full.
   I'm not _____ so much!
5 Your friend left his job because he didn't like working at night.
   He couldn't _____ the schedule.
6 You now have to work twelve hours a day. For you this is no problem. You did it before.
   It's fine! I _____ it!
7 A friend did her first yoga class with you. She's worried it's too difficult to continue.
   You'll be OK! You'll _____ it!
8 You went to a party and only slept for two hours last night. Your friend says you look exhausted.
   You're right. I'm not _____ for only two hours!

GRAMMAR BANK

6C How to ... ask for and confirm information

REFERENCE ◀◀ page 75

confirming understanding or asking for clarification

So you're saying ...
So what you mean is ...
In other words, ...
If I've got this right, ...
So have I got this right, ...?
So let me (just) check ...
I don't get what you're saying.
If I've understood correctly, what you're saying is ...

asking someone to repeat a specific point

Can you (just) say that last bit again?
Could you (just) go through those options again please?
I didn't catch/understand what you said about ...
Can you (just) repeat the bit about ... ?

In a request, we often use the word *just* to sound more polite, or less direct. It is not essential and it doesn't change the meaning of the sentence.

Can I **just** ask you ...?
Could you **just** tell me ...?
Can you **just** say that last bit again, please?

PRACTICE

1 Complete the conversations with the words in the box.

| catch | check | correctly | get |
| options | repeat | right | words |

1 A: There are four different types of tickets you can get: a 24-hour pass, a family ticket, a hop-on, hop-off ticket or a seasonal ticket.
   B: Sorry, could you just go through those .... again please?

2 A: It costs £20 and it's a four-hour non-stop tour.
   B: I didn't .... what you said about the cost.

3 A: The guide is downloadable and comes in eleven different languages.
   B: Can you just .... the bit about how many languages?

4 A: The tour starts at 20.00.
   B: So, have I got this .... ? It leaves at 8 p.m.

5 A: You can't buy food or drink on the boat.
   B: So in other .... , we have to bring our own food.

6 A: You can buy a ticket or just use your bank card, although you might be charged an extra fee for that.
   B: I don't .... what you're saying about the extra fee.

7 A: The boat leaves promptly at 7 a.m., but you need to be here thirty minutes before.
   B: So, if I've understood .... , we have to be here by 6.30 a.m.

8 A: There are no stops on the way.
   B: So let me just .... , the tour is non-stop. Is that right?

2 Choose the correct options (a–c) to complete the sentences.

1 Could you just .... that last bit again please
   a to say   **b** say   **c** saying
2 So, have I .... this right?
   a getting   **b** get   **c** got
3 Could you just .... through those options again please?
   a go   **b** get   **c** going
4 Can you just .... the bit about the prices?
   a to repeat   **b** repeating   **c** repeat
5 If I've understood .... , what you're saying is we're too late.
   a correctly   **b** correct   **c** correcting
6 So what you .... is we have to buy our tickets over there.
   a meaning   **b** mean   **c** to mean
7 So let me just .... that I've understood.
   a check   **b** checking   **c** to check
8 So you're .... that the tour is fully booked.
   a saying   **b** say   **c** telling

3 Find and correct one mistake in each conversation.

1 A: Your best option is to take the number 143 bus or the 746. They both take you to the station.
   B: Sorry, could you just to go through those options again please?

2 A: So let me just checking. We can have a table, but we need to leave by 9.30 p.m. Is that right?
   B: That's correct.

3 A: So what you're mean is we're too late to book a tour.
   B: Yes, I'm afraid so.

4 A: If I've understood correctly, what you say is that we need to download the app before we do anything else.
   B: Yes, that's right.

5 A: You have unlimited travel for twenty-four hours and then you just need to lock the bike up in one of the selected docking stations.
   B: Can just you say that last bit again?

6 A: I don't got what you're saying about the speed.
   B: You need to keep to the speed limits.

7 A: I didn't to catch what you said about the payment.
   B: You'll be charged automatically using the card you registered.

8 A: So, in other word, we need to return the car with a full tank of petrol.
   B: That's right.

124

GRAMMAR BANK

7A reported speech

REFERENCE ◀◀ page 81

When we report what someone said earlier, we use a past reporting verb.

We also often make changes to the original sentence.

'**I'm** in a hurry.'
Feisal said that **he was** in a hurry.

Reporting verbs include *agreed, answered, complained, explained, promised, realised, replied, said, told*.

Tense and pronoun changes: revision

After a reporting verb, the original verb often moves one tense back into the past.

We change the personal pronouns and adjectives (e.g. *he, his, she, her*, etc.)

direct speech	reported speech
present simple '**I speak** Spanish.'	past simple Heidi told me that **she spoke** Spanish.
present continuous '**I'm working** from home.'	past continuous Bianca explained that **she was working** from home.
past simple and present perfect '**We went** to the same school.' 'My new phone **has just broken**!'	past perfect Alan said that **they had gone** to the same school. Hakim complained that his new phone **had just broken**.
past continuous '**We were planning** to go to Japan.'	past perfect continuous They said that **they'd been planning** to go to Japan.
will/would '**I'll call** you back later.'	would You said you **would call** me back later.
can/could '**I can't help you**.'	could Bao replied that he **couldn't help** me.

We can use *that* after the reporting verb or we can leave it out.

We agreed **that** the dinner had been terrible. OR We agreed the dinner had been terrible.

We don't need to change the verb form into the past when we are reporting something that is still true now, or was said recently. In this situation, we usually use the present form of a reporting verb.

'There are over 7,000 languages in the world.'
Our lecturer **tells** us that **there are** over 7,000 languages in the world.

'I'm on my way to meet you.'
Han **says** he**'s** on his way to meet us.

Time phrases and place references

We usually change time phrases and place references in reported speech.

direct speech	reported speech
now	then/at that time
yesterday	the day before
two months ago	two months before
tomorrow	the next day/the following day
this afternoon	that afternoon
here	there

Reported questions

When we report *yes/no* questions, we add *if* or *whether* after reporting verbs/phrases like *ask*, and *want to know*.

We keep the word order the same as for statements.

We don't use the auxiliary verb *do/does/did*, and we don't use a question mark.

Do you speak English?
She asked me **if I spoke** English. NOT ~~She asked me did I speak English?~~

PRACTICE

1 Complete the reported statements.

1 'I really appreciate good food.'
  Gina told me that ....
2 'My mother has thrown out my favourite T-shirt!'
  Ali complained that ....
3 'You can go to the zoo with me next weekend.'
  Our cousin Tom promised us that ....
4 'I was pretending to be in a bad mood yesterday.'
  Katy explained that ....
5 'We'd like to organise a goodbye party for Stefan this afternoon.'
  We told our teacher that ....
6 'You're right. I'm not really enjoying my time here.'
  Ariana agreed with me that ....

2 Write the conversation in reported speech. Use the reporting verbs in brackets.

A: Have we met before? (ask)
B: I'm not sure. (reply)
A: Were you at Sam's party a few weeks ago? (want to know)
B: I don't know anyone called Sam. (tell)
A: Wait, I think I saw you on a bus last week. (say)
B: I never take the bus. (tell)
A: I know! We went to the same school ten years ago! (realise)
B: I still don't remember you. Sorry. (say)

I met my husband in the funniest way. It was about five years ago. He walked up to me in a café and asked me if …

125

GRAMMAR BANK

7B passives

REFERENCE ◀◀ page 85

We use the passive to focus on the person or thing which is affected by an action rather than the person or thing doing the action.

The app has been downloaded over a million times.
(The main focus is on the app. We are not interested in who downloaded it.)

We use the passive when the person or thing that does the action:

- is obvious.
  Jude was arrested at the festival last week.
- is unknown.
  The museum was built in the 1980s.
- isn't important.
  The winner will be announced tomorrow.

In a passive sentence, we are usually not interested in who or what did the action. When it is important, we use *by*.
The play was written by Shakespeare in 1609.

We often use the passive in more formal situations, for example, in academic or scientific writing or in public information. It is also often used in news reports.
The liquid was kept at room temperature overnight.
Her name has been linked to the new film.

We make the passive with *be* + past participle.

tense	passive
present simple	English **is spoken** in most cities.
present continuous	I'**m being helped** by two assistants.
past simple	It **was made** over a thousand years ago.
future: *going to*	We'**re going to be met** at the station.
future: *will*	The school **will be completed** next year.
present perfect	The Taj Mahal **has been called** the most beautiful building ever.

We often use *just*, *yet*, *still* and *already* with the present perfect passive.
Notice The position of these adverbs.
My train has just been cancelled.
The report has already been signed, but it hasn't been sent yet.
I still haven't been paid for last month's work.

We can also use *get* + past participle informally when something is dramatic or unexpected. We often use it for negative situations.
I got stopped by the police last night! One of my lights wasn't working.

PRACTICE

1 Choose the correct words to complete the active or passive sentences.
  1 She **forwarded / was forwarded / has been forwarded** this email to me last night.
  2 Nadya's wedding **will be held / is going to hold / will hold** next June in a hotel near us.
  3 That desk **is using / is being used / has been used** at the moment.
  4 The company **was organised / is organised / organises** conferences.
  5 People **convinced / are convincing / are convinced** that the information is true.
  6 A lot of work **was done / has done / has been done** since 2010 to develop a cure.

2 Choose the correct place (a or b) for the word in brackets. In two cases both are possible.
  1 Simon (a) has (b) been accepted for university. (just)
  2 I (a) haven't been given (b) a definite answer about the job. (still)
  3 Over a million pounds has (a) been spent by the local council (b). (already)
  4 The perfect Bluetooth speaker hasn't been (a) designed (b). (yet)
  5 Monica (a) hasn't been told (b) the truth. (still)
  6 The book title has (a) been chosen (b). (already)

3 A Complete the texts with the correct passive form of the words in brackets.

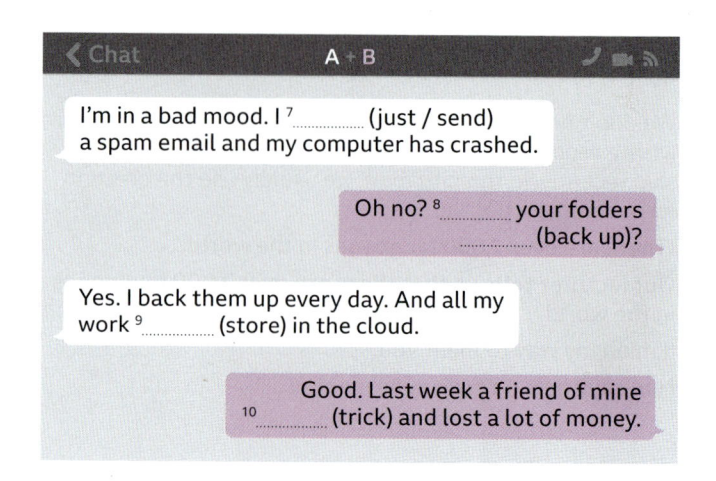

> We take great care with the preparation of the vaccine. As part of the process, the water ¹_____ (measure) exactly before it ²_____ (add) to the mixture. The final liquid ³_____ (test) regularly so as to check for any problems. A new formula ⁴_____ (recently / discover) and tests ⁵_____ (carry out) at the moment. The test results ⁶_____ (publish) in a paper next year.

> **Chat**   A + B
>
> I'm in a bad mood. I ⁷_____ (just / send) a spam email and my computer has crashed.
>
> Oh no? ⁸_____ your folders _____ (back up)?
>
> Yes. I back them up every day. And all my work ⁹_____ (store) in the cloud.
>
> Good. Last week a friend of mine ¹⁰_____ (trick) and lost a lot of money.

B Find a maximum of two places in the texts where it would be natural to use *get* instead of *be*. Why?

126

GRAMMAR BANK

7C How to ... keep a conversation going

REFERENCE ◀◀ page 87

starting conversations and topics

We use these phrases for starting conversations or to introduce new topics in a conversation:

How do you know (name)?
Are you at all interested in (cooking)?
Can you recommend ⎫ a/any (good café/
Do you know ⎭ good restaurants) **near here**?

That's such a great (T-shirt)!
Nice (ring)!

follow-up questions

We can use these follow-up questions to keep the conversation going:

How did you get into that?
What do you mean by ('researching new flavours')?
How does/did that make you feel?
Where did you get it?
Can you recommend a/any (good café/ good restaurants) **near here?**
What's it like?
What was she like?

short (two or three-word) follow-up questions

We use these short questions to ask for examples:

Such as?
For instance/example?
Like what/who?

We use these short questions to ask about reason or purpose:

Why's that?
Why not?
How come/so?
Because?

We use these short questions to ask what happened next:

And then?
And after that?

commenting and showing interest

We use these words and phrases to comment on what the other person is saying and to show interest.

Oh (yes).
Really?
Are you? Do you? Did you? Have you?
That sounds/Sounds (amazing/fantastic/ interesting/lovely/terrible/awful/wonderful)!

PRACTICE

1 Correct seven mistakes in the conversations.

A: Hi, I'm Reggie.
B: I'm Amal. Nice to meet you.
A: How you know Philomena?
B: We worked together a few years ago.
A: You did really? Was it when she was working in London?
B: That's right. We were both starting out.
A: So you're a graphic designer, too.
B: I do user interface animation, actually.
A: Sounds are interesting. What exactly mean you by that?
B: Are you all at interested in graphic design?
A: Yes, very much so. I'm not just being polite.
B: OK, you know the animations you see when you're using a website? That's UI animation.
A: Fascinating. How did you get that into?
B: It was at college actually. Philomena and I both applied for the app design course. She got accepted, but I didn't.
A: How did that made you felt?
B: Terrible of course. But anyway there was only space on the animation course, so I took that. So what do you do?
A: I'm a …

2 Complete the question word webs with the words in the box.

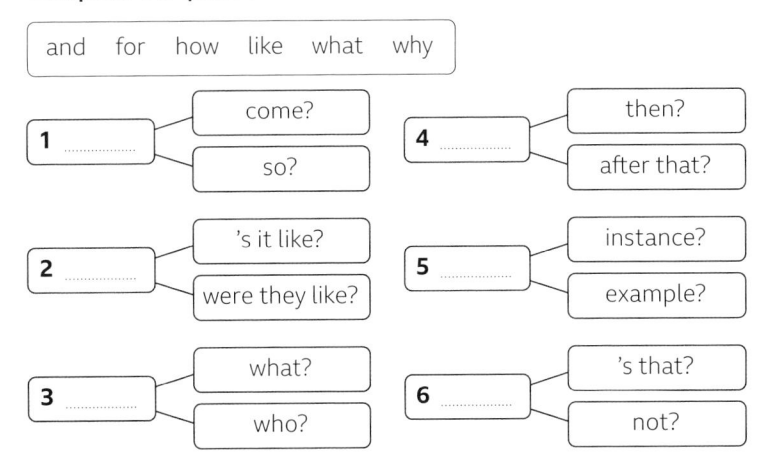

| and | for | how | like | what | why |

1 _____ come? / so?
2 _____ 's it like? / were they like?
3 _____ what? / who?
4 _____ then? / after that?
5 _____ instance? / example?
6 _____ 's that? / not?

3 Complete the conversations with a question or comment from Ex 2. There may be more than one possibility for some answers.

A: Nice scarf!
B: Thanks. I got it from that new market.
A: I haven't been there. ¹_____?
B: It's OK. There are some really interesting shops.
A: ²_____?
B: The food stalls are really good, but I didn't think much of the clothes stalls.
A: ³_____?
B: The clothes were badly made. I bought a T-shirt, saw it was badly made and tried to take it back.
A: ⁴_____.
B: Well, they wouldn't take it back. But maybe they were right.
A: ⁵_____.
B: Because by then I'd worn it several times already.

GRAMMAR BANK

7D avoiding repetition: *so, to, not, be*

REFERENCE ◀ page 88

When we want to avoid repetition, we can use a different word to take the place of other words or we can leave out words.

Auxiliary verbs

We use *do*, *does* or *did* to take the place of a verb in the present simple or past simple.

Q: I think you know John? A: Yes, I **do**. (Yes, I know John.)

Susan thinks Ben doesn't like jazz, but he **does**. (but he likes jazz)

I didn't see John, but Mary **did**. (but Mary saw him)

so and not

We use *think so*, *hope so* and *tell (someone) so* to avoid repetition. We use these phrases to give a positive answer.

A: Are you going to the party?
B: I **think so**. (I think that I'm going to the party.)
A: And is Elena going?
B: I **hope so**. (I hope that she's going.)
A: It's important for her to get out more.
B: Yes, I **told her so**. (I told her that it's important for her to get out more.)

We can also use *suppose so* and *guess so* when we give a positive answer but we don't really want to agree.

A: Can I borrow your phone?
B: I **suppose so**, but I'll need it back in half an hour. (I suppose that you can borrow my phone, but I'm not happy about it.)

For negatives we use *hope not*, *suppose not* and *guess not*.

A: Has Angus gone home?
B: I **hope not**. (I hope that he hasn't gone home.)
A: We're not going to catch the plane.
B: I **guess not**. (I guess we're not going to catch it.)

With *think*, we prefer to use *don't/doesn't think so*.

A: Did Elena finish the video?
B: I **don't think so**. (I don't think she finished it.)

Verbs with *to*

We often use *want to*, *would like to* and *try to* to avoid repetition, particularly of a verb.

A: Would you like to go out for a meal tonight?
B: Yes, I**'d love to**. (I'd love to go out for a meal tonight.)
My parents expected me to go to college, but I **didn't want to**. (I didn't want to go to college.)
A: You need to register online.
B: I**'ve tried to**, but the website keeps crashing. (I've tried to register.)

be

With *be*, we use *want to be*, *would like to be* and *try to be*.

A: Do you want to be a professional actor?
B: I**'d like to be**, but it's not easy. (I'd like to be a professional actor.)

Negatives

For negatives, we use *don't want to* and *try not to* or *don't want to be* and *try not to be*. *Wouldn't like to (be)* is less common.

A: Don't work too hard.
B: I'll try **not to**. (I'll try not to work too hard.)
A: Shall we invite Terry?
B: I **don't** really **want to**, but I suppose we must. (I don't really want to invite Terry.)
A: Sometimes you're too strict.
B: OK, in future I'll try **not to be**. (I'll try not to be too strict.)

PRACTICE

1 Complete the sentences with the words in the box.

| be | do | does | did | so | not | to |

1 I hardly ever go to the gym, but my wife _____ . She goes every day.
2 Megan promised that she'd send me a video of the wedding and she _____ .
3 A: Do you think it'll snow?
  B: I really hope _____ . I have to drive a long way this evening.
4 I didn't take up running. I really wanted _____ but I couldn't find the time.
5 A: Are you intending to buy that car?
  B: I suppose _____ even though it's very expensive.
6 A: You seem like someone who is calm in every situation.
  B: Well, I'd like to _____ , but I'm not.
7 If you see George before I _____ , can you tell him I'm looking for him?

2 Change the conversations to avoid repetition. Use *so*, *not*, *to* and the auxiliary *do*.

A: Oh no, my computer! I've just lost four hours' work.
B: Did you back it up?
A: ¹I don't think I backed it up.
B: Stay calm.
A: ²I'm trying to stay calm!
B: I'm sure the file will be there somewhere.
A: ³I really hope the file will be there somewhere.
B: You'll have to get IT support.
A: ⁴Yes, I suppose I'll have to get them.

A: Is there a lesson next week?
B: ⁵I hope there isn't a lesson next week. I'll be on holiday.
A: Are you going to Scotland again?
B: No. ⁶Andy wanted to go to Scotland, but I said no.
A: Why not? I thought you liked it there?
B: ⁷I'd like to go somewhere different and I told him that I wanted to go somewhere different. So we're going to Spain.

GRAMMAR BANK

8A third conditional and *should have*

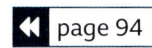

REFERENCE ⏪ page 94

Third conditional

We use the third conditional to talk about imaginary or hypothetical events in the past. These are unreal or impossible situations. We often use the third conditional to talk about regrets (things we'd like to be different about the past).

conditional clause	result clause
If + past perfect,	*would* + *have* + past participle

If I had woken up on time, **I wouldn't have missed** the bus. (It's impossible to change this because the situation has already happened.)
We would have left early **if we'd known** about the terrible traffic. (We didn't know about the traffic, so we didn't leave early.)

We can use *could have* + past participle or *might have* + past participle instead of *would have* to talk about alternative actions in the past. We use *could have* and *might have* when we are less certain of the result of something.

Maybe we **could have won** if we'd played better.
If I'd known she was at the party, **I might have come**.

should/shouldn't have

We use *should/shouldn't have* to talk about regrets (things we'd like to be different about the past).

I should have bought my ticket yesterday. Now there are none left.
I shouldn't have eaten so much. Now I feel ill.

PRACTICE

1 Choose the correct words to complete the sentences.
1 You **had / would have** passed your exams if you'd studied more.
2 If they **had listened / listened** to their parents, they wouldn't have got into trouble.
3 He **had / would have** been a great player if he'd had more opportunities.
4 If I'd known where you were, I **didn't be / wouldn't have been** worried!
5 If you **had / would have** received the job offer, what would you have done?
6 They wouldn't have **known / knew** if she hadn't told them.
7 If you had eaten your breakfast, you **hadn't / wouldn't have** been hungry at 11.00.
8 If I **hadn't lost / didn't lose** my keys, I would have been home earlier.
9 She **might have / had** bought that car if she'd had enough money.
10 If we'd known you needed help, we **could / could have** come earlier.
11 If they hadn't been stuck in traffic, they **might have / had** arrived on time.
12 We **would meet / could have met** for lunch if I'd known you were in town.

2 Write a sentence with *should have* or *shouldn't have* for each situation. Include the words in bold in your answer.
1 You didn't listen to the **teacher's advice**
   You should have listened to the teacher's advice.
2 Her ticket was expensive. She didn't buy **it online**.
3 I'm tired. I went **to bed at 4.00 a.m.**
4 She was thirsty. Next time she'll drink **more water**.
5 I was late because of the traffic. It was a bad idea to leave **at 6 p.m.**
6 They came at a bad time. They didn't speak **to us first**.
7 You failed your exam. You needed to work **harder**.
8 It was too expensive. Why did they pay **so much**?

3 Complete the texts with one word in each gap. Contractions count as one word.

I brought this beautiful book to the beach and it got completely ruined! I fell asleep and a big wave came and everything got wet. If I ¹_____ been awake, I would have seen the wave coming. I ²_____ have taken that book to the beach in the first place.

I owned dogs for years, but my last one was a nightmare. I got her from the dog shelter when she was four months old. If I'd got her earlier, she ³_____ have been such a bad dog. But it's my fault. I ⁴_____ have been stricter with her.

I had two avocado plants outside. I went away for a couple of weeks and they died. I shouldn't ⁵_____ left them outside when the weather changed, but I didn't realise it would get so cold. If I'd known, I ⁶_____ have brought them inside before I left.

129

GRAMMAR BANK

8B would

REFERENCE ◂◂ page 96

would

We can use *would* to talk about past habits. We can also use the past simple.

My father **would** read to me every night. (habit)
My father **read** to me every night.

We don't use *would* to talk about past states.

As a child, I **was** very curious. NOT ~~As a child, I would be very curious.~~

used to

We can use *used to* when talking about past habits or states, which have often changed or are not true now. We can also use the past simple.

As a child, I **used to** love reading. (habit)
As a child, I **loved** reading.
When we lived in New Zealand, I **used to** feel so isolated from my family. (state)
When we lived in New Zealand, I **felt** so isolated from my family.

When we use an adverb of frequency (*often*, *always*, *sometimes*, etc.) with *used to* or *would*, the word order is different.

When we use *would* it goes *before* the adverb of frequency.

We **would always** see them in the afternoon.
We **would often** visit my grandparents during the holidays.

When we use *used to* it goes *after* the adverb of frequency.

We **always used to** see them in the afternoon.
We **often used to** visit my grandparents during the holidays.

PRACTICE

1 Complete the sentences with *would* or *used to* and the words in brackets. Where both are possible use *would*.

In the days before mobile phones ...

1. We didn't have internet banking and apps on our phones – people _____ (go) to the bank in person and queue to get hold of their money.
2. We _____ (always / get) really bored reading terrible magazines while waiting for the doctor or the dentist.
3. When you met someone for the first time, you _____ (ask) for their phone number and write it on a piece of paper, which you quite often lost.
4. When we couldn't remember an important name or fact, we _____ (normally / look) it up in a book.
5. It _____ (be) really difficult to find someone if you arranged to meet them at a music concert or football match. Now, you just call and ask 'Where are you? Oh, there you are. I can see you waving.'
6. We _____ (call) people and actually speak to them, instead of just sending messages.
7. We _____ (keep) people's phone numbers written down in a little book. And we _____ (remember) our own and other people's telephone numbers.
8. People _____ (always / take) a physical map with them to walk around a new city.
9. We _____ (look) in a newspaper to find out what time a TV programme started on the television.
10. People _____ (use) an actual alarm clock to wake up in the morning.

2 Cross out the alternative which is NOT possible.

1. I **used to play / played / play** a lot of chess when I was younger.
2. When I was six, I **would take / used to take / take** the bus to school every day.
3. I **used to live / would live / lived** in New York.
4. When I was at university I always **used to study / studied / would study** at night.
5. As children we **would visit / used to visit / have visited** our grandparents once or twice a month.
6. As a child I **used to love / would love / loved** eating ice cream.
7. I **used to work / would work / worked** for a big company until I had children.
8. When he was a teenager, Frank **used to think / would think / thought** he would become a lawyer.

130

GRAMMAR BANK

8C How to … give a presentation

REFERENCE ⏪ page 99

When we give a presentation, we can use these phrases to help organise our talk. These phrases help the listener(s) to follow the structure of the talk.

starting the presentation

Thanks for coming/joining me …
Today I'm going to/I plan to talk about/speak about …
I'm going to/intend to/plan to begin with (a short story/a few facts) …
To begin with, (I'll describe …)
Can I just get a show of hands for all the people here who … ?

going through the main points

The first point I intend to/I plan to/I'm going to talk about is …
This brings me to my/the first point.
Moving on to my/the next point, …
Turning now to …
As a final point, …
I'd just like to add …

finishing

I'd like to end with …
To sum up, …
Just to recap, …
Does anyone have any comments or questions?

dealing with difficult questions

I'm not sure I can answer that now, but …
I'll get back to you on that. / Let me get back to you on that.
That's (an interesting question/a good question/a tricky question) …
What does everyone else think?

PRACTICE

1 Correct the mistakes in the sentences.

1 Thanks for join me at today's presentation.
2 Can I just get a show of hand?
3 Moving in to the next point, I want to discuss the results.
4 Turning now on the main problems, let's look at the causes.
5 To sum over, this project has been a success for three reasons.
6 I'd like for to end with a summary of the main points.
7 Let me to get back to you on that.
8 That's a question tricky.

2 Complete the presentation with one word in each gap.

FRANKENSTEIN FACTS!

Hi, everyone! Thanks [1]_____ coming. Today I intend to talk [2]_____ my favourite story, *Frankenstein*. Can I just get a [3]_____ of hands for all the people here who have read it, or seen a film of the book? Almost everyone! There have been several misunderstandings about the book and its author and there are some facts that I think a lot of people don't know. I'll go through these one by one.

I'm going to begin [4]_____ the story of how it was written. This first point isn't a misunderstanding, but it's a surprising fact. Mary Shelley, who was only eighteen, was at a party in Geneva, Switzerland, with her husband, the poet Percy Bysshe Shelley, when another poet, Lord Byron, suggested they have a competition to see who could write the best story. She wrote *Frankenstein* and won.

The next point I'm [5]_____ to talk about is a common misunderstanding about the story. Lots of people think Frankenstein is the name of the monster, but it isn't. The monster doesn't have a name. Victor Frankenstein was the man who created the monster.

Moving [6]_____ to my next point, the book was published when Mary Shelley was just twenty. Because her husband was a famous writer, for decades many people thought he'd written it, but they were wrong.

As [7]_____ final point, I want to mention that the book has been popular for over 200 years, with dozens of films, books, comics, art and plays based on it.

Does [8]_____ have any comments or questions? … How many films have been made about the story? That's a good question. I'm not sure. I'd have to check. Let me [9]_____ back to you on that.

I'd like [10]_____ end with a fact you may not know. Mary Shelley didn't only write *Frankenstein*; she wrote other novels, as well as travel books.

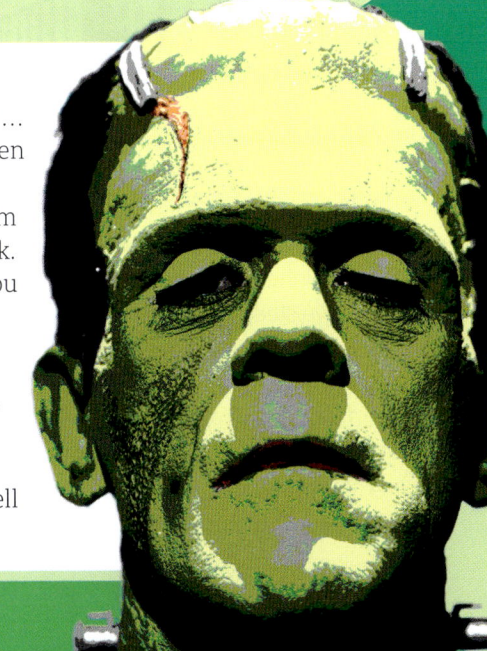

VOCABULARY BANK

1A materials

◀ page 9

1 A Match the type of material (1–12) with the photos (A–L).

It's/They're made of …

1 stone
2 rubber
3 a diamond
4 iron
5 cotton
6 silver
7 denim
8 wood
9 steel
10 plastic
11 gold
12 glass

B 🔊 **VB1.01** | Listen and check.

2 A Complete the sentences with the most suitable material.

1 I've just ordered a new .... jacket online. It's a cool designer jacket at a really good price.
2 She creates beautiful statues using .... imported from the mountains of Italy.
3 She inherited some jewellery, and one of the rings had a huge .... in it. It's worth lots of money.
4 I love sleeping in clean, white .... sheets.
5 He bought a set of .... pans for his new kitchen.
6 The .... is kept in the bank.
7 The shoes on a horse are made of ....
8 The .... of her car tyres left black marks on the road.
9 I dropped the .... bottle on the floor and it smashed.
10 The house has beautiful floors made of .... taken from the local forests.
11 She finished second and won a .... medal.
12 I always recycle my .... bottles.

B Work in pairs. What objects do you own that are made from the materials in Ex 1A?

VOCABULARY BANK

3C negative prefixes
◀◀ page 38

1 A Add the prefixes to make the adjectives negative. Use *in*, *ir* or *un*.

1 _____ appropriate
2 _____ certain
3 _____ clear
4 _____ confident
5 _____ dependent
6 _____ employed
7 _____ enthusiastic
8 _____ expensive
9 _____ fair
10 _____ flexible
11 _____ formal
12 _____ healthy
13 _____ lucky
14 _____ necessary
15 _____ popular
16 _____ professional
17 _____ regular
18 _____ responsible
19 _____ sensitive
20 _____ willing

B 🔊 **VB3.01** | Listen and check.

2 Choose the correct words to complete the rule.

We usually **stress** / **don't stress** the negative prefix.

3 Complete the sentences using a word with a negative prefix from Ex 1A.

1 He doesn't want to do it. He's _____ to do it.
2 I don't have any work at the moment. I'm _____ .
3 That wasn't the right thing to say in that situation. It was totally _____ .
4 You really don't handle change well, do you? You're really _____ .
5 You didn't need to do that. It was _____ .
6 It was gorgeous weather all summer except on your wedding day. That's a bit _____ .
7 He used to be everyone's favourite politician, but now he's really _____ .
8 I'm not sure what will happen next year. I'm _____ about my future.
9 There's no need to dress up. You can wear _____ clothes.
10 I suggested a party, but no one seemed very interested. They were _____ .
11 They left their young kids home by themselves. That's completely _____ .
12 I don't understand everything she says. She's very _____ .

4B films and film-making
◀◀ page 48

1 Read the article. Match the words and phrases in bold with the meanings (1–10).

The film-making process
step-by-step

Have you always wanted to be a **film-maker**? If you want to be a part of **the film industry**, you can start by reading our tips for the film-making process step-by-step.

When you make a film, it's useful to think of the process in three stages:

❶ planning and getting ready to **film**.
❷ **producing** and **directing** the film.
❸ finishing the film and getting it ready to show (post-production).

In the first stage, you need to think about your film-making idea. How will you tell your story? Write down your idea and write a short **script**. Choose a **location** – where you would like to film. Decide who is going to **star** in your film.

Next, make sure you know how to use all the equipment before you start filming. **Shoot** more film than you need. You can always edit later. For a one-minute drama, you might need to shoot between three and five minutes of video. For documentaries, you will need more because you can't predict what people will say.

Finally, look through all the **footage** before you start editing. Maybe do a rough edit first, but make sure you save all the material you cut, in case you want to make changes later. Do you want to add a **soundtrack**? When you're happy with the sound and the video, upload and share your film with the world. Good luck!

1 _____ or _____ : to use a camera to record a story or event so it can be shown on a screen
2 _____ : finding the money to make a film and arranging how it will be done
3 _____ : someone who makes films
4 _____ : recorded film of an event
5 _____ : the words that people will say in a film
6 _____ : appear as a main character in a film
7 _____ : telling the actors/people in a film what they should do
8 _____ : the place where a film is shot
9 _____ : the music and sounds that go with a film
10 _____ : all the people who are involved in the business of making and selling films

2 Work in pairs and discuss the questions.

1 Have you ever made your own film? Tell your partner about it using the words and phrases in Ex 1.
2 What do you think makes a good film?

VOCABULARY BANK

4C the news
◀ page 50

1 A Work in pairs. Match the words in the box with the meanings (1–8).

> announcement   biased   breaking news
> go viral   live feed   subscribe
> trending   updates

1 new information about an event that is happening right now
2 currently popular or discussed a lot online, e.g. on social media
3 supporting one person or group in an unfair way
4 important official statement about something that has happened or will happen
5 when an image, video or story spreads extremely fast on the internet, e.g. through social media
6 the most recent information about a news story
7 a news story you listen to/watch online that is happening at the moment and not recorded
8 arrange (maybe pay) to receive something regularly, e.g. a magazine or access to a website

B Complete the sentences with the words in the boxes.

> biased   go viral   live feed   updates

1 It's impossible to know which stories will .... and be seen by millions.
2 Our news channel provides .... on news stories every hour.
3 Some people say journalists are .... against big business.
4 We now have a .... of the story coming in from Berlin.

> announcement   breaking news
> subscribe   trending

5 Please .... to our YouTube channel to get more news stories.
6 The channel reports .... several times a day.
7 The government made an important .... about the new tax law.
8 This story is .... on Twitter and various websites.

2 Work in groups and discuss the questions.
1 Do you subscribe to any magazines, news websites or media channels?
2 How do you find out about breaking news and updates?
3 What stories are trending at the moment? Do you think they will go viral?

5B money
◀ page 59

1 A Which words (1–10) are connected with the photos (A–E)?
1 bargain
2 charge
3 discount
4 donation
5 fare
6 fee
7 loss
8 refund
9 profit
10 receipt

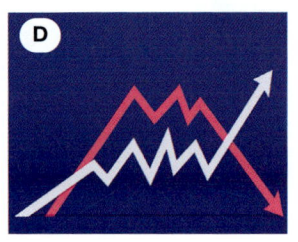

B Match the words (1–10) in Ex 1A with the definitions (a–j).
a money you pay to travel by train, bus, plane, etc.
b something you buy cheaply or for less than its usual price
c money you make when you sell something for more than you paid for it
d money you lose because you sell something for less than you paid for it
e a reduction to the usual price of something
f money you get back because you are not satisfied with a product or a service
g a piece of paper or an electronic message that shows you have paid something
h money you pay for professional services or you pay to do something, e.g. a course
i the amount of money you have to pay for something
j money you give to help an organisation or a person

C Match the words in Ex 1A with the correct word stress (1–4).
1 O   2 Oo   3 oO   4 oOo

D 🔊 VB5.01 | Listen and check.

2 A Choose the correct words to complete the sentences.
1 Is a congestion **refund / charge** to reduce traffic in a city centre a good idea?
2 Have you ever made a **profit / donation** on something you've sold?
3 Do you ever ask for a **discount / fare** when you're buying something in a shop?
4 Should a shop ever give a **refund / bargain** even if you don't have a **loss / receipt**?
5 Do you ever make **discounts / donations** to organisations that help people in need?

B Work in pairs and discuss the questions in Ex 2A.

VOCABULARY BANK

VB

6B idioms

◀◀ page 72

1 A Match the idioms in bold in the sentences (1–6) with the meanings (a–f).

1 When I go on holiday, I prefer to **travel light**. I usually take just one small suitcase and nothing else.
2 It takes eight hours to get there by car, so we'll **break the journey** halfway and go for lunch.
3 Touring with the band was fun. But after twenty different hotels in twenty nights, I got tired of **living out of a suitcase**.
4 On my trip, I had lots of problems with my boat. I was all alone, so I had to **think on my feet**.
5 I couldn't find my passport in my bag so I worried I would **get into hot water** with the airport staff. Luckily, it was in my coat.
6 It's always hard to start a new job, because you have to learn a lot of things quickly. But you just need to **weather the storm**. Things will improve.

a stop somewhere for a short time during a long journey
b stay for a short time in many places, while having only a few possessions with you.
c take only a few things when you travel somewhere
d deal with a difficult situation without being hurt or damaged
e be in big trouble
f react to events quickly, without time to plan

B Complete the blog post with the correct form of the idioms in Ex 1A.

Advice from a traveller

by Nawal Mahfouz

I've travelled to over seventy countries, often backpacking and usually with little money. Here's my advice. Firstly, [1]_____. Take as few possessions as possible. Often you can buy the things you need in the places where you're travelling. This helps the local economy.

Sometimes you'll need to [2]_____. I remember arriving at 3 a.m. in a tiny village and there were no hotel beds available. I didn't want to sleep on the street because you can [3]_____ with the local police. So I rented a hammock, put it up between two trees behind the hotel and got a few hours' sleep.

At times, you'll feel lonely and you'll feel like going home. It's tiring [4]_____ - when you're moving all the time – and it's tough when you don't know anyone and can't speak the language. My advice is to [5]_____. Things often get better quickly after a good meal or when, by chance, you meet someone friendly.

When planning a long trip on foot or by bus, look for places to [6]_____. On many occasions, I've stopped somewhere, thinking I'd be there for just a few hours, and ended up staying for several days because I loved the place.

C Work in pairs and discuss. Which pieces of advice do you like? Why? Have you ever experienced anything similar to the writer's experiences?

VOCABULARY BANK

7A ways of speaking

◀◀ page 81

1 A Which words are in the photos (A–E)? One photo shows two words.

1 read aloud
2 scream
3 shout at
4 speak up
5 talk something over
6 talk to yourself
7 whisper
8 yell at

B Match the words (1–8) in Ex 1A with the definitions (a–g). One definition matches two words.

a say something very quietly, using your breath, not your voice
b say something to someone/something else very loudly and angrily
c say the words you are reading
d say publicly what you think about something
e make a loud, high sound with your voice because you are frightened, angry or excited
f say your thoughts aloud, not speaking to another person
g discuss a problem, often in order to decide what to do

2 Work in pairs and discuss the questions.

1 Did you have to read aloud in school when you were younger?
2 If you have to make a big decision, do you talk it over with anyone first?
3 If someone screamed 'Help!' in the street, would you definitely go to help them?
4 Do you shout at people when you're angry with them?
5 When you're alone, do you ever talk to yourself?
6 If someone whispers to you on the phone (because they have to), do you whisper back even if you don't have to?
7 Would you speak up in a group even if most people seem to disagree with your opinion?
8 Is it effective to yell at children or animals in order to correct their behaviour?

136

VOCABULARY BANK

7B internet words

◀◀ page 83

1 A Match the words (1–10) with the pictures (A–J).

1 icons H
2 download
3 folder
4 inbox
5 network
6 refresh
7 scroll down/up
8 swipe
9 tap
10 upload

B 🔊 VB7.01 | Listen and check.

C Match the words (1–10) in Ex 1A with the definitions (a–j).

a a location in a computer where you keep related documents together
b a set of computers that are connected to each other
c a small picture on a computer screen that is used to open a programme
d hit your finger lightly on a computer screen
e make the screen show any new information that has arrived since you first began looking at it
f move information from a computer network or storage location to a smaller computer
g move information from your computer to a storage location
h move information on a computer screen up or down so that you can read it all
i slide your finger on a computer screen to the left or right to move an object or change screens
j the place in an email program where new messages arrive

2 A Complete the sentences with words from Ex 1A.

1 How often do you .... your files to cloud storage?
2 Does your finger ever get sore from too much .... up and down or .... left and right?
3 Do you give useful names to new .... on your computer? Is it easy to find them later?
4 How many emails are in your .... ?
5 Which of these .... can you name?

B Work in pairs and discuss the questions in Ex 2A.

8B phrasal verbs

◀◀ page 95

1 A Read the text. Then use the phrasal verbs in bold to complete the sentences (1–8).

How to realise your goals

1 Daydream and visualise

The first thing you need to do is use your imagination to **dream up** some ideas. What is it that you really want to do? Think about your 'why?' Why is this important to you?

2 Write it down

Once you know what your goal is, it's really important to **write it down** so that you don't forget. Now you have a chance to **think the idea through**. See if you can **figure out** how to achieve that goal. Can you **break it down** into stages and make a plan?

3 Take action

It's no good just having goals on a piece of paper. Now you need to **follow up** on the plan and take action. **Try out** your idea. Don't worry if it doesn't work the first time. Do something, however small, every day to start making your dream a reality. **Get together** with people who have similar dreams and see if you can help each other.

1 When you understand something or solve a problem, you .... how to do it.
2 When you test a new idea, you .... it ....
3 When you use your imagination to invent a new idea, you .... it ....
4 If you meet together with other people as a group, you ....
5 When you write something on a piece of paper you .... it ....
6 If you take a big idea and split it into smaller sections, you .... it ....
7 When you consider the facts about something in a carefully organised way, you .... it ....
8 When you investigate something further to find out more information, you .... it ....

B 🔊 VB8.01 | Listen and check.

2 Work in pairs. Think about an important goal in your life that you have achieved. Answer the questions (1–5). Tell your partner how you achieved your goal.

1 How did you dream up the idea? Who inspired you?
2 Did you write the idea down and think it through?
3 Did you have to break the idea down in order to figure out how it would be possible?
4 What happened when you first tried out your idea?
5 Did you get together with other people to follow up the idea?

137

COMMUNICATION BANK

1C Ex 6B Student A

Read the notes and prepare to leave detailed messages on voicemail.

1 You're studying late in library. No food in house. Ask flatmate: pick up fast food (give details: type, restaurant).
2 Someone is going to rent your flat. Ask partner: go over instructions with guest (give details: lock door, internet, washing machine, set the alarm, etc.).
3 You're stuck in traffic. Ask work colleague: give document on desk to manager (give details: what document, where on desk, which manager).

3C Ex 9 Student A

Roleplay 1

1 You're a human resources manager. You are interviewing Student B for a position at your company. Look at the list of questions and choose five. Number them in the order that you would like to ask them.
- What are your main strengths?
- What are your weaknesses?
- Tell me about a difficult situation you had, and how you handled it.
- Who do you admire most, and why?
- What motivates you, and what makes you feel demotivated?
- How would a colleague or classmate describe you?
- Tell me about a time that you made a mistake.
- How do you react when you fail at something?
- What do you find most annoying in other people?

2 Roleplay the interview. Make notes of Student B's answers.

3 Look at your notes with Student B. Which parts of the interview went well? Which parts didn't go well?

Roleplay 2

1 A You are a job applicant. Student B is the Human Resources Manager at the company and will be conducting the interview. These are some of the questions that Student B might ask you in the interview. Prepare by thinking about your answers.
- What are your main strengths?
- Tell me about a difficult situation you had, and how you handled it.
- How do you react when you fail at something?
- What motivates you, and what makes you feel demotivated?

2 Roleplay the interview.

3 Look at Student B's notes. Which parts of the interview do you think went well? Which parts didn't go well?

7A Ex 8A-C Student B

1 Read the conversations. Where do they take place? What is the problem in each one?

Conversation 2

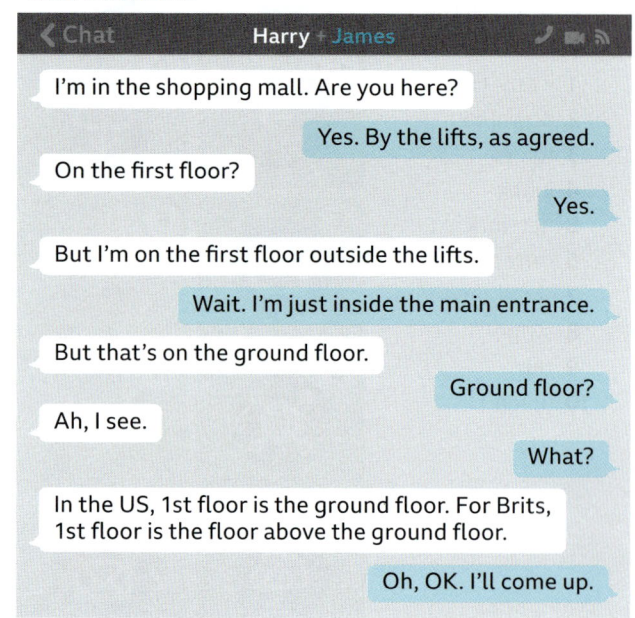

Chat — Harry + James

- I'm in the shopping mall. Are you here?
- Yes. By the lifts, as agreed.
- On the first floor?
- Yes.
- But I'm on the first floor outside the lifts.
- Wait. I'm just inside the main entrance.
- But that's on the ground floor.
- Ground floor?
- Ah, I see.
- What?
- In the US, 1st floor is the ground floor. For Brits, 1st floor is the floor above the ground floor.
- Oh, OK. I'll come up.

Conversation 4

Olivia: Would you like some more dessert, Martin?
Martin: No, thanks. I'm completely fed up.
Olivia: Oh! I'm sorry to hear that. I don't know what to say. Do you want to talk it over?
Martin: Sorry? I don't understand.
Olivia: You said you were fed up. Is there a problem?
Martin: No. The dessert was delicious but I can't eat any more!
Olivia: Oh, I think you mean you're full up.
Martin: Yes. Did I use the wrong word?
Olivia: Yes. 'Fed up' means upset or depressed. I thought you didn't like the food.
Martin: Oh, no! I loved it. Thanks. Full up. I must remember that.
Olivia: That's a relief! You got me quite worried!

2 You are Harry in conversation 2 and Olivia in conversation 4. You are going to tell Student A about the conversations. Write six words or phrases for each conversation to help you remember what happened.

Conversation 2: Lift, 1st floor, main entrance, ground floor, US 1st floor = ground floor

3 Work with Student A. Take turns to tell each other what happened in your conversations. Only use *said* once. Try to use at least three verbs other than *said*.

I had a very funny conversation yesterday. I was …
Something funny happened a few days ago …
I was with …
And then he told me …

COMMUNICATION BANK

1B Ex 1C Student A

Minimalism vs. Maximalism

Zuleya Samova:
'Less is More'

In my work, minimalism refers to designing things in a simple, elegant way. We've seen this trend growing: smartphones and televisions are flat, simple and easy to use. We design homes with clean lines and blank walls, **ideal** spaces for people living thoughtful, creative lives. For minimalists like me, the saying is a way of life: 'Less is more'. It means a simpler world is a better world.

Many people learn about minimalism through the movement made famous by the lifestyle writer Marie Kondo and the Netflix series *The Minimalists: Less is Now*. I think Kondo and the presenters of that Netflix series, Joshua Fields Millburn and Ryan Nicodemus, succeeded in persuading people to stop collecting useless stuff and to throw away the possessions they can **do without**.

One of the main arguments for using less stuff is that it's better for the environment, but it's not only that; it's a way to free yourself so you can **appreciate** the things that matter. If we stop to think about what's really important, we realise that it's people and relationships, not stuff.

1B Ex 1C Student B

Minimalism vs. Maximalism

Richard Mbuya:
'Fill the World with Colour and Light'

My love of maximalism came from a journey I took. When I first travelled abroad, to Mozambique, I was a nervous twenty-year-old. It turned out to be the most important trip of my life. There, I discovered patterns and materials I'd never seen before. I went on to become a designer and I've spent the last twenty years mixing shapes and fabrics from different cultures – my **dream** job.

Maximalism isn't about luxury. It's about joy. My house is filled with treasures, things I love: stones I found in the Alps, shells from a beach in Indonesia, a 1960s typewriter, my children's paintings. They are beautiful to look at and touch. They **give pleasure** to me and my visitors and, for me, they bring back memories. I think you can live a simple life and still enjoy amazing colours and patterns. Or you might live a complicated life but have no furniture. We all have different **tastes**.

Personally, **I'm not a big fan of** minimalism and I wouldn't want to live in a minimalist house without my treasures around me. **It's not for me**. It would be like living in a hospital! My home reflects my work. I believe in creating joyful, bright, colourful designs and I look forward to visiting more street markets and finding objects to inspire my work.

3D Ex 6 Student B

1 Look at the 'This or That' questions. Prepare to ask a question for each one.
   - Shower or bath? Which would you rather have, a shower or a bath?
   - Apartment or house?
   - E-bike or real bike?
   - Alone or in a big group?
   - Travel by plane or by boat?

2 Answer Student A's questions. Use some of the Key phrases in your answers.

3 Ask Student A your questions.

6A Ex 5C Student A

1 Student B has just visited a city you know well. Ask the questions (1–3) and listen to their response.
   1 Did you go to the museum?
   2 Did you visit any of the parks?
   3 Did you eat in one of the local restaurants?

2 You have just visited a city that Student B knows well. Listen to Student B's questions. For each question, complete the prompts to give your answers. Remember to emphasise *so* and *such*.
   1 Yes, there were .... many lovely shops that …
   2 Yes, it's .... a lovely area that …
   3 Yes, the city was .... lively at night that …

COMMUNICATION BANK

3C Ex 9 Student B

Roleplay 1

1 You are a job applicant. Student A is the Human Resources Manager at the company and will be conducting the interview. These are some of the questions that Student A might ask you in the interview. Prepare by thinking about your answers.

- What are your main strengths?
- Tell me about a difficult situation you had, and how you handled it.
- How do you react when you fail at something?
- What motivates you, and what makes you feel demotivated?

2 Roleplay the interview.

3 Look at Student A's notes. Which parts of the interview do you think went well? Which parts didn't go well?

Roleplay 2

1 You are a human resources manager. You are interviewing Student A for a position at your company. Look at the list of questions and choose five. Number them in the order that you would like to ask them.

- How would a colleague or classmate describe you?
- What would be their main criticism?
- Tell me about a time that you made a mistake.
- How do you react when you fail at something?
- Do you have a role model? Tell me about them.
- What do you find most annoying in other people?
- What are your main strengths?
- Tell me about a difficult situation you had, and how you handled it.
- What motivates you, and what makes you feel demotivated?

2 Roleplay the interview. Make notes of Student A's answers.

3 Look at your notes with Student A. Which parts of the interview went well? Which parts didn't go well?

2D Exs 4 and 6A

1 You're hiking on a hill and a lightning storm starts. Your car about is ten minutes away, but there is a house nearby with no lights on.
2 You're swimming in the sea. Someone is on a paddleboard nearby. At some point you notice that the paddleboard is there, but the person is not.
3 You're in the cinema and someone near you has their mobile on. The light is disturbing you.
4 You're at home and you think you hear a strange sound downstairs in the night.
5 Someone's dog jumps into a river and gets into difficulties. The owner is shouting for help.

5D Ex 7A

Read the summary of a meeting. What tasks are the organisers doing themselves? What tasks are they getting someone else to do?

Summary of meeting

Purpose of meeting: to organise the end of year party
Date: 3 July
Attendees: Stella, Giuseppe, Marco, You-Jung

Overview

After some discussion about costs, we decided to get outside companies to provide the food and drinks, as well as the music. We will organise the invitations and the decorations ourselves.

Action points

- Stella and Giuseppe will contact three different catering companies and report back on the prices and services offered. They will email this information to us by the end of day Friday **4th of next month**.
- Marco will contact his friend who regularly DJs at private parties and weddings to see if he is available on 29 September. If he isn't, Marco will investigate other DJs.
- You-Jung will design invitations and have them printed at her brother's printing company. She is sure he will be able to do these at a very reasonable price. She will send us her design by **EOD Friday**.

To be discussed

- Farewell gift for Bob, who's leaving – What's our budget? Who's going to buy it?
- Guest list – Is anyone missing? Do we really want to invite all the staff?
- Clean-up – Should we get the cleaning staff to clean up the venue or should we do it ourselves? (Stella, can you check the cost of the cleaning staff for something like this?)

Next meeting

Monday 7th. 7.30 p.m. at the Cosy Café.

COMMUNICATION BANK

5A Ex 4C

Check the meanings.

1 snapped – broke, particularly a hard material
2 faulty – having a fault or error, often mechanical or electrical
3 outrageous – extremely unacceptable
4 brand new – completely new, as with any product you've just bought
5 warranty – an agreement from the manufacturer to repair or replace a product if there's a problem, usually for a limited time, e.g. two years
6 assured – promised or told someone that something would definitely happen

1C Ex 6B Student B

Read the notes and prepare to leave detailed messages on voicemail.

1 You're in class. Forgot take food out of freezer. Ask partner: go home, take food out (give details: which food, how much, where to leave it).
2 You're walking home. Weather turned cold. You left heating on too low. Ask new flatmate: change temperature setting (give details: where, how, what temperature).
3 You're working late. Ask partner: pick up children (give details: time, location).

6A Ex 5C Student B

1 You have just visited a city that Student A knows well. Listen to Student A's questions. For each question, complete the prompts to give your answers. Remember to emphasise *so* and *such*.

  1 Yes, it was .... interesting that ...
  2 Yes, they are .... peaceful to sit in that ...
  3 Yes, we had .... delicious meal that ...

2 Student A has just visited a city that you know well. Ask the questions (1–3) and listen to their responses.

  1 Did you do any shopping?
  2 Did you walk down by the lake?
  3 Did you go to any nightclubs?

5A Ex 7C Student A

Roleplay 1

1 You are a customer. Read your role card and prepare to roleplay the situation.

> Recently you ordered a new television online. It was supposed to arrive three days ago. You stayed home from work to be there for the delivery, but nothing came. You phoned, and no one answered. The next day, you phoned and they said that they had tried to deliver it but you weren't home, which isn't true. Now you're phoning the online electronics shop to complain.
>
> Remember to complain effectively. Before you call, think about the sentences you will say, and decide what you want to achieve by the end of the conversation.

2 Do the roleplay with Student B.

3 Work in pairs and discuss. How well did you follow the guidelines you wrote in Ex 7A?

Roleplay 2

1 You are the customer service person. Read your role card and prepare to roleplay the situation.

> You work in an online electronics shop. You often receive phone calls with complaints. Read the list of common complaints and your instructions for how to respond.
>
> | Complaint | Response |
> | --- | --- |
> | Brand new product isn't working | Ask if it's within the warranty. If so, tell the customer to send the product back to the address on the website. If not, tell them they can send it for repair, but it will cost a minimum of 50 euros. |
> | New product damage – caused by customer | Remind them that the warranty is not valid if they have used the item wrongly. |
> | Online sales representative is rude | Apologise, ask the name of the sales rep if the customer knows it, and promise to look into it. |
> | Online sales representative lacks knowledge of products | Apologise, ask the name of the sales rep if the customer knows it, and promise to look into it. |
> | Delivery issues: product wasn't delivered on time | Keep customer on hold and contact the delivery department to find out what's happening with the delivery. |
> | Delivery issues: shipment incomplete – something missing from package | Make sure the customer has fully inspected the package. If they don't find the missing item(s), promise to send them a new one. |
>
> If a customer is extremely aggressive or dissatisfied, transfer them to your line manager.

2 Do the roleplay with Student B.

3 Work in pairs and discuss. How well did Student B follow the guidelines you wrote in Ex 7A? What were the differences between this and the previous roleplay you did?

141

COMMUNICATION BANK

5C Ex 8B

1 Look at the information about two backpacks. Make notes about which would be better for the college student and the businessperson in Ex 8B.

Stenson
Laptop Backpack

$70

From the manufacturer's website:
The Stenson Laptop Backpack is a very solid bag with leather straps and metal zips throughout. It has two large compartments, one specially designed for carrying a laptop and documents, the other for other large items such as a water bottle or large headphones. The smaller pockets are ideal for storing your pens, phone, wallet and other items. There's a special compartment in the top for keeping your sunglasses and other easy-to-break items. This practical bag is ideal for everyday use and for weekend trips. Its dimensions meet the carry-on limit for all airlines. Colour: black

Review ★★★★
This is the best backpack ever. I use it for overnight business trips and after a year it still looks brand new. It really does have solid construction. With all my other bags, the zips get broken within a few months, but not with this bag. Even when it's fully loaded, the bag sits comfortably on my back and feels stable. The leather straps are very strong and I think will last for a long time.

The only improvement I can imagine is a bigger side pocket for my water bottle and perhaps a key ring inside one compartment. But those are minor details – I highly recommend this bag.

Bramford
Laptop Backpack

$50

From the manufacturer's website:
The Bramford Laptop Backpack is made of the highest-quality materials. It has three large main compartments and fifteen (that's right, fifteen!) smaller compartments for separating all your things. One large compartment is designed to protect your laptop and is also ideal for carrying documents. The laptop compartment is designed for easy-opening, convenient when going through security at the airport, or just pulling your laptop out at the café. This stylish bag is available in three colours: black and violet, black and dark green and all black.

Review ★★★★
One of the most practical backpacks I've ever had. It has a lot of pockets and for me that's important because I need to carry a lot of different things, and this bag helps me to keep organised. I love the side pockets, great for carrying a water bottle or keys. I use it every day for going to college, and for weekend trips away as well – it's that good!

The only thing I don't like is that the fabric isn't as strong as I'd like. Still, it's a decent bag and good value at $50.

2 Work in pairs and discuss. What similarities and differences did you find between the two bags? Which do you think is better for each person? Why?

3 Work with other students. Tell them your decision, give your reasons and explain how you made your decision.

COMMUNICATION BANK

5A Ex 7C Student B

Roleplay 1

1 You are the customer service person. Read your role card and prepare to roleplay the situation.

> You work as a customer service person at an online electronics shop. You often receive phone calls with complaints. Read the list of common complaints and your instructions for how to respond.
>
> | Complaint | Response |
> |---|---|
> | Brand new product isn't working | Ask if it's within the warranty. If so, tell the customer to send the product back to the address on the website. If not, tell them they can send it for repair, but it will cost a minimum of 50 euros. |
> | New product damage – caused by customer | Remind them that the warranty is not valid if they have used the item wrongly. |
> | Online sales representative is rude | Apologise, ask the name of the sales rep if the customer knows it, and promise to look into it. |
> | Online sales representative lacks knowledge of products | Apologise, ask the name of the sales rep if the customer knows it, and promise to look into it. |
> | Delivery issues: product wasn't delivered on time | Keep customer on hold and contact the delivery department to find out what's happening with the delivery. |
> | Delivery issues: shipment incomplete – something missing from package | Make sure the customer has fully inspected the package. If they don't find the missing item(s), promise to send them a new one. |
>
> If a customer is extremely aggressive or dissatisfied, transfer them to your line manager.

2 Do the roleplay with Student A.

3 Work in pairs and discuss. How well did Student A follow the guidelines you wrote in Ex 7A?

Roleplay 2

1 You are a customer. Read your role card and prepare to roleplay the situation.

> Recently you ordered a new coffee machine. When you ordered, there was a special offer of fifty free coffee capsules. The coffee machine arrived with no capsules. So you bought capsules at a shop, and you want the company to pay you for them, or to send you the free capsules. You're phoning the online electronics shop to complain.
>
> Remember to complain effectively. Before you call, think about the sentences you will say, and decide what you want to achieve by the end of the conversation.

2 Do the roleplay with Student A.

3 Work in pairs and discuss. How well did you follow the guidelines you wrote in Ex 7A? What were the differences between this and the previous roleplay you did?

6C Ex 7 Student B

1 Student A is going to ask you about hiring an e-scooter. Look at the information below and be prepared to answer Student A's questions.

> ### Hire an e-scooter
>
> You must be eighteen years old and have a driving licence.
>
> Use the cycle lanes. You mustn't ride an e-scooter on the pavement. You must keep to the speed limits. Only one person is allowed to ride the e-scooter.
>
> First download the app and register with your mobile number.
>
> Then locate an available scooter near you by using the map.
>
> If you're a beginner rider, activate Beginner's mode so you move slowly until you get used to the accelerator and the brakes.
>
> Scan the QR code to unlock the scooter.
>
> Pay £1 to unlock the scooter and then 20p per minute for your ride.

2 You want to find out about quick car hire. Look at the prompts and think about the questions you need to ask. Then ask Student A for information. Make sure you check the information you hear and ask for clarification when you're not sure.

- find a quick car hire near you
- book in advance
- minimum length of hire (24 hours?)
- how it works
- rules
- cost
- pay for insurance
- fuel
- where to leave the car at the end of the journey

143

COMMUNICATION BANK

6C Ex 7 Student A

1 You want to find out about e-scooters. Look at the prompts and think about the questions you need to ask. Then ask Student B for information. Make sure you check the information you hear and ask for clarification when you're not sure.

- the nearest place to hire an e-scooter
- book in advance
- cost of e-scooter to hire
- how it works
- rules
- OK if you have never ridden an e-scooter before
- where can you ride the e-scooter
- can two people ride at the same time

2 Student B is going to ask you about hiring a car. Look at the information below and be prepared to answer Student B's questions.

Quick car hire

Find, book and unlock your quick car hire using the app.

We pay for fuel, parking, congestion charges and insurance – so you don't have to pay for any of those. You need a driver's licence and a credit card.

Download the app.

If there is less than a quarter of a tank of fuel when you finish your trip, fill the car up before returning it to the parking spot.

You can rent cars or vans by the minute, by the hour or by the day for a basic price of £10 per hour.

You must leave the car clean.

3D Ex 6 Student A

1 Look at the 'This or That' questions. Prepare to ask a question for each one.
- Sweet or salty? **Which taste do you prefer, sweet or salty?**
- Hotel or campsite?
- Swimming pool or lake?
- E-book or real book?
- Be able to fly or be able to disappear?

2 Ask Student B your questions.

3 Answer Student A's questions. Use some of the Key phrases in your answers.

4C Ex 6A Student B

1 Read the story below and prepare to tell it to Student A. Use these phrases.

> Did you hear … ? Basically, …
> What happened was … And apparently, …

Lizard in supermarket

A video showing a giant lizard climbing up supermarket shelves has gone viral. A giant lizard, more than 1.8 m long, scared shoppers in a supermarket outside Bangkok when it walked in and started climbing up the shelves and knocking boxes and packages onto the floor. Staff and customers were laughing and shouting as they watched the lizard climb the shelves until it reached the top where it appeared to rest. Luckily, nobody was hurt as lizards are not usually dangerous. Experts believe the lizard probably climbed out of the nearby canal where it may have had trouble finding food.

2 Listen to Student A's story and respond. Use these phrases. Then tell your story to Student A.

> What happened? I had no idea. I can hardly believe it.
> Oh no, that's terrible/really funny! That sounds …

8D Ex 4B

1 Plan your pitch. Think about the questions below and make notes.
   1 What is the story behind your product/service? How did you get the idea? (Invent a history of the product/service.)
   2 What is special about your product/service? Who is it for?
   3 What are your future plans for the product/service (e.g. new markets or new products)?
   4 How much money will you ask for and what share of your company will the investor get (5%? 10%? More?)?

2 Work in groups.

   Student A and Student B: You are entrepreneurs. Follow steps 1–3.
   1 In pairs, make your pitch in three minutes or less.
   2 Answer the investors' questions.
   3 If an investor makes an offer, discuss with your partner: will you accept it or negotiate? If there is more than one offer, choose one. Make a note of the final outcome.

   Student C and Student D: You are investors. Follow steps 1–3.
   1 As you listen to the pitch, think of a question.
   2 After the pitch, ask your question(s).
   3 Individually, decide if you will make an offer. Explain your offer to the entrepreneurs.

3 Now swap roles. Student A and Student B: You are investors. Student C and Student D: You are entrepreneurs. Repeat step B.

MEDIATION BANK | SPEAKING

1C We're really busy right now

SPEAKING OUTPUT | a work-based discussion
GOAL | agree on the best way to fix a work problem
MEDIATION SKILL | inviting contributions

WARM-UP

1 Work in pairs and discuss the questions.
   1 How do you prefer to contact companies: by phone or by the chat service on their website?
   2 When you call a company, what kind of automated messages do you often hear while you're waiting to talk to someone?
   3 Is there anything you don't like about the experience of contacting customer service on the phone?
   I don't like the music. It's really annoying.

PREPARE

2 🔊 **MB1.01** | Read the Scenario and listen to the messages. Why does Janel want to talk about the automated message system?

> **SCENARIO**
>
> Janel sends you this message:
>
> Hi everyone.
> I looked at our feedback yesterday and everybody hates our automated messages on the customer service system! It has a rating of two stars out of five and people say it's really unfriendly and annoying. Can you listen to it and have a look at the script (see below) and think about how we can change it? Then we can talk about it in next week's meeting.
> Thanks!
> Janel
>
> **Automated message**
> You've got through to Well Gym. Press 1 to book a personal trainer. Press 2 to book the pool. Press 3 to speak to someone.
> *[If no one is free to help the customer when they choose an option:]*
> We're really busy right now. Continue to wait or maybe call back later. While you're waiting, why don't you leave us a five-star review online?
> *[Music plays: heavy rock]*
> *[Repeat message every 15 seconds.]*

3 A 🔊 **MB1.02** | Listen to three people discussing the messages. What problems do they discuss?
   - the person's voice
   - the music
   - too many options
   - the content of the messages

B 🔊 **MB1.02** | Listen again. Which things (1–4) does Janel do to help her colleagues give their opinions?
   1 say how the conversation will be organised
   2 ask people's opinions
   3 say something funny to help everyone relax
   4 ask people to say something about other people's opinions

4 Read the Mediation Skill box. Which phrases did Janel use? Listen again and check.

> **MEDIATION SKILL**
> **inviting contributions**
>
> When you are trying to solve a problem in a group, it is good to organise the conversation so that everyone has a chance to share their ideas. Here are a few ways you can do this.
>
> Say how the conversation will be organised
> **Can we share one idea each about** how we can change this?
> **Let's talk about** the music first, **then we can talk about** the messages.
>
> Ask the whole group
> **OK, what does everyone think?**
> **How do we feel about these ideas?**
>
> Ask individuals
> Lesley, **what are your thoughts on** it?
> Rich, **how do you feel about** Lesley's **idea**?
>
> Ask people to build on other people's opinions
> Rich hates the music – **what are your thoughts on it**, Lesley?
> I think the guy's voice is a bit boring. **What does everyone else think?**

5 Complete the conversation with sentences from the Mediation Skill box.
   Janel: So, we've got two possible plans to fix the problem. ¹ _____ ?
   Lesley: I think plan A is better, it's cheaper and easier to do.
   Janel: ² _____ .
   Rich: I think Lesley's right, it is easier.
   Janel: OK, so Les and Rich think plan A is better. ³ _____ ? Tom? Chris?

6 Look at the Scenario again. Make some notes about how you can make the message more friendly and less annoying.

MEDIATE

7 Work in groups. Discuss the issue from the Scenario and decide how you will improve the system.

MEDIATION BANK | WRITING

2C
Well-being Week

WRITING OUTPUT | a written summary
GOAL | summarise an article
MEDIATION SKILL | summarising skills

WARM-UP

1 Work in pairs and discuss the questions.
  1 What are some of the main reasons that people argue with their colleagues or classmates?
  2 What's the best way of stopping an argument becoming a big problem?

PREPARE

2 Read the Scenario. What do you think 'Well-being Week' is?

SCENARIO

You receive this message:

> As you all know, it's Well-being Week soon, and I'd like us all to do some research about how to look after our mental health in the team. I'll send you all some links to look at later today. Let's use them to make our 'Top four ways of dealing with anger in a team' blog.

3 Work in pairs. Student A: Read Text A. Student B: Read Text B. Which of the topics in the box are mentioned?

> knowing your own behaviour
> pretending things are OK
> taking a different point of view
> writing something down

Text A
How to deal with anger at work

Because I work in a stressful job, I understand what it's like to feel angry at work. Here's some advice for dealing with it.

❶ It's totally normal!

A lot of people want to calm down straight away when they're angry and just forget about what made them angry, but often this is not possible. Sometimes, you just have to accept it, and also remember that anger is a normal emotion – you're not a bad person just because you feel mad at someone or something. Pretending that you're calm when you're not can actually be pretty dangerous – you still have a lot of stress inside you, and it's very easy for you to get angry again, especially if the situation happens a lot. In my first job I often had coffee with colleagues who I was really angry with, pretending everything was OK, but in the end the bad feeling always came out and there were some really ugly situations that I could have avoided.

❷ It's not the end of the world

Sometimes when we're really mad, it can feel like the end of the world, and our relationships with people on our team are permanently broken. When you feel like this, try to remember previous problems with people at work. Did you fix the situation? The answer is almost always 'yes', and if this was true before, it's also true now – it will be possible to find a way to make things better. I remember two of my colleagues who used to fight a lot, and they've been happily married for ten years now!

❸ Space is good

Sometimes the best thing you can do when you're really angry with someone is walk away. Take a walk outside, take some deep breaths and let some of the stress go. It's better than staying in a bad situation because things can just get worse and worse. In my last job I always wanted to have the last word when I was mad at my colleague (and she did with me, too!), and it always made things worse when we kept arguing. If we spent a little time apart, we were usually just fine.

❹ There are warning signs

You know yourself. You know when that feeling of anger is getting stronger and stronger. It's like traffic lights: when your feelings reach yellow, don't wait for them to get to red, do something before it gets really bad. In my last job, I knew my colleagues really well, and I could see the warning signs. That was the time to go for lunch and talk about things in a friendly way or take some time away from each other, before it got really bad.

MEDIATION BANK | WRITING

Text B
Tips for beating anger at work

OK, guys, today's blog is my top four tips for dealing with stress with other people on your team.

1 See it both ways

So, you're getting angry with a colleague for some reason. Imagine a stranger coming in and looking at the situation. What would they think? Would they see a different way of looking at the issue than you? It's a real skill to look at a situation through another person's eyes, and a really good way to help you calm down. Sometimes, we feel that other people are trying to make us angry, but when you think more carefully about the reasons for their actions, you can start to understand why they are doing the things they are doing. Sometimes when I look at my own behaviour from a strangers' point of view, I feel quite embarrassed and I can't stay angry.

2 Take out a pen and paper

If you're the same as me, I find it very hard to explain how I feel when I'm angry. I focus on the emotion and I find it really difficult to explain the details that will help people understand why I'm angry, well, because I'm just too angry! When I write down what the problem is, I start to understand myself better, and I can stop, think and edit what I've written so that I can explain things better. I can also edit the angry language that I write at the beginning and replace it with calmer words. For example, I remember writing: 'Carl is such an idiot. He never listens to anyone because he always thinks he's right.' Later on, I thought about the situation and wrote: 'Carl is very confident about his opinions, but maybe he needs to listen more.'

3 Focus on the answer

Yes, you want to talk about how you're feeling, and that's important. However, you need to do more than that. You need to be part of solving the problem and you need to be open to suggestions from other people. If you only concentrate on why you're angry and you're not interested in talking about solving problems, then it's difficult for the situation to improve.

4 Take care

There are some things you can do to make your general mood better, which makes an argument with a teammate less likely. Some of the key things are: getting enough sleep, doing regular exercise and controlling things like caffeine and alcohol. It's difficult to be in control of all of these things all the time, but you need to do your best for your sake and for your colleagues', too. A few years ago, I promised myself that I would get a minimum of eight hours sleep per night, and it changed my mood a lot. Give it a try!

---

4 Read the Mediation Skill box. What kind of information can we sometimes remove when we write a summary?

MEDIATION SKILL
summarising skills

When you write a summary of a text, there are a few useful steps:

First, decide what information you need. Read the text and for each paragraph decide what the most important point is. For example:

I think an important thing to think about is how much sleep you're getting, and it's something that people don't talk about enough, because **if you don't sleep well, it's going to be very easy for you to get angry with people around you**. I remember when I had a really bad argument with a colleague because I had slept badly. It all happened just because I was tired. I said sorry later, but the argument caused a problem for months.

Then think about what information you don't need, such as long introductions to the topic and examples.

Use bullet points to help keep your summary short.

When you finish writing, check your summary against the article.

We can also use certain helpful phrases to help us summarise:
The article/blog/writer says (that) …
One of the main points is …
The writer recommends + -ing
The article says that it's very easy to get angry with other people if you don't sleep well.

5 Look at your article (Text A or Text B) again. Find the key information that you would include in a summary.

MEDIATE

6 A Read the Scenario again. Write a short summary of your article, using the ideas from the Mediation Skill box to help you.

B Work in pairs. Give your partner your summary and allow them some time to read it. Take turns to ask and answer any questions you have about your partner's summary.
Why is sleep so important?

C Choose the top five tips you would include in an article about avoiding anger in a team.

D Work with another pair. Share your top five tips and your reasons for choosing them. Do you agree?

MEDIATION BANK | SPEAKING

3C The volunteers

SPEAKING OUTPUT | a meeting
GOAL | choose a candidate for a position
MEDIATION SKILL | asking people to explain their reasons

WARM-UP

1 Work in pairs and discuss the questions.

1. Have you ever worked as a volunteer or do you know anyone who has? What did you/they do?
2. If you volunteered, what type of organisation would you want to work for?

   I'd love to work with animals. I feel so sad when I see dogs with no homes.

2 Read the text about what makes a good volunteer. Work in pairs and answer the questions.

1. Which of the qualities mentioned in the text do you think is the most important for a volunteer?
2. Do you think you have the right qualities to be a volunteer? Why/Why not?

What makes a good volunteer?

Sometimes people think that it's easy to volunteer. They say things like 'Well, they don't get paid, so the work they do probably isn't so difficult.' It makes me sad, because I know how hard it is to find great volunteers. Here are some of the most important qualities I look for when I need to find volunteers for my organisation.

1 Passion

This is the most obvious one, maybe, but perhaps the most important. A volunteer needs to care about the project they are working on. Sometimes people volunteer for the wrong reasons – maybe because they want to take photos for social media to show people how interesting their life is or so they can tell their friends what good, kind people they are because they are volunteering. These people usually give up first. The project is the king!

2 Communication

Volunteer teams are usually a real mix of people who have had different experiences in their lives, have lived in different places and studied different things. It's important that volunteers work well together, and to do that they need to be able to listen to each other and understand different opinions, even opinions which are very different from their own. This is also true when volunteers talk to members of the public about the project – sometimes people don't understand why you are volunteering and think you are wasting your time! It's important to be able to listen to people, explain what the project is trying to achieve and, at the same time, show respect.

3 Never giving up

Volunteering can be tiring and make you feel depressed sometimes. Some days it's raining and you don't want to leave the house, after all they're not paying you, are they? Maybe you're trying to raise money for a charity, which is so important, and everyone you ask to help says no. You spend the whole day with people saying no to you and at the end of it you feel that haven't helped the charity at all. A good volunteer understands that days like these happen and they don't give up, even when they have a bad day. They know the project is important and they keep going because they believe in it.

4 It's not about you

Let's be honest - not everybody gets the most interesting jobs when they volunteer. I remember the first volunteer role I had: I picked up rubbish from the beach every weekend for a year, and it was so boring sometimes. Other people in the charity had much more interesting jobs, talking to local businesses and organising events, but when I felt bad about it I tried to remember that my work was important, too – it's about helping the project, not about having the coolest job. The best team players make the best volunteers.

5 Creative thinkers

When you're raising money for a charity, there are many ways to do it, not just standing in the street with a bucket, and it's always good to have volunteers who have new ideas about how we can get people to give to the charity. One of my favourite volunteers, Sam, had a great idea to promote our project to protect local wildlife – we dressed in animal costumes and went to the zoo. We raised a lot of cash doing that!

MEDIATION BANK | SPEAKING

PREPARE

3 Read the Scenario. What do you need to decide in the next meeting with your team?

SCENARIO

You work for a volunteer group which raises money for local charities, including clubs for young people and social activities for older people. You are looking for a volunteer to raise funds. Their main duty will be to approach people in the street to tell them about the charities and ask for their support.

Additional details about the role:
- The applicant should be available as soon as possible.
- They should be very flexible with their schedule if possible.
- Long-term applicants are preferred.
- No salary or expenses to be paid if possible. No current volunteers receive any payment.

You have interviewed three people. Here are your notes.

Trent Dillon

| No previous experience |
| Free 3 days a week |
| Cares a lot about the project |
| Seems very motivated, talks a lot, friendly |
| Note: Free now. Leaving for university in 6 months |

Bella Cheeve

| A lot of experience with various charities, including working with older people |
| Free 5 days a week |
| Has led teams of volunteers before |
| Very serious, determined person, not very 'smiley' |
| Note: Free now. Would like to get paid a small amount for expenses |

Laura Appleby

| Some experience with animal charities |
| Free 7 days a week |
| A little shy and nervous, but believes strongly in the project |
| Note: She's only free in 3 months |

You are going to meet with the rest of the team next week and decide who should get the role.

4 🔊 **MB3.01** | Listen to three extracts from conversations about the applicants. Which candidate does each woman prefer? What reasons do they give?

5 A 🔊 **MB3.01** | Read the Mediation Skill box. Listen again and note down two more questions the man uses to ask for reasons.

MEDIATION SKILL
asking people to explain their reasons

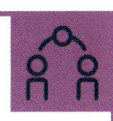

When making decisions in a group, it is a good idea to encourage other people to say what they think and to explain why they think it.

What were your reasons for choosing Laura?

You can also use questions like these when someone has already given you some information, but you want more details. You can add phrases to show that you are interested in the other person's opinion, too.

A: OK, so I think Bella is the best person for the role.
B: Ah I see. Why exactly do you think that?
A: Well, I would choose Trent.
B: OK, he's an interesting choice. Can you explain why you picked him?

B Practise the conversation. Replace the word *Why* with a phrase from the Mediation Skill box.

A: What do you think of Tom? I liked him.
B: I don't think he's a good choice.
A: **Why?**
B: To be honest, he's a bit strange.
A: Well, I think he's a good candidate.
B: **Why?**
A: He's very serious about helping people.

MEDIATE

6 A Work in groups of three. Look at the Scenario again. Discuss who should get the role, asking your partners to give reasons where necessary. Come to an agreement.

Student A: You want Trent to get the role.
Student B: You want Bella to get the role.
Student C: You want Laura to get the role.

B Who did your group choose, and why? Did every group choose the same person?

MEDIATION BANK | WRITING

4C Newsflash!

WRITING OUTPUT | a social media post
GOAL | report a news story
MEDIATION SKILL | writing in note form

WARM-UP

1 Work in pairs and discuss the questions.
   1 Where do you prefer to read the news?
   2 Do you ever read the news on social media? Why/Why not?
   3 Why do some people prefer to read news in a short text and not a full story?

   I read the news online, usually. I prefer short texts because I can see all the main stories quickly.

PREPARE

2 Read the Scenario. Which story do you think people will find the most interesting?

3 A Work in pairs. Look at the news story below. How can it be made shorter?

> A report that we have received from the Met Office says that this is the warmest November for one hundred years in all parts of the UK. The reason for the very mild weather is not completely clear, but experts believe it might possibly be related to global warming.

B Look at the online post of the same story. How did the writer make it shorter?

> Posted by wevgirl99 | 02/07 | 12:24
>
> Met Office report says this is warmest November for 100 years. Reason is not clear. Might be related to global warming.

SCENARIO

You work for a social media news channel and you share news 24 hours a day. You post short news summaries for your followers. Your posts need to be 25 words or fewer.

Your researcher has scanned some local, national and international news sites for stories. Look at the notes they have written for you.

Cow walks onto motorway

One interesting story that I was sent today is about a cow that walked onto the M25 motorway near London yesterday. The young cow escaped from her small field and stopped all the traffic on the giant motorway during rush hour. Lots of furious motorists who were trying to get to work were delayed in their journeys by more than an hour. The police arrived on the scene and caught the cow, whose name is apparently Daisy, and returned her safely to the field.

Giant potato

OK, you're going to love this. I've received an amazing news report from New Zealand today which says that the world's largest potato has been grown there by a farmer in a small town called Hamilton, which is on the North Island just south of Auckland. This monster potato weighs an absolutely unbelievable eight kilograms and it was discovered by local farmer Colin Craig Brown last week. His wife Donna said, 'We couldn't believe it. It's huge!' They have called the potato 'Doug'.

MEDIATION BANK | WRITING

Lost hiker ignores rescue team

Here's a really crazy story. It's about this hiker who got lost on Mount Elbert in Colorado. They ignored lots of phone calls from a really desperate rescue team because they didn't recognise the numbers which were calling them! The hiker, whose name has not been revealed, was reported as missing on 18 October at 8 p.m. and was found the next morning by Lake County Search and Rescue (LCSR). The LCSR officials gave this information on 21 October.

Sleep bus

So, I've got a report here from Hong Kong which describes a new kind of bus tour that has been designed for people who are having problems sleeping. There are a lot of tired, stressed people in the city of Hong Kong who find it very difficult to sleep well in their homes, but for some strange reason they find it easy to sleep when they are on public transport. The unusual bus tour is forty-seven miles long and lasts for five hours. It stops at some famous places so that people can take photos if they want to. Customers receive free sleep masks, too.

4 Read the Mediation Skill box and check your answers to Ex 3B.

MEDIATION SKILL
writing in note form

There are certain apps where posts have a maximum number of characters, which means we may need to write in a short form. Here are some techniques we can use to help us.

Remove information that is not necessary to understand the basic idea.
~~We have received an interesting report that says~~ Scientists have found a new planet.

Remove small words where possible (like *the* in the superlative or when something is mentioned for the second time).
… report says this is ~~the~~ warmest November for 100 years.
… and hit a car. ~~The~~ Car was driven by Isaac Solomson.

Remove *that* after phrases with *say*, *tell* (*me*), etc.
Police said ~~that~~ the man was carrying a yellow umbrella.

Remove adjectives and adverbs that do not give us information about the story.
It's not ~~completely~~ clear why they took this ~~strange~~ route.

Use numbers, not words.
~~Three thousand~~ 3,000 sheep were lost last week in Wales.

Remove conjunctions like *and*, *but* and *because*.
The reason for the very mild weather is not completely clear. ~~but~~ Experts believe it might be related to global warming.

Use the active voice not the passive voice.
~~Information has been received by the police.~~
The police received information.

5 Look at the texts in the Scenario again. Find the words you think that you can cut to reduce the length of the texts.

MEDIATE

6 A Rewrite the news stories for your social media channel. Do not exceed the 25-word limit.

B Work in pairs and compare your stories. Compare the techniques you used to make the stories shorter.

151

MEDIATION BANK | SPEAKING

5C The next big thing

SPEAKING OUTPUT | a spoken proposal
GOAL | explain something clearly to sell an idea to other people
MEDIATION SKILL | selling an idea

WARM-UP

1 A Work in pairs and discuss the question. In what ways can the products in the box be annoying?

> bottles of sauce   car alarms   headphones   pet food
> plastic bags   shoelaces   socks   umbrellas

It's annoying when car alarms go off during the night.

B If you could fix any of the problems with these products, which of your ideas would make you the most money?

I hate the smell of cat food. It's horrible. I think people would pay a lot of money for cat food that smells nice.

PREPARE

2 Read the Scenario. Which product ideas are the most interesting?

SCENARIO

You work in the product design department of a company, and your job is to come up with exciting new products that solve people's day-to-day problems.

Look at the list of proposals for new products below. You are going to choose one product from this list and promote it. You need to decide which one will be the most successful and make the most money.

1 Washable keyboard – a keyboard that you can take off your laptop and wash in order to keep it clean.
2 Socks that make a pleasant electronic noise when you put the correct pair together.
3 A coffee cup that plays lively music when it's full of coffee to help you wake up.
4 Talking recycling bin – it tells you if the thing you put in it is the correct material for recycling in that bin.
5 Glasses with a torch – your glasses have an automatic torch which provides light when it's too dark to see.
6 A sauce bottle that has a special coating on the inside to make the sauce come out more easily.

3 A 🔊 **MB5.01** | Listen to the beginning of a presentation about one of the products. Which one are they talking about?

B 🔊 **MB5.01** | Listen again and complete the sentences.
1 So, it's _____ when you don't know what you can recycle, isn't it?
2 It _____ like a lottery – maybe this can go in the recycling bin, maybe not.
3 Well, you can stop this situation from _____ with our new product.
4 The bin is a _____ like those checkout machines in the supermarket that can recognise products.
5 It's also _____ to the supermarket machine because it speaks.

4 Read the Mediation Skill box. Match the sentences (1–5) in Ex 3B with the headings in the box.

MEDIATION SKILL
selling an idea

When you are presenting a new idea, it's good to make it easy for people to understand and see why it's a good idea. You can achieve this by doing the following.

Show that you understand other people's experiences
So, you know when you can't leave work early and you have to take the train at rush hour …
It's like when you have too much shopping in your bag, it's going to break.

Show how your idea fixes a problem
You can avoid this by making it out of plastic.
This design has two sections, so you don't have to only use one.

Make comparisons to other experiences to explain how something works
It's like that, but you use two different bottles.
It works in the same way as paying with your phone.

5 Work in pairs. Choose a product idea from the Scenario to propose as the next big product for your company. Discuss how you can:
- show that you understand other people's experiences.
- show how your idea fixes customers' problems.
- make comparisons to explain how the product works.

MEDIATE

6 A Work in groups. Take turns to present your idea, explaining why you think your product will be a big success.

B Vote for the product you think the company should make next.

152

MEDIATION BANK | SPEAKING

6C Getting around

SPEAKING OUTPUT | a radio phone-in
GOAL | discuss a proposal
MEDIATION SKILL | collaborating on a task

WARM-UP

1 Work in pairs and discuss the questions.
   1 How do people travel around your town or city?
   2 What are the good things and bad things about your town's transport systems?
   3 What's the best transport system you've ever used?
   I loved using cable cars in Japan – it was so exciting!

PREPARE

2 Read the Scenario and tick any of the transport solutions you would like to have in your town or city. Work in pairs and compare selections. Explain why you have chosen them.

SCENARIO

Your town is planning to improve its transport system, and there are some different proposals about how to do this. You read about some of the proposals on the local government website.

There's a radio phone-in programme today to discuss the best idea. You decide to call in and give your ideas.

As we all know, our town has several key problems with public transport at the moment:
- the cost of public transport
- the town centre is crowded
- there are a high number of traffic accidents

There are three main ideas to help us solve some of these issues:

Self-driving buses Because you don't need a driver, self-driving buses can allow the town to run 24/7 and also allow us to offer people very cheap public transport. In addition, they use a mix of gas and solar power, so they are environmentally friendly.

Skyways Another idea is skyways – walkways built high above ground level. These allow people to move around comfortably, without needing to wait to cross dangerous roads.

Smart roads These are made of a special material that absorbs solar energy. They can use this power to heat roads when it's cold so that ice and snow melt and the roads are less dangerous. The energy can also be used to power street lights at night and even cars. In addition, any proposal that will make the town more attractive to tourists would also be very positive.

3 🔊 **MB6.01** | Listen to part of a radio phone-in programme. Which of the three transport ideas do they discuss?

4 🔊 **MB6.01** | Read the Mediation Skill box. Then listen to the recording again for any other useful phrases you hear which fit the three headings in the box.

MEDIATION SKILL
collaborating on a task

When discussing proposals in a group, there are several things you can do to help the conversation develop in a positive way and to explore different ideas.

Respond to other people's ideas
That's very true.
Well, I'm not sure about that.
It could work.

Ask other people if they agree
Do you feel the same?
[Tina], do you share the same opinion?

Make alternative suggestions
We could do that, but we could also …
Another idea is to …

5 Work in groups of three. Choose a topic from the box and discuss it. Then change roles.

> The best thing to do on a sunny day in your town/city
> The best place to eat lunch in your town/city
> An area of your town/city you'd like to change

Student A: Give your idea about the topic.
Student B: React. Ask Student C how they feel.
Student C: React. Make an alternative suggestion.

6 Look at the transport solutions in the Scenario again. Make notes about which of the town's transport problems you think they will solve.

MEDIATE

7A Work in small groups. You are going to take part in a radio phone-in programme to discuss the different transport solutions and try to decide which one your town should choose. Decide who will be the host and who will call in to the show. The host begins.

Hello, and welcome to the show. Today we are discussing our town's transport problems and some possible solutions. My first caller today is …

B Tell other groups which solution you chose and your reasons for choosing it.

MEDIATION BANK | WRITING

7C Invasion of the chatbots

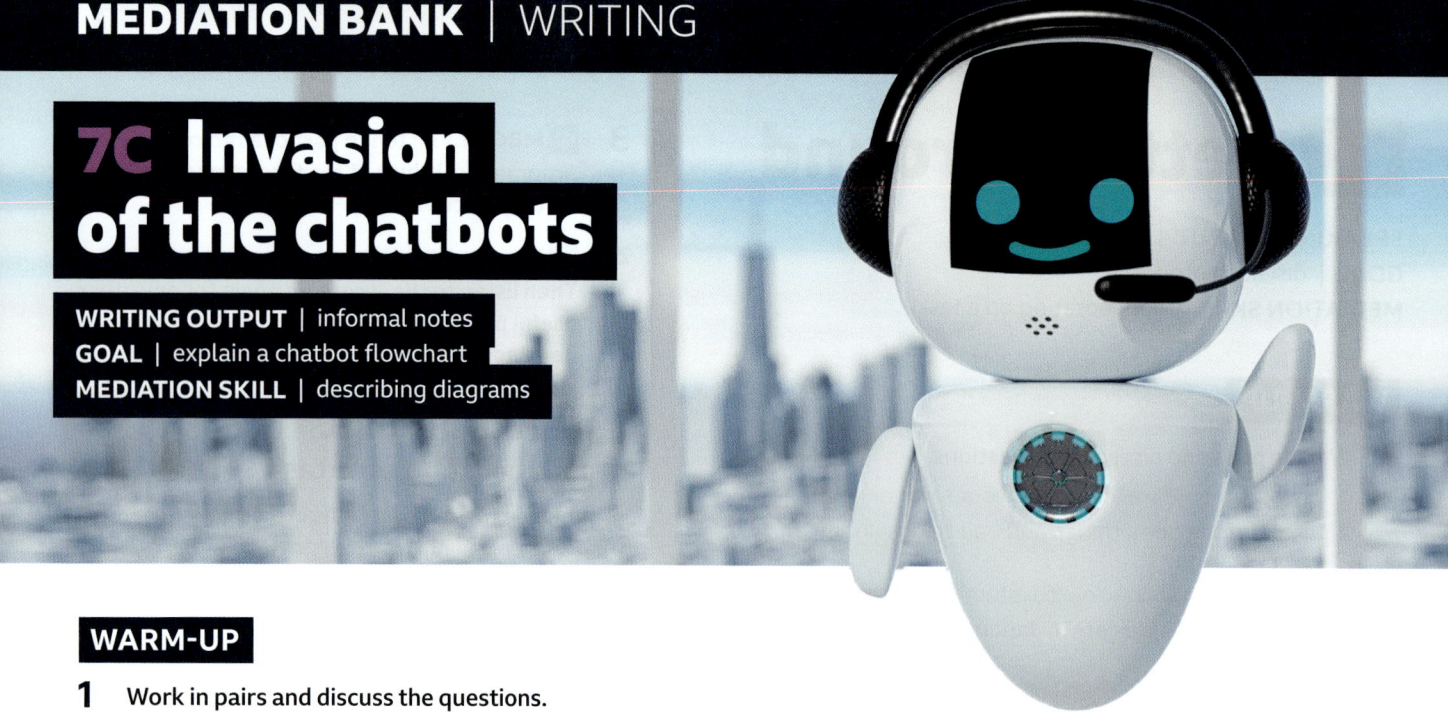

WRITING OUTPUT | informal notes
GOAL | explain a chatbot flowchart
MEDIATION SKILL | describing diagrams

WARM-UP

1 Work in pairs and discuss the questions.
  1 How do you prefer to access customer service? Why?
    a by email
    b using a chatbot (a website's automated chat service)
    c on the phone
  2 What are the good and bad things about using each method?
    I use chatbots a lot when I'm talking to my bank. It's the quickest way to get information, but they are annoying sometimes when they don't offer the help you need.

PREPARE

2 Read the Scenario on page 155. Why does your friend need your help?

3 Look at the flowcharts in the Scenario. What type of company are they for? Do you think they are good systems? Why/Why not?

4 Read the Mediation Skill box. Tick the example sentences that might describe the flowcharts in the Scenario.

MEDIATION SKILL
describing diagrams

When we are describing a diagram, we often need to explain what the objects and colours in the diagram mean, the sequence of actions/events and also the relationship between different actions.

Describing objects in a diagram
The arrow shows the direction of the conversation.
The boxes represent the different flight times.
[Blue] indicates the customer.

Describing a sequence
It starts by greeting the customer.
Then you choose how many you want.
After that, you find out how many people they want to bring.

Explaining the relationship between different actions
When the customer has chosen a size, **we ask them** what colour they want.
If they can't find a date they want for that person, **then they can choose** someone different.

---

5 Look at the chatbot flowchart. Then complete the description using the language from the mediation box to help you.
  1 The arrows show you ....
  2 The boxes represent ....
  3 Green boxes indicate ....
  4 Grey boxes indicate ....
  5 The bot starts the conversation by ....
  6 Then the bot asks ....
  7 If the customer says yes the bot ....
  8 If the customer says no to help, then ....

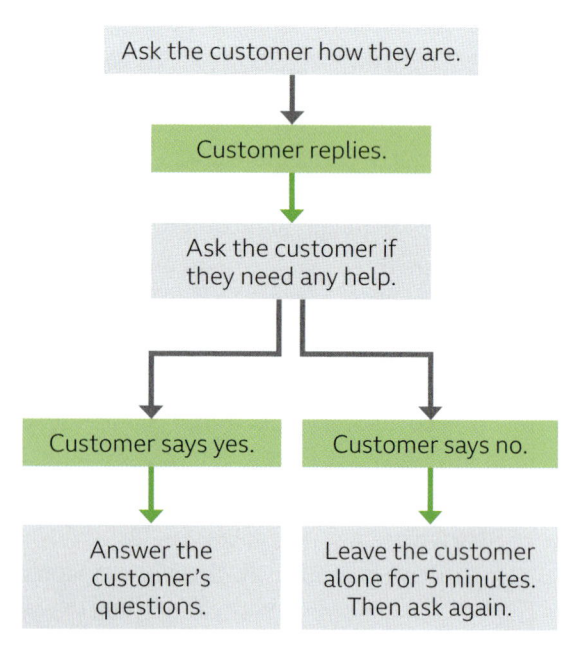

```
Ask the customer how they are.
          ↓
    Customer replies.
          ↓
Ask the customer if
they need any help.
       ↙      ↘
Customer says yes.   Customer says no.
      ↓                    ↓
  Answer the          Leave the customer
  customer's          alone for 5 minutes.
  questions.          Then ask again.
```

MEDIATE

6 Write notes about the chatbot diagrams in the Scenario to help your friend explain how they work to her boss.

7 Work in pairs. Compare your notes and check if they included anything that you didn't. Add anything useful to your own description.

154

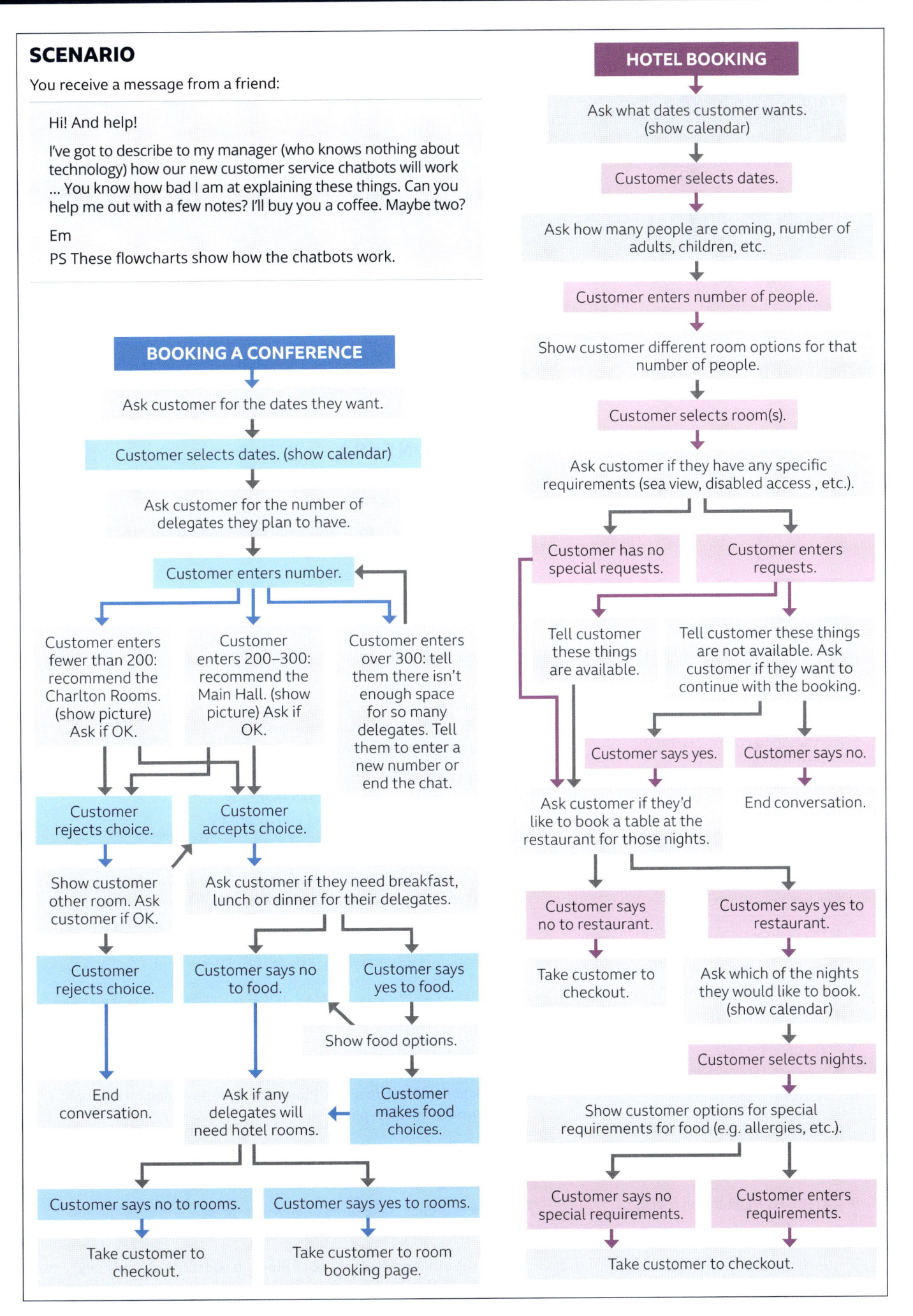

MEDIATION BANK | WRITING

SCENARIO

You receive a message from a friend:

> Hi! And help!
> I've got to describe to my manager (who knows nothing about technology) how our new customer service chatbots will work … You know how bad I am at explaining these things. Can you help me out with a few notes? I'll buy you a coffee. Maybe two?
> Em
> PS These flowcharts show how the chatbots work.

BOOKING A CONFERENCE

- Ask customer for the dates they want.
- Customer selects dates. (show calendar)
- Ask customer for the number of delegates they plan to have.
- Customer enters number.
  - Customer enters fewer than 200: recommend the Charlton Rooms. (show picture) Ask if OK.
  - Customer enters 200–300: recommend the Main Hall. (show picture) Ask if OK.
  - Customer enters over 300: tell them there isn't enough space for so many delegates. Tell them to enter a new number or end the chat.
- Customer rejects choice. → Show customer other room. Ask customer if OK.
  - Customer rejects choice. → End conversation.
- Customer accepts choice.
- Ask customer if they need breakfast, lunch or dinner for their delegates.
  - Customer says no to food.
  - Customer says yes to food. → Show food options. → Customer makes food choices.
- Ask if any delegates will need hotel rooms.
  - Customer says no to rooms. → Take customer to checkout.
  - Customer says yes to rooms. → Take customer to room booking page.

HOTEL BOOKING

- Ask what dates customer wants. (show calendar)
- Customer selects dates.
- Ask how many people are coming, number of adults, children, etc.
- Customer enters number of people.
- Show customer different room options for that number of people.
- Customer selects room(s).
- Ask customer if they have any specific requirements (sea view, disabled access, etc.).
  - Customer has no special requests. → Tell customer these things are available.
  - Customer enters requests. → Tell customer these things are not available. Ask customer if they want to continue with the booking.
    - Customer says yes.
    - Customer says no. → End conversation.
- Ask customer if they'd like to book a table at the restaurant for those nights.
  - Customer says no to restaurant. → Take customer to checkout.
  - Customer says yes to restaurant. → Ask which of the nights they would like to book. (show calendar)
- Customer selects nights.
- Show customer options for special requirements for food (e.g. allergies, etc.).
  - Customer says no special requirements.
  - Customer enters requirements.
- Take customer to checkout.

155

MEDIATION BANK | SPEAKING

8C Tell me more

SPEAKING OUTPUT | discussion following a presentation
GOAL | ask follow-up questions after a presentation
MEDIATION SKILL | asking someone to elaborate on what they said

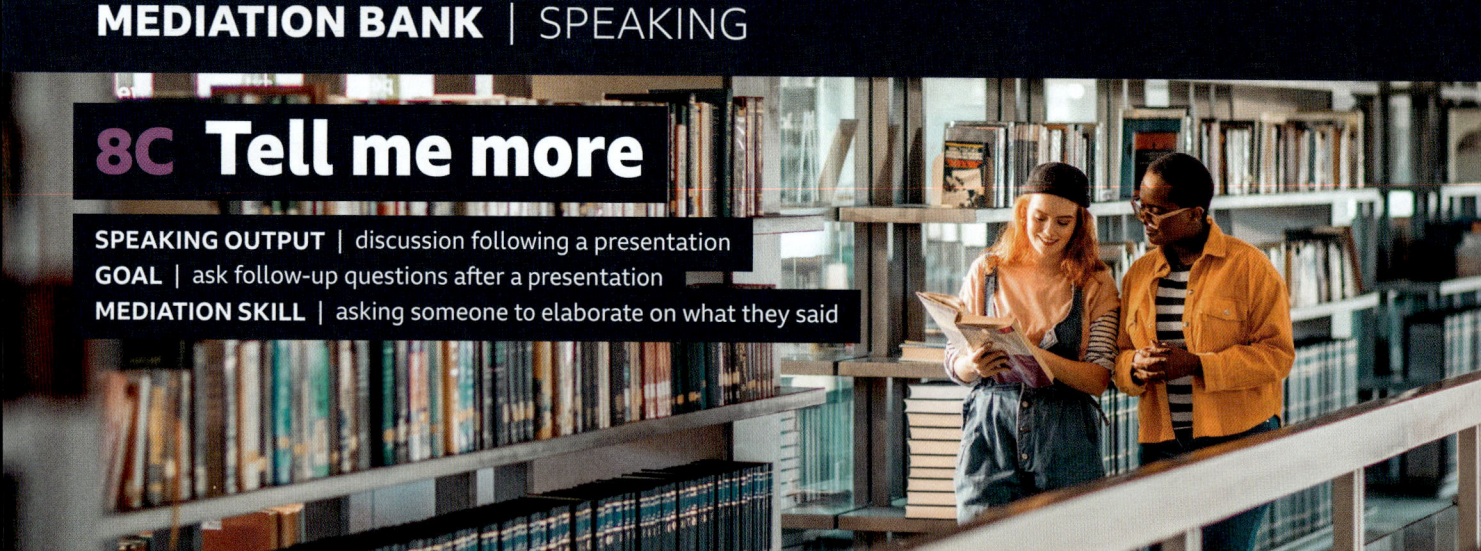

WARM-UP

1 Work in pairs and discuss the questions.

1 Do you learn the most important lessons inside or outside the classroom? Why?
2 Do people learn more from bad experiences or good experiences? Why?

PREPARE

2 Read the Scenario. What kind of situations might people talk about?

SCENARIO

You have been asked to give a presentation to your group on the following topic:

'An important life lesson you learnt'

Describe:
- the situation where you learnt the lesson.
- what you learnt.
- why it was so important.

3A Read some questions that were asked after a presentation. What do you think the presentation was about?

1 In your presentation you talked about how disappointed you felt. Did that feeling help you in some way?
2 Can you tell me a little more about what you did after you left the course?
3 You said that you realised you wouldn't be a great doctor. Can you tell me why you felt that?

B 🔊 **MB8.01** | Listen and check.

4 Read the Mediation Skill box. Complete the example sentences with your own ideas.

MEDIATION SKILL
asking someone to elaborate on what they said

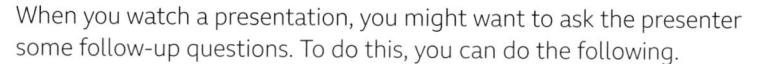

When you watch a presentation, you might want to ask the presenter some follow-up questions. To do this, you can do the following.

Refer to what the speaker said
Do you feel the same?
In your presentation/talk, you spoke about …
You said/told us that you …
You described your …

Ask for more details
Can you explain why … ?
Can you say a little more about your … ?
Can you explain your reasons for … ?

Ask for clarification
When you said …. , did you mean that … or … ?
I'm not sure I understood what you meant by … ?

5 Look at an extract from a presentation. Refer to it and ask for more details. Use the phrases in the Mediation Skill box to help you.

I guess I learnt an important lesson when I finally decided to stop going to dance clubs with my friends and to stay at home and do something that I preferred instead. At that moment, I realised that I don't need to copy other people's behaviour all the time. Everyone in my group of friends loved to dance, but I just didn't and every time we went to a club, I sat by myself while everyone else was having fun. When I thought about it, I realised I did the same thing in so many different areas of my life, always following the crowd.

6 Look at the Scenario again. Plan a short presentation on the topic. Make notes on each point.

MEDIATE

7A Work in groups. Take turns to give your presentations. While you listen to other presenters, write follow-up questions for them.

B Ask the other presenters your follow-up questions. Answer any questions they have for you.

AUDIOSCRIPTS

LEAD-IN

Audio L.01
1. should, wood
2. weight, late
3. build, filled
4. white, height
5. though, show
6. were, fur

UNIT 1

Audio 1.01
M = Marta   T = Tim

M: I've worn silver rings all my life. I got this ring in a street market when I was living in Italy for a few months. I bought it to replace a similar one that I'd lost. This one belonged to my mother and I inherited it when she died. It's not worth a lot, but it's very special to me.

I borrowed this leather jacket from a friend when I was studying at university and I never gave it back. It's a genuine 1980s leather jacket. When I was wearing it, I always thought it looked really cool. It's a bit damaged now, but I still love it.

I have a beautiful lemon tree that a friend gave me as a birthday present. I'd told her that I'd always wanted to live in a house with a lemon tree, so to make my dream come true, she bought me one. I was having a party to celebrate my thirtieth birthday, and in the middle of the party my friend arrived and gave me the lemon tree in a pot. So, now I grow my own lemons!

T: I bought my Spanish guitar in a famous guitar shop in Madrid. Even when I open the case today, I can still smell the wood of the shop. I remember trying it out in a corner. I was quietly playing my favourite piece of music as I didn't want to draw too much attention to myself. However, to my horror, the shopkeeper had listened to me playing and he asked me, 'Are you a professional?' Naturally, I bought the guitar quite soon after he'd asked that question! Six months later I returned to the shop to buy some new strings and there was someone else trying out a guitar. He was playing a piece of music I knew, but he wasn't playing very well. The same shopkeeper was there and said to the man, 'Wow, you must be a professional!' Suddenly, I understood.

I enjoy doing long-distance walks, preferably with friends. I bought these boots while I was travelling around New Zealand. I was about to head off for the Milford Track, quite a challenging four-day walk, and my old boots fell to pieces. I had one day to find a new pair. Years later, I still have those boots. They're not in very good condition and they're heavy, old, leather boots, but they're still comfortable and they're like old friends. I've had such great times with friends and family walking, talking and exploring.

And this? It's an Italian moka coffee pot. A friend gave it to me at university because he had watched me making instant coffee without much care or thought. He said, 'The small ritual of a good coffee is too important to give up.' We used to laugh at him for being so serious about things we thought were unimportant, but now every time I use the pot I realise that he was right. If you can't enjoy little things, then you will never be happy.

Audio 1.02
1. I was travelling around Australia.
2. We were living in China.
3. He was studying at university.
4. I bought a new leather jacket to replace the one I had lost.
5. My mother had given the ring to me.
6. He had seen me making coffee.

Audio 1.03
1. I believe in living a simple life.
2. He succeeded in finding his dream job.
3. You should think about tidying your stuff.
4. Concentrate on appreciating the simple things.

Audio 1.04
1
A: You've reached Café Roma. I'm afraid we're busy at the moment. Please leave a message and we'll get back to you.
B: Hello. This is Marcelo Fagundes. I'm calling about my jacket. I was having dinner in your restaurant an hour ago and I left my jacket. Do you think you could have a look for it for me? It's the leather jacket hanging on the hook by the stairs. Can you call me back? You can reach me on this number – 0779542867.

2
A: You've reached Sam's mobile. Please leave a message.
B: Hi Sam. It's Mum. Could you check that the garage door is locked? I think I might have left it open. The key's in the kitchen. You'll find it on the table next to the window. Also, before you leave, will you take out the rubbish please, and make sure you turn the heating off? Thanks. See you later.

3
A: I'm sorry I can't take your call at the moment. Please leave a message
B: Hi Riccardo. It's Gemma. I've got a guest coming to stay in the apartment later. Would you explain the alarm system to her? You'll need to unlock the box and show her how it works. That would be really helpful. Thanks.

4
A: Hi, you're through to Jacob. I can't take your call right now, but if you leave a message with your name and number, I'll get back to you as soon as I can.
B: Hi Jacob, it's Patricia here. I wonder if you could bring my folder to the meeting? You'll find it on my desk in the office. The meeting starts at 4 p.m., so we'll need to be there at least fifteen minutes earlier. Could you please let me know that you've got this message? Thanks.

5
A: Noelie, it's Pete. Listen, I was going to cook, but there's no food in the house. Do you think you'll be able to pick up some pizzas on the way home? There's a great place just on the corner by the station. You choose the toppings. That would be great. Bye.

6
A: Thank you for calling Smiths and Co. Our office hours are 8 a.m. to 6 p.m. If it's urgent, please leave a message with your name and number and we'll contact you as soon as possible.
B: Hello. This is Natalie Ivanov. I'm calling because we have a broken pipe in our house and the water is going everywhere! I need someone to come and fix it, please. Will you please call me back as soon as possible? It's urgent. You can reach me on this number.

7
A: Hi, you're through to Teresa. Please leave me a message and I'll call you right back.
B: Hi Teresa, it's Yumi. I'm calling to ask a favour. I'm going away in a couple of weeks. I wonder if you'd mind watering the plants for me, like you did last time. I can leave the key with my neighbour. That would be so kind. Let me know. Bye.

Audio 1.05
1. You've reached Café Roma.
2. Please leave a message and we'll get back to you.
3. Thank you for calling Smiths and Co. Our office hours are 8 a.m. to 6 p.m.
4. I can't take your call right now, but if you leave a message with your name and number, I'll get back to you as soon as I can.
5. This is Marcelo Fagundes calling about …
6. It's Patricia here …
7. You'll need to unlock the …
8. You'll find it on the table next to the …
9. Can you call me back?
10. You can reach me on this number.

Audio 1.06
1. Would you explain the alarm system to her?
2. I wonder if you could bring my folder to the meeting?
3. Could you please let me know that you've got this message?
4. Do you think you'll be able to pick up some pizzas on the way home?
5. I wonder if you'd mind watering the plants for me.

157

AUDIOSCRIPTS

Audio 1.07
1 I wonder if you could bring my folder, please?
2 Would you walk the dog, please?
3 Do you think you'll be able to come today?
4 Will you pick up some food on the way home?

UNIT 1 VOCABULARY BANK

Audio VB1.01
A They're made of glass.
B It's made of wood.
C It's made of a diamond.
D It's made of plastic.
E They're made of cotton.
F It's made of silver.
G It's made of denim.
H It's made of rubber.
I It's made of steel.
J They're made of iron.
K It's made of gold.
L It's made of stone.

UNIT 1 REVIEW

Audio R1.01
The House that Jock Built
When Elizabeth finally saw the house, it had been part of her family legend for 200 years. It had been built by Jock Phillip, her distant ancestor who had left Scotland for America aged sixteen, with nothing but the clothes on his back. Five years after arriving, he discovered a hidden treasure in California: a seam of gold, which he later mined. He had succeeded in changing his fortunes, and with his earnings he built his dream home.
It was the ideal house, large and beautiful, a house to pass down from generation to generation. It belonged to his children, then his grandchildren, and so on. When Elizabeth was young, she remembered hearing stories about it. For this reason she had always dreamed about visiting the house. Finally, her chance came.
While she was driving there, she suddenly felt a sense of sadness. She arrived and saw immediately that the house was badly damaged. The walls, made of stone, were falling down, and the windows were long gone. Birds had made their homes in the roof.

UNIT 1 MEDIATION BANK

Audio MB1.01
You've got through to Well Gym. Press 1 to book a personal trainer. Press 2 to book the pool. Press 3 to speak to someone.
We're really busy right now. Continue to wait or maybe call back later. While you're waiting, why don't you leave us a five-star review online?
We're really busy right now. Continue to wait or maybe call back later. While you're waiting, why don't you leave us a five-star review online?

Audio MB1.02
J = Janel   R = Rich   L = Lesley
J: So, everyone hates our automated message. Can we share one idea each about how we can change this?
R: I think it's the music. It's so stupid. It's just the same thing again and again and again …
J: OK, Lesley, what are your thoughts on it? Does the music need changing?
L: Yes, Rich is right, it's so annoying and it doesn't help people relax while they're waiting.
J: Agreed. Also, I think the guy's voice is a bit boring. What does everyone else think?
R: I like his voice.
L: I agree with Janel, and he speaks reeeally slooowly, too.
J: OK, so that's the music and the guy's voice, now let's talk about the actual messages. How does everyone feel about …

UNIT 2

Audio 2.01 and 2.02
1 How long have you been studying English?
2 I've been studying since I was ten.
3 Have you been living in the same place for a long time?
4 I've been living there for five years.

Audio 2.03
1 A: Help you with your work? Well, I'm a bit busy but … sure, I can help.
   B: He's …
2 A: Can I say something? Erm, well, your hair looks great, but the jacket is horrible.
   B: She's …
3 A: My phone … Where is it … ? I can't find it! Oh no, what am I going to do without my phone?
   B: He's …
4 A: I'm having a bad day. Go away! Leave me alone!
   B: She's …
5 A: Oh, I really want to go dancing. Come on, let's go dancing!
   B: He …
6 A: I'm so sorry. It's my mistake. I feel so bad that I've hurt you.
   B: She's …
7 A: No, no, no, I agree with you, really! Really, no need to discuss it, you're right!
   B: He's…
8 A: It's so easy to talk to you. I'm totally relaxed whenever we have a conversation.
   B: She …

Audio 2.04
G = Greta   C = Colin   A = Anna
G: Am I a people pleaser? Well, when someone asks me to do them a favour, I almost always say yes. For instance, last week when my manager asked me to stay and work late, I just said yes without thinking. And I do that all the time. I'm always the person who stays late or does extra work.
I think the problem is that I care too much about what other people think of me. Like when I buy a new dress and wear it for the first time. I know it's crazy, but I don't really feel comfortable until someone says something nice about it. And it's even better if I don't know the person saying it. And if someone makes a negative comment, I get really upset and I might never wear that dress again.
C: I'll do anything to avoid an argument. I just listen to other people's opinions or what they want and agree with them. It's just easier that way. Like when my friend says, 'Let's go and get a pizza' and I feel like having sushi. I just do what he wants. We always have pizza.
One of my friends recently said I don't seem to have my own opinions. He isn't the first person to tell me that. It's true, when I'm in a group of classmates at college and we're discussing something, I don't say very much. I listen, and then I basically agree with the majority. For example, last weekend I was out with some friends. We were talking about a film we'd just seen and my friends really liked it. I thought it was boring, but I didn't say so. I don't know why. It makes life easier, I suppose.
A: It's important to me that people like me. But I think people who care too much about other people's opinions are wasting their time. For example, on social media I don't pay attention to comments that are negative. I don't get upset. It's not my problem. Maybe the person is just in a bad mood.
Yeah, basically, I'm a very positive person, but I don't go with the crowd. Like at work in a meeting. If someone has an idea and I think it's terrible, I'm the first person to say, 'I really don't think that will work', even if everyone else thinks it's a good idea.

Audio 2.05
1 & 2 I try to avoid people who lie.

158

AUDIOSCRIPTS

Audio 2.06
1. I'm someone who feels comfortable talking to big groups.
2. The person I always ask to help me with problems is my brother.
3. One situation I really hate is when I forget someone's name.
4. I'm usually the first person to give my opinion.
5. The thing I love most about my country is the weather.
6. I think people living in foreign countries should learn the language.

Audio 2.07
A: Sorry I'm late. I had a really bad journey.
B: Why? Were there a lot of people on the train?
A: No, not many, but it's just the way some people behave. I can't stand it.
B: Why, what happened?
A: Everything. First I had to queue to buy a ticket because the ticket machines were broken.
B: I hate it when that happens.
A: And of course people were jumping the queue, saying they were in a hurry and could they please go in front of me.
B: Maybe they **were** in a hurry.
A: Right. Like I wasn't?
B: All right.
A: Then I got on the train, sat down – there were lots of empty seats – and this guy sat down next to me, took out a burger and started to eat it.
B: Yuk! People are always doing that on trains! I expect it smelled bad.
A: Yeah, the smell was terrible! It really got on my nerves. I kept looking at him, you know like this, but he didn't react. **So** annoying.
B: Sometimes it's better if you don't react.
A: You mean do nothing? Maybe. Anyway, after two stops he got off … but then three teenagers got on and they were watching a football match. Really loud.
B: You really did have a bad time.
A: And then one of them opened some windows and it was like a tornado. It blew my hair all over the place.
B: I know what you mean, without asking anyone?
A: Yeah, it really annoys me when they do that.
B: You're always getting so upset about things. And you're here now.
A: But that sort of behaviour really bugs me. And I'm not finished.
B: There's more?
A: I was so annoyed that I didn't pay attention to where we were, and I missed my stop.
B: It really doesn't matter. Look, let's get something to eat.
A: OK, sorry …

Audio 2.08
1. B: Were there a lot of people on the train?
   A: No, not many, but it's just the way some people behave. I can't stand it.
2. A: First I had to queue to buy a ticket because the ticket machines were broken.
   B: I hate it when that happens.
3. B: People are always doing that on trains. I expect it smelled bad.
   A: Yeah, the smell was terrible! It really got on my nerves.
4. B: I know what you mean, without asking anyone?
   A: Yeah, it really annoys me when they do that.
5. B: You're always getting so upset about things. And you're here now.
   A: But that sort of behaviour really bugs me.

Audio 2.09
1. I can't stand it when people take a long time to pay.
2. It annoys me when they try to sell me something I don't want.
3. It drives me crazy when people eat food while shopping.
4. I hate it when I can't reach something on the top shelf.
5. I can't bear it when food is packaged in too much plastic.
6. People are always jumping the queue.

Audio 2.10
A: These are really interesting questions.
B: Yes, I thought so, too.
A: But in some of these situations you could just run away.
B: So, in which situations would you run away?
A: If I saw a snake in my bedroom. I would … I'd freeze actually.
B: And then what?
A: Then I'd move very slowly to get to the door and then run away, as fast as I could. You?
B: It depends how big the snake is.
A: Here's another question. You're alone at a friend's house and it's winter. Someone knocks on the door. It's ten o'clock at night.
B: Well, do I have a choice of answering or not?
A: How do you mean?
B: I could just ignore it.
A: Is that what you'd do?
B: Yes, I suppose so. How about this one? You're on a train and the person opposite you drops their empty drink can on the floor.
A: That's a tricky one. I'm the kind of person who … well, I'd like to say that I'd immediately say something, but … You know …
B: I don't quite get what you mean.
A: I mean that I could say that I'd ask them to pick up their rubbish, but I think that in real life I'd hesitate.
B: Why's that?
A: Maybe the person would get angry. And it depends on whether they're with their friends or if they're bigger than me.
B: Do you mean that it might be better not to say anything?
A: That's what I mean I guess. I'd probably get up and walk away. I might give them a hard look! Like this. What would you do?
B: Oh, no question in my mind. I would definitely …

UNIT 2 REVIEW

Audio R2.01
Taking the pain out of the wait
Waiting in a queue drives most people crazy, and that's bad for business. So businesses make a lot of effort to solve this. When high-rise buildings became common, waiting for the lift was frustrating for anyone who was in a hurry and there were lots of complaints. So mirrors were put next to the lifts, and complaints dropped because it gave people something to look at while waiting. An airport was constantly getting complaints about the long wait for baggage. When they moved the arrival gates further away, complaints stopped, and no one got upset about the longer walk. When a new electronic product comes out, there can be long queues, and people camping outside a shop can be a real problem. Danish researchers found a solution: serve the last people to arrive first. That way there's no reason to show up early. As far as we know, no other countries are planning to try out the Danish solution – we can guess how people might react to it. Most people would probably stick to their belief that first-come, first-served is fair, and anyone jumping the queue is just behaving rudely.

UNIT 3

Audio 3.01
1. A: How was your day?
   B: Great, I got a lot done. I finished my essay, had lunch with a friend, went to an online seminar and then played tennis.
2. A: This homework is really difficult. I'll do it later.
   B: No, do it now. You should get it out of the way.
3. A: What time will lunch be? I need to tell the people in the café.
   B: Sorry, we're a bit late. We've fallen behind schedule by about fifteen minutes. So I think it'll be at quarter past one.
4. A: Is your new job hard?
   B: Yes, but I enjoy dealing with a challenge.
5. A: You look good. Where have you been?
   B: For a swim. I always keep to a routine: 6 o'clock get up, 6.30 go for a swim.
6. A: Is it OK if I turn the TV on?
   B: Well, not really. I'm trying to avoid distractions. The sound of the TV would bother me.

AUDIOSCRIPTS

7 A: What's wrong?
B: It's that music from next door. It's making me lose concentration. I can't think!
8 A: We've only got two days to finish the report!
B: Yes, do you think we'll meet the deadline?

Audio 3.02
1 got a lot done.
2 get it out of the way.
3 fallen behind schedule.
4 dealing with a challenge.
5 keep to a routine.
6 to avoid distractions.
7 lose concentration.
8 meet the deadline.

Audio 3.03
A = Andrea   P = Paul   C = Cybil

A: … and that's one of the dangers. It's not true of all gig work, but with some jobs, where you're working for a big company, you still have a boss, and there's a possibility that they will exploit you – get you to work extra hours and for low pay. Gig workers aren't very well protected, and many of us involved in the industry feel that something needs to be done about the rights of gig workers.
And now we're going to hear from two of our special guests, Paul and Cybil, both of whom have been doing gig work for some years now, but with very different stories. Paul, give us a quick summary of how you ended up doing gig work, and what it is that you actually do.
P: So, two years ago I lost my job at a marketing company, couldn't find another one, so I started delivering online orders for a supermarket. I was surprised, it was actually fun at first. I enjoyed driving, and I learnt to deal with a lot of different people and handle different problems! The money wasn't great – I couldn't rent a flat so I had to move back in with my parents for a while.
A: So the money side isn't so good?
P: Not for me, no. I've picked up a few more gigs – I drive for a ride-hailing company, and I deliver furniture for a big store. I like it because you're allowed to choose when you work, but you have to work long hours to earn enough money. And you feel pressure to do all the work they offer you. I feel as if I've got to say yes to every offer that comes along … so I do.
A: So if you were offered a permanent job, would you take it now?
P: I really don't know. It would depend, probably on the money!
A: Thanks Paul. A lot of people end up doing gig work because it's the only option they have. Other people choose gig work as a sort of lifestyle choice. You're one of those people, aren't you Cybil?
C: Yes, I've always had three or four jobs, so gig work is normal for me. I don't even call it gig work, it's just work. When people ask me what I do, I'm not sure where to start, so I say 'This and that'. Then they always want to know more, so I give the list – I'm a dog walker, a babysitter … I love working with kids so I do children's parties, you know face painting, organising games … Sometimes I teach art in schools, but as a one-off, not a steady thing. A friend of mine has a catering business, and she hires me for day jobs now and then. I don't love all of the work, but I do enjoy some of it.
A: So it's necessary to find a balance, to do enough work that you actually like doing.
C: Yes, you've got to make sure that at least some of the jobs really suit you. And still leave yourself time for what you really love doing outside of work.
A: Let me guess. Is that art?
C: Yes! My real passion is painting, so I do that when I get time.
A: And what's a typical day or week like for you?
C: My days are completely unpredictable. I have weeks when I work seven days, and very long days, then weeks with nothing. That's when I paint! The regular work, the dog walking and babysitting, doesn't bring enough money to pay for all the basic things, and that can be a problem. After a few weeks I get stressed if other work isn't coming through. I can't get sick – no work, no pay – and I don't get paid holidays. It's essential to have savings for times like this, for going on holiday or if I get ill. I try and organise things so that I always have some savings.

A: Where do you see yourself in, say, five years?
C: You know, some of my friends ask me that question and my parents ask it a lot. People act like you're supposed to have a big goal in life, a work-related goal, to earn so much money and climb to the top of the ladder. That's not for me, I'm OK with what I do. I just need enough to live on and to give me time for my painting.
A: I completely agree with you Cybil, thank you for making that point. So now we'll open the webinar to questions. Please type your questions – for me, Paul or Cybil, in the comments box, and we'll answer them as best we can.

Audio 3.04
1 Something needs to be done about the rights of gig workers.
2 I like it because you're allowed to choose when you work.
3 I feel as if I've got to say yes to every offer that comes along.
4 It's necessary to find a balance, to do enough work that you actually like doing.
5 It's essential to have savings for times like this for going on holiday or if I get ill.
6 People act like you're supposed to have a big goal in life.

Audio 3.05
2 I like it because you're allowed to choose when you work.
3 I feel as if I've got to say yes to every offer that comes along.
6 People act like you're supposed to have a big goal in life.

Audio 3.06
1 confident
2 enthusiastic
3 flexible
4 independent
5 professional
6 responsible
7 sensitive
8 willing

Audio 3.07
A: Hi, how are you today?
B: Very well, thank you.
A: Have a seat.
B: Thank you.
A: So, tell me a bit about yourself.
B: Oh, erm, where should I start?
A: Let's keep it work-related.
B: All right. I've always loved working with computers, and doing coding. I get an idea for a new app, and I sit and create it. I'd love to show you some of my work.
A: So you like to work alone.
B: Not really, and this is what I wanted to say, that I think I'm not a typical IT person in that I like being with people, working as part of a team. It's important to me to have personal contact, even if the work itself is sort of … solo work.
A: So why are you here today?
B: How do you mean?
A: Why do you want **this** job?
B: I've done some research about the company and I think it's doing the best work in app development. I want to be part of that, and I think I have a lot to offer.
A: OK, so what will you bring to the company?
B: I think one of my main strengths is that I have a problem-solving mind, and I bring in a lot of creativity in solving problems. And I'm a fast learner. I've learnt most of what I know just by doing. And as I said, I like working in a team.
A: Tell me about a time you had a problem with a co-worker. How did you handle that?
B: Hmmm … Can I use an example from university?
A: Sure.
B: At the end of my last year, we were doing a team project that was basically my thesis. There were four of us. Developing a prototype scheduling app. And the other three people kind of let me do all the work. That made me angry.
A: And how did you deal with that?

AUDIOSCRIPTS

B: I don't think I dealt with it very well. I didn't confront them. I just did the work, and they took part of the credit.
A: How do you think those three classmates would describe you?
B: Oh, good question.
A: So … ?
B: You know, in the end I think they respected me. I think they would say I'm professional and responsible, that I get the job done and do it well. They would definitely call me independent. That can be a good thing, I think.
A: Is that all they would say?
B: Are you asking what criticisms they might have?
A: You could put it that way.
B: I suppose they would say I'm not very flexible. In that situation, I had a clear idea of how the work should go. I wanted everyone to follow that.
A: And is it true?
B: Is it true that I'm not very flexible?
A: Yes, that's what I'm asking.
B: Well, I think I've grown up a lot since then. I think people would say that I've become more open to others' ideas.
A: OK. I have more questions, but let's turn things around for a bit. What questions do you have for me?
B: About the job?
A: About the position, the company, anything.
B: Well, first of all I'd like to ask …

Audio 3.08

1 A: So, tell me a bit about yourself.
   B: Oh, erm, where should I start?
   A: Let's keep it work-related.
   B: All right.
2 A: So why are you here today?
   B: How do you mean?
   A: Why do you want **this** job?
   B: I've done some research about the company and I think it's …
3 B: I want to be part of that, and I think I have a lot to offer.
   A: OK, so what will you bring to the company?
   B: I think one of my main strengths is that I have a problem-solving mind …
4 A: I have more questions, but let's turn things around for a bit. What questions do you have for me?
   B: About the job?
   A: About the position, the company, anything.

UNIT 3 VOCABULARY BANK

Audio VB3.01

1	inappropriate	11	informal
2	uncertain	12	unhealthy
3	unclear	13	unlucky
4	unconfident	14	unnecessary
5	independent	15	unpopular
6	unemployed	16	unprofessional
7	unenthusiastic	17	irregular
8	inexpensive	18	irresponsible
9	unfair	19	insensitive
10	inflexible	20	unwilling

UNIT 3 REVIEW

Audio R3.01

Remote working on the rise
Working from home is no longer only for the self-employed. Based on the experience of recent years, companies have discovered that some employees are happier when working remotely. The employee works from home, a favourite café, wherever they want, but it's essential that they're connected all the time, in case a colleague wants to reach them. They take responsibility for keeping to a routine so that they meet their deadlines and don't fall behind schedule in their work. The company saves on the costs of renting office space, and the employee saves the cost of commuting. There are downsides too, of course. Remote workers can feel isolated, unless they have regular contact with someone. And they have to find ways to avoid distractions. A person who isn't independent might prefer working in an office, but if a person is flexible and willing to deal with the challenge of turning their home into their workplace, it's ideal.

UNIT 3 MEDIATION BANK

Audio MB3.01

1 A: OK, so you chose Laura, right?
   B: That's right.
   A: And what were your reasons for choosing Laura?
   B: She just seems like a nice person.
   A: Bella has more experience. Why not Bella?
   B: Because she wants to get paid and none of the other volunteers do.
2 A: So, who did you prefer?
   C: OK, so I think Bella is the best person for the role.
   A: Ah, I see. Why exactly do you think that?
   C: It's obvious, she has the most experience.
   A: But she wants to be paid. Laura and Trent don't want that.
   C: Yes, I know, but I think she's worth it.
3 A: Any thoughts?
   D: Well, I would choose Trent.
   A: OK, he's an interesting choice. Can you explain why you picked him?
   D: I thought he was a very positive person, that's important.
   A: What about Laura?
   D: Hmm, not for me.
   A: Can you explain your thinking?
   D: She seemed a little nervous. Maybe it would be hard for her to talk to strangers.

UNIT 4

Audio 4.01

1	scheme	4	answer
2	doubt	5	would
3	sign	6	listen

Audio 4.02

1 Can I ask what you think of this documentary?
2 Could you tell me when the film starts?
3 Do you know where I can see it?
4 Isn't that the documentary you were telling me about?
5 Didn't you watch it?

Audio 4.03

P = Presenter   A = Amy   D = Dave
P: Hello and welcome to the Documentary Podcast, where today we're looking at the power of a documentary to change the way we think about the world. We have two guests with us in the studio and they're going to tell us about some of their favourite documentaries. Let's start with you, Amy.
A: Hello.
P: First of all, Amy could you tell us what your documentary is called?
A: Yes, I'm going to talk about *My Octopus Teacher*.
P: OK, so what's it about?
A: It's the extraordinary story of a diver who makes friends with a wild octopus over the period of a year.
P: That sounds unusual. And can you explain what you found so interesting about it? What did you learn?
A: Well, the film-maker, Craig Foster, was basically suffering from stress at work, so he decided to spend some time freediving to get close to nature. And he spotted this wild octopus and then decided to go back to the same spot and film every day for a year. The underwater filming is very dramatic. I'd never seen anything so beautiful on screen. But it also gives us these amazing insights into the life of an octopus. I learnt a lot about how these creatures live.

161

AUDIOSCRIPTS

P: Aren't octopuses supposed to be really intelligent?
A: Yes, they are. And that's the point. As we watch, we see how Foster gets to know this one octopus really well. And the octopus starts to recognise him, to get to know him. When he arrives, the octopus comes out to play. As the year progresses, Foster starts to learn about himself from his relationship with the octopus. He starts to think about his relationships with people and how he could improve them.
P: Hence the name *My Octopus Teacher*.
A: Exactly. He starts to look at the world differently because of the time he spends underwater. It's a very intelligent film in that it makes you realise just how important our oceans are and how we need to protect them. And the whole film is really enjoyable. My family loved it.
P: That sounds great. Definitely one to watch.
D: I don't know if I should say this, but I saw *My Octopus Teacher*, and I found it a bit disappointing.
A: Oh no!
P: Really? Didn't you like it? Why not?
D: It was really slow. A lot of the film just shows footage of the octopus. I found it a bit boring.
A: Didn't you think that was amazing to watch? I thought it was beautiful …
D: No, I just didn't find it very exciting. Maybe it's not my kind of thing.
P: Right, isn't it interesting how we can have different reactions to the same documentary, Dave? So, can you tell us about one you did enjoy? Isn't your documentary also about nature?
D: Yes, I'm going to talk about *The Salt of the Earth*.
A: Oh, wasn't that the one about the photographer? Um … Salgado?
D: That's right, yes.
P: Excellent. Could you tell us about it?
D: Well, it's a really powerful documentary about the life and work of photographer Sebastião Salgado. Salgado travelled the world taking photographs and documenting the different natural environments and also the people who live in them.
P: So wouldn't you say it's more about people than about nature?
D: Well, I think it's both. With his beautiful photography he encourages us to think about some of the biggest problems facing humanity. He tells the story of the shocking conditions that many people around the world often have to live in. So, it forces us to examine human nature and try and learn from our mistakes instead of repeating them again and again.
P: That sounds fascinating. And it's obviously such an important topic.
D: Yes, absolutely. I thought it was a wonderful documentary that really makes you think about the world.
A: That's exactly what I thought about *My Octopus Teacher*. I loved *The Salt of the Earth* too, though. I thought it was stunning, very powerful. You can't watch something like that and not come away with a different viewpoint. The way it …

Audio 4.04
Conversation 1
A: Have you seen that story about the kid in the zoo?
B: No, what happened?
A: Haven't you seen it? It went viral. Look, I'll show you. Oh, my battery's dead. So there was this little kid in the zoo with his parents, right?
B: Yeah.
A: So, basically, what happened was that he was feeding the giraffe and the mother was filming him. So he holds up a big leaf to feed the giraffe. And the giraffe takes the leaf and pulls his head upwards, really high, and the kid is still holding onto the branch with the leaf, so the giraffe lifts the boy up into the air, really high. It's hilarious!
B: Oh no! That sounds scary.
A: No, the kid was fine – the dad pulls him down. It's just really funny …

Conversation 2
A Have you heard about the fire?
B: What fire?

A: In town. Didn't you see the smoke?
B: No, what happened?
A: The supermarket caught fire. It's all over the news.
B: Really?! I had no idea. How did that happen?
A: I don't know. It seems there might have been an electrical fault or something.
B: Was anyone hurt?
B: No, everyone's fine. Luckily, the supermarket was closed, so it was empty at the time.
A: Oh, that's a relief!
B: But the whole building pretty much burned down.

Conversation 3
A: Did you hear the news about Sean Davies?
B: No. What happened?
A: He's quit his job as manager.
B: Really? I had no idea!
A: Yes. I saw it on the news. He was less than two months into his contract. I can't remember the details, but basically, it seems like he's going to manage a different team.
B: Wow, that's quite a scandal, after all that money he was paid!

Conversation 4
A: Have you seen what's happening at the airports?
B: No, what do you mean?
A: Loads of flights have been cancelled because of the weather. Apparently, thousands of people are stuck at the airport. It's on all the news channels.
B: That reminds me of that time we got stuck in Athens. Do you remember?
A: Yes, we had to wait all night in the airport. It was awful …

Conversation 5
A: Are you following the news about the protests?
B: Yes, it's received a lot of coverage. It's terrible. Apparently, the protesters have taken over the university buildings and they're refusing to leave.
A: I know. It all happened so quickly. I can hardly believe it.
B: Yes, there was an announcement that if they didn't leave, they would all be arrested.
A: That's unbelievable!

Audio 4.05
1 So, basically, what happened was …
2 Apparently, thousands of people are stuck at the airport.
3 Basically, it seems like he's going to manage a different team.
4 Apparently, now the protesters have taken over the university buildings.

Audio 4.06
N = Nikolas   J = Jade
N: Hi, Jade – is that you?
J: Wow, Nikolas! How amazing to see you!
N: This is crazy … How long is it since we've seen each other?
J: Oh, I don't know … about … um …
N: Maybe five years or so.
J: Yeah, probably. I thought you were living in New Zealand.
N: That's right, but I moved back a while ago.
J: OK. Are you still working for that film company?
N: Ah … no, actually, I'm freelance now. I'm still a director, but I work for myself.
J: Wow, that's amazing.
N: Yeah, I can't complain. How about you?
J: I'm still in the bakery.
N: Really?!
J: Yes, I love it there. It's such a nice team of people to work with.
N: So do you still see Rob at all?
J: Yes, he lives around here. I see him all the time. You know he's married now.
N: No! Is he really? Wow.
J: Yeah, he's got two small kids.

162

AUDIOSCRIPTS

N: Really?! I can't believe it!
J: I know! How about you? Are you married, in a relationship?
N: Uh, no. No, I'm … you know … it's just me.
J: And do you still ski?
N: Yes, whenever I can. You know I passed my exams to be a ski instructor?
J: Really?! That's great. You always said you wanted to do that.
N: Well remembered. Yes, I did. I took the course last year, so now I can teach during the ski season.
J: That's brilliant. I'm so pleased to hear that. It's amazing bumping into you. We should maybe get together sometime, and catch up properly.
N: Yes, I'd really like that. Perhaps we can get Rob to come, too.
J: Great idea. I'll send him a message telling him I saw you. Have you still got the same number?
N: Yeah, I have … you should have it.
J: Ah yes, here it is. I'll send you mine. It's really great to see you again.
N: Yes, you too.
J: Stay in touch.
N: I will. See you soon.

UNIT 4 REVIEW

Audio R4.01

Facts and fiction: when Hollywood gets it wrong

The film industry exists to tell us stories and sell us dreams. But are films supposed to tell the truth? Aren't they a mixture of fact and fiction? Read these examples of Hollywood getting the details wrong and judge for yourself.

A scene from *Apollo 13* is set in April, 1970. Astronaut Jim Lovell's daughter holds The Beatles' album *Let It Be*. It's a good scene, but can anyone explain how she had this album, which didn't come out until May, a month later?

In *Raiders of the Lost Ark*, set in 1936, a map appears on screen, showing Indiana Jones's journey. We read the name Thailand. You might ask, 'Is this a problem? Wasn't this possible?' The journey certainly was, but Thailand wasn't named 'Thailand' until 1939. It was Siam before that.

Occasionally, the director makes deliberate mistakes. Sofia Coppola's *Marie Antoinette* is all about the queen of the same name, who was born in 1755. In one scene, there's a pair of Converse trainers. (The shoe company was founded in 1908.) Coppola thought this would be a way to show how young Marie Antoinette was.

UNIT 5

Audio 5.01

1 calm, shy
2 patient, pleasant
3 direct
4 confident, sensible
5 aggressive

Audio 5.02

Conversation 1
A: Good morning. How can I help you?
B: Good morning. I'm here to make a complaint about a chair I bought from you.
A: OK. I'll need some details. Can I have your name?
B: Yes, it's Elinor McDonnell. That's M-c-D-o-n-n-e-l-l. Capital D.
A: Ms or Mrs?
B: Mrs.
A: So Mrs McDonnell, can you explain exactly what happened?
B: Yes, I bought one of your office chairs for my son's work desk, and yesterday he was sitting in the chair … He leant back and it broke. The metal piece holding the seat just snapped, and the whole seat fell off. He almost broke his arm!
A: I'm sorry to hear that. When exactly did you buy it?
B: It was about three years ago.
A: Three years. Could you give me the exact date?
B: I don't know the exact date. But that's not the point. The design's obviously faulty. It's not normal for a chair to break.
A: We *will* need the receipt so as to check the date when you bought the chair. If it's over three years ago, we won't be able to help.
B: But that's outrageous! My son could have been seriously hurt. This shouldn't happen even if the chair's not brand new.
A: I'm sorry, but there's nothing I can do about it. The warranty is for three years.
B: This isn't good enough. I want to speak to your manager.
A: My line manager isn't here at the moment. He should be back in an hour. If you give me your number, he can give you a ca–
B: What do I have to do in order to get someone to help me? Listen, get me your supervisor right here, right now or I'm going public with this. On social media.
A: Just a moment. I'll give him a call.

Conversation 2
C: Good morning. Customer Service. Francisca speaking.
D: Hi Francisca. My name's Filip. Look, I'm really not happy with the situation with my luggage. I was wondering if you could help.
C: Can you give me your full name?
D: Of course. My name's Matas, that's M-A-T-A-S, Filip Matas.
C: And the nature of your complaint?
D: Well, my luggage got lost two days ago. I flew in from Lima and had a stopover in Madrid, but my suitcase never arrived here. I spoke to one of your colleagues yesterday and he assured me it would be here today, but it hasn't arrived.
C: I'll need to take the flight number so that I can check what has happened.
D: Of course. It was ESE1472.
C: Let me check the record on this … Oh yes. It says the suitcase was delivered to your address this morning.
D: Well, then we have a huge problem here, because it wasn't delivered. I've been here all day. Look, I know it's not your fault, but this really isn't good enough. Do you think you could find out exactly what's happening?
C: Yes, it does sound wrong. I'll phone the delivery company this morning.
D: Is it possible to do it now? I can hold on so as not to waste time. I really need to know what's happening.
C: Just a minute, I'll put you on hold.
D: Thank you so much. I really appreciate your help.

Audio 5.03

1 snapped – He leant back and it broke. The metal piece holding the seat just snapped, and the whole seat fell off.
2 faulty – The design's obviously faulty. It's not normal for a chair to break.
3 outrageous – But that's outrageous! My son could have been seriously hurt.
4 brand new – This shouldn't happen even if the chair's not brand new.
5 warranty – I'm sorry, but there's nothing I can do about it. The warranty is for three years.
6 assured – I spoke to one of your colleagues yesterday and he assured me the suitcase would be here today.

Audio 5.04

1 The best ever advert I've seen was one for jeans.
2 TV ads are becoming more and more like mini films.
3 Phones are getting cheaper and cheaper.
4 The more I buy the better I feel.

Audio 5.05

A: So have you made up your mind?
B: Well, yes and no. I messaged Sam and he had some good advice. And I've read a lot about e-bikes, you know, reviews and websites, everything.
A: So, what did Sam say?
B: Well he was really helpful. From what he says, it depends on what you want to use it for. I just want a bike to get to work and do the shopping, so I thought a commuter bike would be perfect.

163

AUDIOSCRIPTS

A: But?
B: But Sam made a good point, that if I ever want to use the bike outside the city, go into the forest or something, I'd be better off with a commuter bike that's also good off-road.
A: What about a mountain bike then?
B: The only thing is that a mountain bike is no good for carrying things like shopping, and according to Sam, it's quite heavy. So anyway, he recommended two models that would be good for both things and I'm trying to decide which one.
A: Let me see. They both **look** nice. Wow, they're not cheap. Which one's better, do you think?
B: Not sure. There are a few things I need to think about. Like how much power the bike has, how much range …
A: How much range?
B: Yeah, how far it goes before it runs out of electricity. I hadn't thought of that before I started looking. Anyway, the Dorith has a better range, and it also has more power going uphill. Long story short, it's a better bike.
A: So it's a matter of whether you want to pay more for more range and a better uphill ride?
B: Yes, in the end, it's a question of how much I want to pay.
A: Have you read any reviews?
B: Yes, tons. All in all, reviewers of both models were happy with their bikes, though one said the Wells Rider didn't have the range he expected.
A: So they didn't help.
B: They did, I guess. They made me think about things like range and power, but I don't really need those to be amazing. It all comes down to the price, really, if I'm deciding between these two models. I don't mind spending more, but is it worth it?
A: Well, just because something's less expensive, it doesn't mean it's not good.
B: Yes, taking everything into account, I think the Wells Rider is good enough for me.
A: Well, let's go get it then!

Audio 5.06
1 From what he says, it depends on what you want to use it for.
2 The only thing is that a mountain bike is no good for carrying things like shopping.
3 According to Sam, it's quite heavy.
4 Long story short, it's a better bike.
5 So it's a matter of whether you want to pay more for more range and a better uphill ride?
6 Yes, in the end it's a question of how much I want to pay.
7 All in all, reviewers of both models were happy with their bikes.
8 It all comes down to the price.
9 Well, just because something's less expensive, it doesn't mean it's not good.
10 Yes, taking everything into account I think the Wells Rider is good enough for me.

Audio 5.07
1 From what he says, it depends on what you want to use it for.
2 According to Sam, it's quite heavy.
3 Long story short, it's a better bike.
4 In the end, it's a question of how much I want to pay.
5 All in all, reviewers of both models were happy with their bikes.
6 Taking everything into account, I think the Wells Rider is good enough for me.

UNIT 5 VOCABULARY BANK

Audio VB5.01
1 charge, fare, fee, loss
2 bargain, discount, refund, profit
3 receipt
4 donation

UNIT 5 REVIEW

Audio R5.01
Shoppers beware!
Every consumer knows about pricing tricks like putting 99 at the end of the price, but what about other things a shop does to get you to make a purchase? One example is the location of products. Even if you don't have a particular brand loyalty, you're more likely to buy things because shops put them at eye-level so that you see them first. In supermarkets, the essential things (milk, bread, etc.) are at the back of the shop so as to make you pass everything else on the way.
And shops also pay attention to your senses to influence you. Take music, for example. The slower the music, the calmer you feel and the more time you spend shopping.
And in the end, shops know that price is king and everyone's a bargain hunter at heart, so you'll find products on offer in almost every part of a shop. After all, who can say no to a good deal?

UNIT 5 MEDIATION BANK

Audio MB5.01
So, it's frustrating when you don't know what you can recycle, isn't it? It feels like a lottery – maybe this can go in the recycling bin, maybe not … You put things in, then you take them out again, you do this for hours. Well, you can stop this situation from happening with our new product which tells you if the things you put in the bin can be recycled or not. The bin is a bit like those checkout machines in the supermarket that can recognise products – it has a camera which can 'see' the products and decide if they're OK. It's also similar to the supermarket machine because it speaks. It will say something like 'I'm sorry, you can't recycle this'. Your life will never be the same again when you have this product in your home – you'll help the planet and feel good about yourself.

UNIT 6

Audio 6.01
L = Logan   C = Cecilia   A = Amy
L: There are so many diverse neighbourhoods in Toronto. However, I'll go with the one that's just nearby my house because I go there so often. It's Rosedale. It's a very wealthy neighbourhood just to the northeast of the city centre (it's about a ten-minute walk). It has these huge tree-lined avenues, with these historic century-old houses, each one different to the next, so the architecture is really interesting and unique. The streets wind around, with different street lamps and sidewalk styles. And the tall trees offer shade, so it's a lovely spot for walking. One thing I love about this area is that there are no restaurants or stores or high-rise buildings; there are plenty of them back in the centre. The east side is entirely surrounded by a deep valley, where Torontonians jog, walk their dogs, or just stroll by the river. There's a really relaxed atmosphere. It's so peaceful that you hardly realise you're still in the city.
C: The Barranco district is one neighbourhood I always try to visit when I travel to Lima. It was an area where wealthy residents used to enjoy the beach. So it has these historic old summer houses, but the area became very run-down, and then lots of artists moved in, so now the whole district is covered with these amazing colourful murals and street art. It's so beautiful to walk around. The houses are painted in different colours and there are lots of little bars and coffee shops to enjoy. There's a busy market where local artists sell their work, and you can buy jewellery or hand-made Peruvian arts and crafts. The area has become so popular that it's quite a tourist spot now, but it is still a great place to wander around. It has such a friendly, welcoming atmosphere and there are lots of things you can do, like maybe visit an art gallery, or enjoy a delicious meal with a fantastic view of the ocean. Or you can visit in the evening because it has such lively nightlife, too.

AUDIOSCRIPTS

A: One of my favourite neighbourhoods has to be Yarraville, in Melbourne, Australia. In fact, it was named as one of the coolest neighbourhoods in the world. It's a wonderful place to live because it has such a great sense of community. There's so much to do in Yarraville. There's an amazing Art Deco cinema and there are lots of lively music venues and fun places to shop. There's an amazing bookshop called the Sun Bookshop, and there are organic food shops, bakeries, things for your house, plant shops. It has a busy farmer's market where you can find lots of local produce or get a great coffee in one of the coffee shops. Yarraville is also a fantastic place to eat and drink. You can get Mexican burritos or Japanese noodles. You can enjoy restaurants with delicious food from all over the world. Or you can listen to live music or enjoy a bit of culture. Basically, Yarraville has everything you need – you don't need to go anywhere else. I love it.

Audio 6.02
1 It was so interesting to learn about the history of the place.
2 It was such a lovely place to visit.
3 The food was so delicious that we decided to go back the next day.
4 The neighbourhood had such a welcoming atmosphere that we didn't want to leave.

Audio 6.03
1 I'm used to travelling alone.
2 We're used to the ocean.
3 I got used to the cold.
4 We're getting used to living on a boat.

Audio 6.04
B = Boris   T = Tonya

B: OK, so Tonya, could you tell us the best way to see the London sights using public transport? What do you think is our best option?
T: Yes, absolutely. As I was telling you earlier, I'd recommend you take the Thames Clipper river boats. I mean, there are lots of different river boats, but the cruises designed for tourists are much more expensive. The Thames Clipper is really good because basically it's public transport.
B: So what you're saying is the Thames Clipper is cheaper, right?
T: Cheaper than a cruise, yes, that's right. And the great thing about it is that you don't need to buy a special ticket as it's part of London's public transport system. You don't need to book in advance, you can just use your travel card to tap in and tap out. And it's easy to get on a boat. You just go to the nearest tube station.
B: Sorry I didn't catch what you said about 'tap in and tap out'.
T: Oh, yes of course. You can use your travel card or your bank card and just tap the ticket machine and it automatically takes the fare for your journey. You also have to tap out at the end of the journey.
B: I see. So we don't have to book in advance or buy a special ticket that is valid just for the boat?
T: That's right.
B: OK, that's great. And where would you suggest we get the boat?
T: Well, there are two different routes – one which goes up the river and one which goes down. You can hop on and hop off at any point, just like you do with the bus or a train. But a very popular option with visitors is to get the boat from Westminster Pier. You take the tube to Westminster and it's signposted from there.
B: Sorry, can you just say that last bit again? Where do we take the tube?
T: To Westminster. You can walk to Westminster Pier from there.
B: OK.
T: And you take the boat right along the river all the way to Greenwich.
B: So let me just check I've got this right. So, we can take the boat from Westminster Pier to Greenwich.
T: Yes. And on the way, the boat passes many of London's famous landmarks – you see the Houses of Parliament, London Bridge, Tower Bridge, you go past the Globe Theatre and the South Bank.
B: Oh, in other words, we see nearly everything. That sounds great. And what's the boat like?
T: The boat itself is quite big, and you can sit inside. You can sit outside, too, but it gets a bit crowded and it can be windy. So if you go inside, there's a café and toilets. It's very comfortable. And there's no tour guide explaining everything, you can just get hold of a tourist map with information about all the landmarks and learn about them as you go along.
B: So, have I got this right? There isn't a guided tour.
T: That's right, but you can find out all the information and have it on your phone.
B: Yes, I think we prefer that.
T: It's a really fantastic day out. I'd thoroughly recommend it if the weather is good.

Audio 6.05
1 So what you're saying is the Thames Clipper is cheaper.
2 I didn't catch what you said about …
3 Sorry, can you just say that last bit again?
4 So let me just check I've got this right.
5 In other words, we see nearly everything.
6 Have I got this right? There isn't a guided tour.

Audio 6.06
1 Could you just go over those options again, please?
2 So let me just check, …
3 Can you just say that last bit again, please?

Audio 6.07
I'm going to talk about my adopted city of Oviedo in the north of Spain. It has wonderful cultural traditions – its music, language and food – and these traditions have stayed the same for many generations.

An example of the culture is Oviedo's architecture and public art. The old town is famous for its medieval buildings and structures such as the archaeology museum and La Foncalada Fountain. There are also many sculptures in public places – in the parks and streets. One of the best-known is a sculpture of a mother and child by the Colombian artist Fernando Botero. But really, as I said, anywhere you go in the centre you'll find sculptures and statues.

Oviedo is also famous for its traditional food. So, for example, let's take fabada. Fabada is a dish made of beans and meat, like a type of stew. It's absolutely delicious. Another speciality of the region is rice. There are some amazing rice dishes, such as rice with octopus or with shrimps. So I'd say fabada and the rice dishes are the best specialities to try in Oviedo.

The city also has its own culture and language. Many people in Oviedo still speak Asturian, which is similar to Spanish. And when it comes to music, the region even has its own musical instruments. There's one that is similar to a Scottish bagpipe. You can hear it at the many festivals that celebrate the regional culture and history.

UNIT 6 REVIEW

Audio R6.01
Astronaut
They drive the crew to the launchpad. You stand and look up at this spaceship seventeen storeys high, with its huge rocket boosters on each side. You feel fear and excitement. Before, you were so busy training that you didn't have time to feel scared. You didn't think you were risking your life. Now it becomes real.

You take a lift to the launch platform thirty metres in the sky. You go into a white room and put on your equipment. Next, you look into a camera and say goodbye to your family. The other astronauts become your new family. You're used to them and their habits; you've been training together for months.

You enter the shuttle. Inside it's tiny. It's one of many things you have to get used to. You are strapped in and you check your equipment one last time.

Space is silent, but the rocket isn't. The engines make such a loud noise you can't hear yourself think. Soon you're travelling at 17,500 miles per hour. After eight and a half minutes, you've left the Earth's atmosphere. Suddenly, the noise stops. You remove your helmet, let it go, and watch it float. You trained for these conditions. Everything is familiar. Yet nothing will ever be the same after you've been in space.

AUDIOSCRIPTS

UNIT 6 MEDIATION BANK

Audio MB6.01
A = Art   M = Melinda   G = Georgina

A: Well, obviously it needs to be the smart roads idea, really. There are so many traffic accidents at the moment, and anything we can do to reduce that number is good.
M: Yes, good point, and smart roads would definitely help with the problem, especially with the heavy snow in winter, but another way to fix the problem is to have fewer people in cars in our city. Does everyone agree with that?
A: It's a nice idea Melinda, but I feel it's going to be very difficult to make people leave their cars at home.
M: OK, let's bring in a new voice to this discussion. Georgina.
G: Hey there, Melinda
M: Georgina, what do you think? Do you see it the same way as I do? Fewer cars? Maybe we should charge people for driving into the city centre?
G: Well, yes, Melinda, we need fewer cars on the road, but I'm not sure about charging people. Another possibility is to make it cheaper to travel on public transport. The self-driving buses would help us with that.
A: But maybe people just prefer their cars. They feel more comfortable in their own space, not sitting on a crowded bus …
M: But it's not a question of if they are comfortable, Art. People need to be taught to use a new system, and we shouldn't worry if they get a little upset about changing how they behave. That's normal. Don't you think that people need to grow up and stop doing things which hurt our city, hurt the planet?
A: I understand how you feel, but I think you don't understand how people's minds work. They're not going to change their behaviour just because you get angry with them, they need to choose to do the right thing.
M: OK, let's bring in Roger, now. Roger, what …

UNIT 7

Audio 7.01
H = Host   L = Luisa   R = Rich   J = Josh   E = Ela

H: What's in a word? Well, it depends on who says it, and what they mean. Many of us believe that most conflicts in relationships are the result of miscommunication, and so often this comes down to language. Sometimes just one word. Take the word 'invite' for instance.
L: A few days before my friend's birthday, she sent me a message saying that she wanted to invite me to her birthday party. It was in a private room at an expensive restaurant. I knew the place, but only from the outside. But I messaged her back and replied that I'd be there. I bought her a present, and when the day came, I went. At the end of the meal, when the bill came, it was clear all of the guests were expected to pay our part of the bill. I was really upset. She should have been clearer. It cost me a whole week's salary. It was such an expensive place.
H: Well that can't have been good for your friendship. And what about other types of relationship? Maybe workplace ones? Rich has a story from his workplace.
R: I was in my first month on the job and my manager said she wanted to talk to me and could I come to her office. I felt really nervous. She had a very serious style, kind of scary. I walked into her office, and sat down. She was actually really nice. She wanted to know if I liked the job. Then she asked whether I'd had any problems with colleagues or anything. I answered her and we had a good conversation. Then she started checking her computer and she said, 'OK, could you close the door?' I got up, closed the door – on the inside – and stood there. My manager kept looking at something on her computer, and there was dead silence. Finally, she looked up and said, 'Oh, are you still here?' I was so embarrassed.
H: That **is** embarrassing! At least next time you'll know what to do. If there is a next time. And speaking of next time, when is next weekend? Sometimes it's not so clear, like in Josh's story.
J: Not long ago my friend Endre called me on a Wednesday night and asked me if I was doing anything the following Saturday – he said, 'Are you doing anything next Saturday?' and I said no. He said he was giving a surprise party for his wife, Moni, and asked me if I could come. I said yes. Endre told me that I'd be in trouble if I told her! I promised that I'd keep it a secret. Anyway, it was at their house, and the plan was for me to go there at 7 p.m. on Saturday and set things up, then the other guests would arrive at 8 p.m., and Endre and Moni would come back from a restaurant at nine. So three days later, on Saturday at 7 p.m., I drove over to their house and knocked on the door. Moni answered the door, and said 'Josh, what are you doing here?' I just said, 'What happened to the party?' Endre walked up behind her and looked at me with an angry expression and said, 'I told you, it's **next** Saturday.' I basically ruined the whole thing.
H: Very awkward. I would have been pretty angry with you, too. Meanwhile, we have time for one more, and this one's a reminder to all of you learning a foreign language to pay close attention to your grammar. Here's Ela.
E: So, I was having a coffee with a Scottish woman who I met at the college, and at the time my English wasn't as good as it is now. We were sitting chatting, getting to know each other, and at one point the conversation went a bit quiet. So I said, 'I'm sorry, I've been talking too much. Are you boring? Shall we leave?' A very simple mistake, I know, but as I said at the time my English wasn't great, and I didn't even realise my mistake. She said OK, asked the waiter for the bill, and when we said goodbye I noticed she looked a bit uncomfortable. After that we didn't meet again. I didn't realise what I had said until much later, during an English lesson about adjective endings. I still feel really bad when I remember that.
H: Well, maybe she **was** boring. We'll never find out! We'd love to hear more of your experiences though, so write in the comments or send me an audio message with your story of how a misunderstanding affected one of your relationships. Thanks for listening and we'll be back with more next time!

Audio 7.02
1 I messaged her back and replied that I'd be there.
2 She wanted to know if I liked the job.
3 She asked whether I'd had any problems with colleagues.
4 My friend Endre asked me if I was doing anything the following Saturday.
5 He said he was giving a surprise party for his wife Moni.
6 He asked me if I could come.
7 He said I'd be in trouble if I told her
8 I promised that I'd keep it a secret.

Audio 7.03
1 Are you going out tonight?
2 I can't do it.
3 You'll all get wet.
4 I'm leaving tomorrow.
5 Did you stay at home yesterday?
6 Do we have to speak English?

Audio 7.04
1 answer, argue, mention, promise, wonder
2 agree, complain, confirm, convince, enquire, explain, reply

Audio 7.05
1 I've just been tagged in a photo.
2 I haven't been messaged yet.
3 I was given my phone case by a friend.
4 My phone got damaged recently.
5 I'm being sent a lot of spam at the moment.

Audio 7.06
P = Paul   D = Denise

P: Hi. Nice party.
D: Yes, yes, very nice.
P: I'm Paul.
D: I'm Denise.
P: So, do you know Celia?
D: Yes, I do. We went to college together.
P: Sorry, I just saw someone I know. So, from college?

AUDIOSCRIPTS

D: Yes, that's right.
P: Oh … erm, this is a nice party.
D: Yes, I think so, too. It's my first time…
P: Hey Sharon! Hi Jez! Sorry. So, nice weather, isn't it?
D: Yes, very.
P: Very. Erm …
D: Oh, I've just seen someone I know. Nice to meet you.

Audio 7.07
P: Hi. Nice party.
D: Yes, yes, very nice.
P: I'm Paul.
D: I'm Denise. Nice to meet you.
P: And you. How do you know Celia?
D: We went to college together.
P: Oh yes, were you on the same course as her?
D: Yes, we both did food technology.
P: How did you get into that?
D: My mother was a chef, so I suppose I just thought it was a good idea.
P: You know, I've always wondered, what exactly is 'food technology'?
D: Well, obviously you learn a lot about cooking, but it covers all sorts of other things.
P: Such as?
D: Well, how food is produced, erm, researching new flavours.
P: That sounds interesting. What do you mean by 'researching new flavours'?
D: Well, different ice cream flavours or crisp flavours.
P: Crisp flavours! That's unusual. So, for instance?
D: Well, I once developed a banana-flavoured crisp.
P: Sounds terrible. What was it like?
D: My tutor said it was the most disgusting thing she'd ever tasted.
P: I'm not surprised! It sounds awful.
D: It was! What about you? How do you know Celia?
P: I used to work with her, at the café. I was a waiter there, but I left.
D: Really? Why's that?
P: I liked the people I was working with, but I didn't like some of the customers.
D: How come?
P: Well some of them were quite rude to the waiters. They got very impatient if we didn't serve them immediately. They were always complaining.
D: How did that make you feel?
P: Pretty angry, actually. But you can't lose your temper with customers.
D: Yeah, I can imagine. But you like food?
P: Yeah. I love food. This food's extremely good.
D: Yes, isn't it? This salad's particularly nice. How about you? Are you at all interested in cooking?
P: I love cooking, but I'm a terrible cook! I'm more of a restaurant person.
D: Oh, so am I, but I'm fairly new to this area. Can you recommend any good restaurants near here?
P: What sort of food do you like?
D: Indian, Mexican, and I quite like …

Audio 7.08
D = Denise   P = Paul
D: I'm Denise. Nice to meet you.
P: And you. How do you know Celia?
D: We went to college together.

D: Yes, we both did food technology.
P: Oh. How did you get into that?

D: Well, obviously you learn a lot about cooking, but it covers all sorts of other things,
P: Such as?

P: That sounds interesting! What do you mean by 'researching new flavours?'
D: Well, I once developed a banana-flavoured crisp.
P: Sounds terrible! What was it like?

P: I was a waiter there, but I left.
D: Really? Why's that?
P: I liked the people I was working with, but I didn't like some of the customers.
D: How come?

P: They were always complaining.
D: How did that make you feel?

Audio 7.09
P = Paul   D = Denise
1
P: It covers all sorts of other things.
D: Such as?

2
P: I used to work with her, at the café. I was a waiter there, but I left.
D: Really? Why's that?

Audio 7.10
1 Because?
2 What's it like?
3 How come?
4 For instance?

UNIT 7 VOCABULARY BANK

Audio VB7.01
A scroll down, scroll up
B tap
C swipe
D download
E folder
F refresh
G network
H icon
I upload
J inbox

UNIT 7 REVIEW

Audio R7.01
Imperfect inventions
They say that necessity is the mother of invention – if there's a need, then the solution will be found. But there seem to be some needs for which the perfect solution hasn't been developed yet. Here are some of your ideas.

Earplugs that work
More and more people live in noisy environments, and many said they had been waiting for years for the perfect ear plug. 'I'm often woken up by the neighbours, and nothing I've tried has worked.'

No-jam printer
Many of you asked if it was possible to invent a printer that never jammed. 'It's particularly annoying when I'm in a hurry and I get a pop-up with a jammed icon.'

Scratch-proof sunglasses
What can make you angrier than when you drop your expensive sunglasses and they get damaged? 'When I spend a lot of money on sunglasses, I expect no scratches – zero.'

Self-labelling computer filing system
'It shouldn't be too hard – the program could scan the documents in a folder and choose a label that fits.'

167

AUDIOSCRIPTS

UNIT 8

Audio 8.01
1 I should've been nicer.
2 You shouldn't've paid any attention to him.
3 If I'd known, I'd've done things differently.
4 If we'd known, we wouldn't've been so worried.

Audio 8.02
When my father came home from work in the evening, he always smelled of coffee. He worked in a roasting shed at Lindvalls Kaffe in Uppsala. That's how I came to love the scent of coffee long before I began to drink it. I watched out for him cycling along the street and I'd ask the same question every time: 'Did you find anything today?'

When the sacks of green coffee beans arrived for roasting, they were tipped onto a conveyor belt and screened by a powerful magnet. The idea was to remove any metal objects that might have ended up in the sack during the drying and packing. Pappa would bring these things home and tell me a story about every one of them.

Sometimes he brought a coin. 'Look, this is from Brazil,' he'd say. 'Brazil produces more coffee than anywhere else.'

He'd let me sit on his lap, open up the world atlas in front of us and tell the story: 'It's a large country and very hot. This coin turned up inside a sack from Santos,' he'd explain, pointing at the Brazilian port city.

He'd describe the working men and women, links in the chain that ended with people in Sweden sipping their coffee. Early on, I realised the coffee pickers got the poorest pay.

My powerful longing to understand the world began with Pappa telling me about the coins in the coffee sacks and showing me all those countries in the atlas. This longing grew into a lifelong passion.

Audio 8.03
1 I watched out for him cycling along the street and I'd ask the same question every time: 'Did you find anything today?'
2 Pappa would bring these things home and tell me a story about every one of them.
3 He'd let me sit on his lap, open up the world atlas in front of us and tell the story: 'It's a large country and very hot.'
4 'This coin turned up inside a sack from Santos,' he'd explain, pointing at the Brazilian port city.
5 He'd describe the working men and women …

Audio 8.04
1 I'd wait for him every evening.
2 He'd always answer my questions.
3 He'd explain where Santos was on the map.
4 He'd point to the Brazilian city.

Audio 8.05
P = Presenter   AM = Audience Member

P: Today I'm going to talk about five things that you need to know about people if you want to give a good presentation. When a speaker gives a presentation, they need to understand their audience. The more the presenter knows about how people think and listen, the easier it is for them to give a presentation which informs, inspires and motivates the audience.

So, to begin with, can I just get a show of hands for all the people here who have had to listen to a long presentation with lots of facts and figures and they've found it difficult to stay focused? Right. Lots of you. This brings me to my first point. People learn best in twenty-minute chunks. After that time, it becomes difficult to keep your concentration. So, if you're giving a presentation, it's best to keep it short. Think about TED Talks. Most of them are twenty minutes long. If your talk is longer, maybe an hour, then divide the talk into three sections, each of twenty minutes. In between the sections try to have a short break or activity.

Next, my second point. People can listen and watch at the same time, but only if the visual information is easy to read and helps us to understand what is being said. If the visual information is too complicated, people will start trying to read and they'll stop listening to the speaker. So it's important not to put too much text on your slides. Only use a visual where it clearly illustrates your idea and helps the listener to understand.

Moving on to the next point, it's important to remember that what you say is only part of your message. The audience will be looking at your delivery. How are you standing? Do you look confident? Do you look like you know what you're talking about? We get a lot of information from just looking and listening to **how** the speaker talks, before we listen to the actual words they say.

Turning now to what you want people to do when they listen to your presentation. Do you want them to buy a product, or sign up to your website? If you want people to do something, it's important that you tell people exactly what to do at the end of the presentation. This is called a 'call to action'.

As a final point, think about your emotions. People will copy your emotions and your feelings, so be enthusiastic about your subject, be passionate about what you're saying and then your audience will feel the same.

So, just to recap. 1 Keep your presentation short – less than twenty minutes. 2 Keep the visuals very clear. 3 Think about your delivery. 4 Include a call to action. And finally, number 5, be enthusiastic. I think that's it.

Does anyone have any comments or questions? Yes, thank you.

AM: What do you do if the technology doesn't work and you can't show your presentation? Do you have any advice?

P: That's a very good question. I'm not sure I can answer that now. Obviously, it depends on the presentation, but one thing I suggest is that …

Audio 8.06
1 To begin with, …
2 The first point …
3 Moving on to …
4 As a final point, …
5 To sum up …
6 Just to recap ..

Audio 8.07
D = Dan   M = Melissa   J = Jack

D: Hello. My name is Dan Barnet.
M: And I'm Melissa Barnet.
D: We are entrepreneurs and together we run a business called Live Your Life Adventure Holidays.
M: Years ago we realised we didn't like spending our holidays just lying on a beach doing nothing. We're both very active and like to be out of our comfort zone, so we started organising adventure holidays for ourselves.
D: And then our friends asked us to do the same for them. Pretty soon we were arranging ten to fifteen holidays a year, so we realised it was a business opportunity.
M: We organise holidays in various locations around the world. Our holidays are a mixture of physical activity, stunning natural environment and cultural experiences. For example, you can stay on a farm in Romania, climb mountains in Turkey, or walk along the Italian coastline and then learn to make fresh pasta with an Italian chef. We also offer riskier activities where you need some training. Examples include caving, rock climbing and trekking.
D: What's special about Live Your Life is that we work very closely with our clients to arrange the perfect holiday for them, and also we've personally tried out every trip that we offer.
M: Adventure tourism is a very large tourism sector. The market for global adventure tourism is worth nearly $500 million and it's forecast to grow steadily over the coming years, so this is a huge market. Our turnover figures for the last three years have been €70,000, €100,000 and €150,000.
D: We'd like to expand our business to cover more countries in Asia and South America and to reach new clients in these parts of the world. We're hoping that an investor will have business experience in these areas and useful contacts that can open doors for us.

AUDIOSCRIPTS

M: And we're asking for €100,000 for a ten percent share of the business.
J: The idea's great, but I have a couple of questions. Who is the target market for these adventure holidays? Is it mostly families, couples, individuals?
M: All of the above. We tailor the holiday to the client's needs.
J: OK. So can you tell me about your social media strategy?
M: Yes, of course. We have several social media channels so we try to make sure that there's a constant stream of photos and videos of people enjoying their adventures on social media and then …

UNIT 8 VOCABULARY BANK

Audio VB8.01

1 When you understand something or solve a problem, you figure out how to do it.
2 When you test a new idea, you try it out.
3 When you use your imagination to invent a new idea, you dream it up.
4 If you meet together with other people as a group, you get together.
5 When you note something on a piece of paper you write it down.
6 If you take a big idea and split it into smaller sections, you break it down.
7 When you consider the facts about something in a carefully organised way, you think it through.
8 When you investigate something further to find out more information, you follow it up.

UNIT 8 REVIEW

Audio R8.01

Inventing a Better World

Ann Makosinski grew up in Canada, but she didn't have a lot of toys as a child. Her first toy was a box of electronic parts. Later her parents bought her a hot glue gun. Should her parents have bought her more toys? She doesn't think so. Having these 'toys' encouraged her to collect things around the house and piece them together to make new 'inventions'. These inventions rarely worked, but she was never afraid to do something new. She had discovered her love for dreaming up new ideas and inventing things, and this became her lifelong passion. Motivated by the story of a friend in the Philippines who had failed her school exams because she had no electricity, Ann took time to work on inventing a light source that didn't need batteries. At fifteen, she won the Google Science Fair with a torch powered using only the heat in your hand. Two years later, she invented her eDrink coffee mug, which uses the heat from a drink to charge your phone. Ann pays attention to the world around her, so is always inspired and never runs out of ideas. It's possible that if she'd had more toys as a child, she wouldn't have been so creative in her free time, and she might never have become an inventor. She also didn't own a mobile phone when she was a teenager, but she doesn't think her parents should have let her have one. She enjoyed being different to the other kids and it gave her a chance to deepen her interest in her inventions.

UNIT 8 MEDIATION BANK

Audio MB8.01

I was studying medicine, in my second year at university, and everyone was so happy, so proud of me, our son is going to be a doctor type of thing. Except, I had a different feeling. I didn't share the excitement about being a doctor, in fact I couldn't imagine myself as a doctor. Not a good one anyway. I tried to ignore the feeling, but it just didn't work. In the end, I left the course, and obviously everyone was disappointed, and I was the most disappointed person of all – I was going to be the one in the family that everyone was proud of, and I'd let everyone down. For a few months I thought about what I really wanted to do with my life and decided on a new direction, and here I am ten years later and I'm a very successful accountant. And a happy one, too. Some people are born doctors, and I'm a born accountant.

VIDEOSCRIPTS

UNIT 1

Opener: BBC Vlogs
1. The best present I've ever received was a laptop because after I received my laptop I was able to start working online and that changed my life.
2. The best present I've ever received was my engagement ring.
3. The best present I ever received was a puppy. I was three years old. This meant we grew up together and were always the best of friends.
4. My favourite present was my saxophone. My parents gave it to me when I was ten for my birthday. I'd wanted one for ages and when I opened the present I was so excited.
5. The best birthday present I've ever had was my son who was born on my birthday.
6. The best present I ever received was a new set of golf clubs, er, because golf is my passion and these clubs made me a better golfer.
7. The best present I've ever received is a music studio, built into my own house.
8. I think the best present I ever received was a holiday to South Africa to go on safari, and it's something I had wanted to do, um, since I was a child.
9. The best present I have ever received was a car that my husband bought me because he really wanted me to learn to drive. It was an old car and it was really beautiful.
10. The best present I've ever received I think must be a camera that I got for my tenth birthday. It was quite a basic camera, but it led me to a great interest in photography and I still love taking photographs today.

1D: BBC Street Interviews
Exs 2A and 2B

Rory: I think I could live without all my gadgets apart from my phone, because it's so important to me, because I use it for my emails, for university, for school work, and to keep up with news and my friends.

Connor: I'm a musician and I play guitar so my favourite kinds of gadgets are guitar pedals 'cause I can change the way my guitar sounds.

Catherine: I could live without the iPad. Umm … I could live without a … um … a home computer, but I do like a laptop, and I absolutely – I hate to say it – I love my phone.

Marc: I would say my laptop is a pretty important thing, er, for work, in general, and I just can't live without it. In terms of gadgets that I could live without, I'd say my smartwatch.

Joshua: Er, I love my phone. I use it all the time. Um … I even use it in bed. I'm just pretty much never off it.

Shannon: Um … I love my laptop. I couldn't really live without it 'cause I attend university and everything is now online, so we all rely on our textbooks online and all our lectures and our teachers teach us from our laptops.

Josh: So I love a range of gadgets from my Xbox and my laptop, but I could live without all of them except for my phone, and that's because I use it for everything: my work and in my free time.

Ex 2C

Rory: I think they do, but I think in this day and age it's needed to look at screens, and I think that a lot of people couldn't do without the screens so I think that's why a lot of people do it. But I do think some people do it too much.

Connor: I do think people spend too much time looking at screens. I think when you spend so much time looking at a screen, you lose the face-to-face contact and that emotion that you get from that interaction.

Catherine: I do think people spend too much time on the screens. I think people are addicted to screen time, er, needing information or entertainment more immediately at their hands. Um … I think people, younger generation, might have more difficulty just being with themselves, on their own.

Marc: I would agree with that. People certainly look at their phones too much. It might even be the first thing in the morning. Um … I wake up, check my emails and might as well be the last thing in the evening, where I do the same thing, or check the news, or things like that.

Joshua: Um … I do, especially like nowadays everything is online, everything's on technology, whether it's phones or computers.

Shannon: Um … I think people probably spend too much time on their phone. But I only really use my laptop to study, and I use my phone just to contact my friends.

Josh: I think so, because it prevents you from being able to talk to people in person, and I think that the recent use of phones, even more so than in the past, has aided that problem.

UNIT 2

Opener: BBC Vlogs
1. I think one of my best habits is eating healthily. When I was a child, my mum would make sure that my sister and I didn't eat sweets or soft drinks or cakes and biscuits unless it was a special occasion and I've tried really hard as an adult to keep up with this habit.
2. I try to meditate almost every evening. I think it's a very healthy habit. It helps me relax and it clears my head after a busy day.
3. My best habit is definitely being punctual. Whether it be to meet a friend or starting work, I always like to arrive on time.
4. I think one of the good habits I have is try to have a great breakfast every morning, and also drink plenty of water and finally take a walk every day.
5. So I think I've got two really good habits, erm. The first one is cycling, so I try and cycle every day for 15 minutes, either to the shops or, or to the office. And the second one is, is reading before bed, erm, I always read before bed and it, it helps me relax and, and have a good night's sleep.
6. What I really like is playing chess. It helps me to concentrate and make a good decision in real life.
7. A good habit that I have is that I try to go swimming every week, um, outside. So, I go swimming in a lake and, depending on the time of year, it can be really cold, but I've heard that cold-water swimming is really good for you.

2D: BBC Documentary
Exs 2A and 2B

If you are small, finding the right tree can mean a home for life. He's a Draco lizard. He's only the size of a pencil and he eats ants. This one tree could provide him with all he will ever need, a conveyor belt of food. It's a perfect place to settle down. Well, it would be, but there's already someone here. This larger male is the tree's owner and Dracos don't share. The owner's flag is a warning – trespassers won't be tolerated. The owner's not only intimidating, he's prepared to battle. A dead end. Safety is a long way away. Now he must choose – fight or flee. Only in the jungle do you find lizards that can soar like dragons. He can travel over 30 metres in a single leap. It's a very fast and efficient way to move through the jungle. Maybe this new tree will have food and no resident owner.

UNIT 3

Opener: BBC Vlogs
1. I'm a PhD student at Bilkent University. I work best in the library at the university because it's nice and quiet, and when I need books for my assignments I can find them easily.
2. I'm a university student. I don't like working in libraries. I prefer working in cafés because I like the background noise, and I can buy coffee and cake.
3. I prefer to work from home. I spend a lot of my time on video calls with my colleagues in overseas offices, and sometimes, actually a lot of the time, these calls happen at very short notice, and in the office it's really difficult to find a quiet space to make calls at short notice, so it's, it's much better for me just to be at home.

VIDEOSCRIPTS

4 I way prefer working in the office than at home. I really enjoy having my friends from work and my colleagues around me – whether that's just to have a chat with a coffee or to talk about some important work, erm, it's a lot easier, and I find it a lot more of an interesting environment to be in.
5 I really prefer to work from home. I have everything here that I need, including a nice cup of my favourite coffee in the morning.
6 These days, I'm, I'm working from home. My favourite spot is the living room. I like it because it's spacious, erm, and it's good because I like to stretch out a bit and have short breaks in between tasks, and it has a nice view as well.
7 So, I prefer working from home. Um, I'm a writer, so I like waking up when I want to, switching my computer on when I prefer, and also getting the food and drink from the fridge when I want to, and it's a much more comfortable environment for me.

3D: BBC Street Interviews
Ex 2
Dara: When I was growing up, I wanted to be a PE teacher.
Monica: I wanted to be a lot of things. I think I wanted to be a doctor at some point, a lawyer as well, and … an astronomer.
Des: So I wanted to be a footballer who played for Chelsea.
Tian: Erm, I think I wanted to be an actress.
Eva: I wanted to be a fashion designer.
Daniel: When I was four, I wanted to be an astronaut. Erm, then I wanted to be a doctor when I was about twelve.
Sky: I wanted to be a movie star, so bad. I wanted to be on TV, and television, just red carpet, all of it. I wanted to be a movie star.
Rohan: I always wanted to be an electrician, but more I wanted to be a musician. A reggae singer.
Anais: I wanted to be a photographer because my dad got me into photography growing up, so it kind of just came from that, and I just really liked it.

Exs 3A and 3B
Dara: Out of a teacher and a chef, I would rather be a teacher because I like children and I'm quite used to working with children, so I think that job would fit me quite well.
Monica: An actor or a journalist. I'd rather be a journalist because I'm very interested, at, with what's happening with the world, um, and I love to learn what's happening in society and other countries, so I think that's what I would rather be the most.
Des: I'd rather be an author, and I'd rather be an author than an engineer because, erm, I think I could reach more people by writing books and I could work from home.
Tian: Farmer or a politician.
Eva: I think I'd rather be a politician, no, wait, no, a farmer because I don't like arguing with people.
Tian: I'd rather be a politician because I like arguing with people.
Daniel: If I was to choose between being a teacher and a chef, I think I would prefer to be a chef, erm, probably because I do my own cooking and I really enjoy it. It's one of my hobbies. So I'd like to work in a kitchen sometime.
Sky: I'd prefer to be a farmer 'cause I like being outside in nature, and I don't think I would be a very good politician.
Rohan: Um, an author or an engineer. I'd definitely go for an author because I love stories and I would love to share a good story as well.
Anais: I think I'd prefer to be a chef over a teacher. Erm, I think it would just be pretty cool to make some cool dishes. I don't think I'd really like to teach.

UNIT 4

Opener: BBC Vlogs
1 True stories are really interesting, but I prefer fiction. I like the challenge of having to read between the lines, and really trying to understand what the author's trying to say.
2 Erm, I read both I think. I read, er, non-fiction for work, which is most of my time, er, but when I go on holiday I love to read, erm, detective stories.
3 I prefer true stories over fiction. I prefer watching documentaries over films. My favourite subject at school was history.
4 I prefer reading fiction, er, particularly poetry, but I like watching documentaries.
5 I prefer reading non-fiction books, especially letters or memoirs. You can really learn a lot about the daily lives of famous people from these.
6 I like to read the news online, er, every evening, because I like to see what's going on in the world, and, er, I also like to read biographies; particularly about musicians and sportspeople, because I find them inspiring, and I like to find out more about their lives.
7 I think I probably prefer fiction. I just love being taken away to new worlds and, you know, growing with the characters and finding out what happens to them. Um, but I do read lots of non-fiction, and I do really enjoy documentaries as well.
8 When I was younger, I definitely preferred fiction – I used to love getting lost in stories – but, as I get older, I definitely prefer more true stories, especially historical stories or biographies of interesting or famous people.

4D: BBC Entertainment
Exs 2A and 2B
Holly: Adam!
Adam: Holly?
Holly: Wow, that's …
Adam: Whoa, this is … crazy!
Holly: I know!
Adam: Er, how long's it … ?
Holly: Oh, years. Seven years. Um, I thought you were living New Forest way?
Adam: Yeah, I moved back a few months ago. Er, long story. You look good.
Holly: So do you.
Adam: Wow. God, I never thought I'd, er … This is madness!
Holly: Well, give me a hug!
Adam: Oh, er. Ha ha! So, do you live round here, or … ?
Holly: Er, not far. I have an apartment.
Adam: Right.
Holly: You?
Adam: Yeah. Er, bought a place. Nothing special. Cathedral Road?
Holly: Nice. Where are you working?
Adam: Porter Collins? For my sins.
Holly: Still making a living out of others' misfortune?
Adam: Hey, ever since I was a little boy, I said, 'When I grow up, I want to be an insurance loss adjuster'.
Holly: Ha ha ha! Mm …
Adam: You?
Holly: I'm a manager. This online sports place.
Adam: Wow!
Holly: Yeah, 150 staff.
Adam: Amazing!
Holly: I, er, can't complain. I mean, it's long hours, lot of responsibility, but, you know, I like it, I like managing people, you know, making sure I get the best out of my team.
Adam: Um … It's amazing bumping into you. We should … catch up, or …
Holly: That would be great. … If it's not weird for your wife? I mean, you know, ex-girlfriend alert.
Adam: I'm sure she'll be fine, especially as we're separated and she lives with a guy called Zane.
Holly: Shall we swap numbers?
Adam: Great, yeah. Er, punch yours in here. I'll call you.
Holly: I'll just … um, make sure I've got yours. It … minute … There we go.
Adam: Er, it's good to see you again.
Holly: You too.

VIDEOSCRIPTS

UNIT 5

Opener: BBC Vlogs

1 A few weeks ago, my dishwasher broke down, erm, and I realised it once the dishwasher was full, and it just would not work. So, I had to take everything out and wash everything by hand. It was very, very annoying.
2 Last week, we had a problem with our broadband connection. It kept dropping out, which was really frustrating when we were trying to watch television or when my son was gaming.
3 Before I left on vacation, I went to a car rental agency and I reserved a car. But when I got here, they told me there weren't any cars available. They had all been rented. Ugh!
4 Yes, I, I recently had a problem with the person who delivers, er, milk to my house, because sometimes he just doesn't deliver the milk, erm, and sometimes he leaves it in the wrong place. Erm, so yeah, I'm not going to use him anymore. I'm going to buy it from the shops.
5 The last time I had a problem with a product or a service was actually with these glasses. I had an eye test back in January, um, and they made up some new glasses for me, but for some reason they weren't right. So, I went back, had another eye test; again, they made some new glasses, they still weren't right, and this continued for months and months and months. It was really annoying.
6 I like to order food delivery online. It's so convenient! I usually don't have any problems, but last week I had a problem – my food didn't arrive. I can track where my food is on the app. I asked them to leave it by my doorway, it even showed me a picture of when it arrived. But, when I opened the door, my food wasn't there.

5D: BBC Street Interviews
Exs 2A and 2B

Dean: I always do the washing up myself because, er, I used to work in a café, in a restaurant, and, er, I, I know how to do it the best. And it annoys me when I see people do it wrong so I always make sure that I do it so that it's perfect every time.
Imogen: Yeah, I mean I always do the dishes, er, and like the general kind of cleaning, we don't have a cleaner. Erm, I actually always cut my own hair. Yeah, find that a lot, er, cheaper.
Rory: Er, I always try and sort of fix things that I've broken myself. So for example, when I was living at uni I broke the cupboards to my, in my kitchen, and I really didn't want to call a handyman to get it done, so I really tried to fix that myself.
Eden: Oh, interesting. I always clean my own room, I make dinner on a Tuesday … Uh, what else do I do? Think that's about it. Yeah.
Jane: I always walk the dog 'cause no one else in the house will do it.
Elpida: I do the housework myself. I don't pay a cleaner to do it.
Sagar: Erm, I always try and do the DIY in the house, so I try and fix broken shelves and cupboards, erm, and I always try and fix my own car myself.
Aisha: I do my grocery shopping by myself rather than getting it delivered.

Exs 3B and 3C

Dean: Um … so we have a gardener, so we always get our grass cut for us. Um … I'm too lazy to do it and he does the best job, so it's worth the money.
Imogen: Erm, yeah I always have my car cleaned. Erm, … I think that's probably it, yeah.
Rory: Yeah, I, I always get my hair cut professionally, because I would not trust myself or anyone else to do it for me 'cause I want to look good.
Eden: So, I get my food delivered, I get my hair coloured and I get my nails painted.
Jane: We get our windows cleaned every month by a professional window cleaner.
Elpida: Um … I get a mechanic to check my car every year, to see if it's working properly, and pass the MOT test.
Sagar: I would always have my hair cut by a professional. Um … Yeah, that was it, yeah.
Aisha: I'd get someone to colour my hair rather than do it myself.

UNIT 6

Opener: BBC Vlogs

1 My favourite city is Katowice in Poland. I really love that city. The architecture is just beautiful, and it's not too big, it's not very small. It's a very friendly city.
2 I would choose Rio de Janeiro in Brazil as my favourite city from the ones that, erm, that I know. It has magnificent energy, er, people are very friendly. You have the sea, you have the, the mountains, you have forests. Actually, you have the biggest forest in a city in the world – it's there. Er, it has football, it has music – it has samba. Erm, it's really the place to go and visit.
3 My favourite city is Valencia in Spain because I absolutely love Spanish culture, and I love the traditional and modern architecture.
4 My favourite city is Lisbon. It has wonderful architecture and amazing food, and it's so easy to get around.
5 My favourite city might be Istanbul. I love it because it is very beautiful, full of history, and it really is a point where East meets West.
6 My favourite city has got to be York, which is in the north of England. It's so old and has a very rich history. And it's beautiful in any season – spring, summer, autumn, winter – it doesn't matter. There's beauty everywhere.
7 My favourite city is Paris. I lived there for two years after I left university. And it is so beautiful, it's so human, it's so full of life, and it's definitely my second home now.

6D: BBC Documentary
Exs 2A and 2B

Reggie: Shenzhen, China's 'Miracle City'. This entire region used to be farmland and fishing villages, home to just 30,000 people. But in just four decades, it's become a teeming metropolis of over 12 million and the epicentre of China's tech revolution. They say if you want to see the future of the human race, you want to come here. But what draws people to this extraordinary city?
Reggie: Hello.
Reggie: Among Shenzhen's population are a growing number of expats – tech entrepreneurs who could work anywhere in the world, and they're choosing this city.
Reggie: Hello. Hi, er, Reggie.
Duncan: Hey, how's it going? Welcome to HAX.
Reggie: Duncan? Nice to meet you.
Reggie: Duncan is a Brit who essentially runs his own Dragons' Den.
Reggie: What is it about China specifically over somewhere like the UK?
Duncan: Right.
Reggie: What's keeping you here?
Duncan: It's just, like, the speed of change here. It's … It's actually addictive, like, you realise, 'cause I go back to the UK fairly often, how things really haven't changed that much. Whereas here, you blink and everything's completely different.
Reggie: Innovators from all over come here with their ideas. This team have created glasses that can talk to your ears. Tap 'em and they start telling you things – from what's in your diary to the weather. This company is making robots for car parks. And these two are seriously into their ping pong. The pace of change here is undeniable. So much so, it even has its own name: 'Shenzhen Speed'.
Reggie: This monument … You've got these years, er, on this monument which reference different years of importance clearly to the area, and '78, '79 is around about the time when things really started to change here in Shenzhen, and, erm, '82 is the year before I was born. So, you know, this is pretty much my lifetime. When you compare the changes in the area that I was raised in versus here … I mean, in my lifetime, we've had some nice new roads laid, er, there's a shopping centre that's gone up. It's unbelievable.

172

VIDEOSCRIPTS

UNIT 7

Opener: BBC Vlogs
1 I love words that sound a bit like what they mean, erm, like, er, 'lazy'. That's a good one, because it's got a 'zzz' in the middle, which is a kind of sleeping sound. So, 'lazy', mm, yeah, that's one of my favourites.
2 My favourite word is a Scottish word and it is 'wheesht', and it means 'be quiet'. And there's a variation of that, which is 'hold your wheesht', which means pretty much the same thing: 'hold your tongue', 'hold your silence'.
3 My favourite word in the English language might be 'petrichor', er, which is the smell of earth after it rains. I just think it's very nice.
4 I really like the word 'giggle', er, because it makes me smile and, erm, sometimes it makes me giggle, and it's good to laugh.
5 My favourite word is to 'groke'. It means to stare at people who are eating in the hope that they will give your some of their food.
6 One of my favourite words is a Japanese word, 'yosh', and it means 'OK' or 'all right'. And, let me give you an example: In English if I'm going to pick up something really heavy, I say 'OK, all right, I've got this'. But in Japanese, all you have to say is 'yosh!' It sounds great!
7 My favourite word is 'mangelwurzel' because it sounds funny. A mangelwurzel is a vegetable that grows underground like a potato. Erm, in the fields near my house there are a lot of mangelwurzels.

7D: BBC Street Interviews
Exs 2A and 2B
Zoe: I hope so. I think I'm quite friendly, so I feel like I can talk to people quite easily.
Joshua: Yeah I think I'm good at communicating but there's, there's certain situations where I struggle a bit.
Janine: Yes, I think so. With my line of business and work, I have to work with lots of people across lots of platforms and yes, that's definitely a key requirement.
Monica: I think I am a good communicator. I may ha … , make some mistakes with grammar since I'm from Spain, but I would like to think that people can understand what I'm saying.
Pear: I would say I am a good communicator, if I'm having a good day, but if I'm having a bad day, I think my communication is lacking.
Lily: I'd say I'm a good communicator but only through speaking. I'm not great at communication through writing. Does that make sense?
Michael: Um, I could be a better communicator, is what I would say.
Hannah: I think I'm quite a good communicator. I'm quite honest, so I feel like someone knows if they've done something wrong or if I like them.
Yiannis: I believe that I am a good communicator. Um … I do a lot of public speaking and debating, and I enjoy talking to people, so yes, I think I am a good communicator.
Raihan: I do not think I'm a good communicator. I get shy when I speak to a large audience.

Exs 3A and 3B
Zoe: When there's conflict I try to stay out of it, definitely.
Joshua: Yeah, er, so do I, and, erm, in large groups I find that quite difficult as well.
Janine: I think online, generally, um, it's easier to work face to face with people. Um, I think it's more, um, creative.
Monica: I think probably when I'm public speaking, I get a bit nervous, so I, I want to practise a lot before I do it, erm. But yeah, practice makes perfect.
Pear: I think it can be difficult to communicate when I am feeling sad, because … or angry, because I am busy thinking about myself, so I'm not thinking about how I'm coming across to other people.
Michael: Um, communication I would say under pressure, that's, that's definitely um, when you're under pressure, choosing the right words can, can be difficult.
Hannah: Um, I think if I'm angry I'll find it quite difficult to communicate. I can't find the words to explain why I'm angry.
Yiannis: I have difficulty communicating with girls, 'cause it's very hard to talk to them sometimes.
Raihan: So do I. Especially when I like them, it makes me all nervous.

UNIT 8

Opener: BBC Vlogs
1 It's actually a piece of advice that my husband was given by his boss. It's very simple and yet very important: er, good enough is good enough.
2 Don't go supermarket shopping when you're hungry because you will buy lots of food that you don't need, and you will probably buy snacks like chocolate and crisps.
3 The best advice I was given is to work hard, erm, always look after your health, er, try to join a gym, because health is wealth.
4 The best piece of advice I ever got was from my coach, who told me that you learn more from your mistakes than you do from your successes.
5 I think the best advice that I ever got was to get a dog. Erm, er, my dog is my best friend, and he has been for the last eleven years. Erm, I absolutely love him.
6 The best piece of advice that I've ever been given came from my mother. She told me to go and eat a banana when I can't sleep at night. It's brilliant! Works like magic!
7 The best piece of advice I've ever been given, er, was by a colleague of mine a few years ago when I was thinking about the next steps in my career. And at the time I was overthinking it and overanalysing it. And what my colleague told me at the time is to, to just follow my heart and see what feels good for me, what feels right for me. Er, and that's what I did. And it proved to be the right thing.

8D: BBC Entertainment
Narrator: Next to face the Dragons is entrepreneur, Jacob Thundil, with his food and drink business. But will any of the Dragons want to invest?
Jacob: Hello, Dragons. I'm Jacob Thundil, chief nut at Cocofina – the coconut experts. We produce coconut products to eat, drink and cook with. I was born in a place called Kerala, and Kerala means in Sanskrit, 'land of coconuts'. Cocofina was my destiny. As a young boy, I was fascinated with the amount of uses out of coconut and today I use coconut products every day. The market for coconut oil and coconut water alone in the US is worth around £750 million and, in the UK, £50 million pounds, and doubling annually. Our turnover figures over the last three years has been £1 million, £600,000 and £300,000. I'm offering 5% for £75,000. I would welcome you to try our products.
Narrator: It's a confident pitch from Jacob Thundil, who's asking for £75,000 for a 5% share of his business. With a wide range of coconut products, from water and milk, to snack bars and oils, Jacob has a lot to offer. But will any of the Dragons be interested?
Dragons: Thank you.
Narrator: First up its Touker Suleyman who wants to know more about the business structure.
Touker: Describe your organisation to me.
Jacob: So, there's me and then there's a lady that started with me. Er, she's a 50% shareholder of the business.
Peter: What's her name?
Jacob: Er, Manisha.
Nick: Can we meet her?
Jacob: Yeah, sure. She's, er, she's downstairs.
Narrator: Jacob's business partner, Manisha Solanki, is a little camera shy. But as she owns 50% of the business, the Dragons are keen to meet her.
Dragons: Hello.
Jacob: This is Manisha.
Manisha: Hi Dragons.
Nick: Manisha I apologise for dragging you out at, er, with no notice, but er, it's obvious that you're a very important part of this business. What I'd like to understand is how you divide the roles.
Jacob: I'm sales, marketing, purchasing. Manisha is all operations, so logistics, all the deliveries, everything like that.
Tim: Great.
Manisha: So, basically, once he has made the sales, I take care of everything.

173

VIDEOSCRIPTS

Narrator: The Dragons now have a clear understanding of the business. But will anyone make an offer?

Deborah: So, I'm going to make you an offer. And I'm going to offer you all of the money. I want 20% of the business. And I want 20% of the business because there is, a – obviously the contacts that I can bring, but I think the development side … there's a little bit of work that needs to be done on that. But I think we are the team that can do it, so that's my offer to you.

Narrator: Deborah's sudden offer is a good start for Jacob and Manisha. But she wants 20% of their business – a lot more than they want to give away. Can online expert Nick Jenkins do any better??

Nick: Well, I think I might pitch in with an offer as well. I love the passion you have for the product. So, I'm going to match the offer. All of the money for 20%.

Narrator: Sarah Willingham, who owns several successful restaurants, is also interested.

Sarah: So, I'm going to match the offer. All of the money for 20% of the business.

Narrator: Jacob and Manisha now have the same offer from three of the Dragons. But Jacob has a question of his own.

Jacob: If we were to buy the shares back from you for double the money in three years' time, would you give up 10% back to us?

Narrator: Jacob wants the option to buy back 10% of the business when it starts making money. But will any of the Dragons accept?

Nick: I don't have a problem with that.

Narrator: Nick is happy to sell 10% of the business back to Jacob after one year. And Sarah is still interested, too.

Sarah: I would just want to add one thing, that I would very much be prepared to split it with another Dragon.

Nick: Sarah, would you be prepared to split it on the terms that I suggested?

Sarah: Yes, I would. I would be prepared to split it with Nick.

Nick: I think between the two of us, you get two for the price of one!

Jacob: I don't think we need to discuss further.

Nick: Right, OK.

Sarah: Brilliant.

Nick: Brilliant. Great.

Jacob: Thank you very much, sorry.

Sarah: Hug! Oh, brilliant.

Narrator: Jacob and Manisha have done it. They've given up 20% of their company but will be mentored by two Dragons.

IRREGULAR VERB TABLE

Verb	Past simple	Past participle
be	was	been
become	became	become
begin	began	begun
bite	bit	bitten
blow	blew	blown
break	broke	broken
bring	brought	brought
build	built	built
buy	bought	bought
catch	caught	caught
choose	chose	chosen
come	came	come
cost	cost	cost
cut	cut	cut
deal	dealt	dealt
do	did	done
draw	drew	drawn
drink	drank	drunk
drive	drove	driven
earn	earned/earnt	earned/earnt
eat	ate	eaten
fall	fell	fallen
feed	fed	fed
feel	felt	felt
find	found	found
forget	forgot	forgotten
freeze	froze	frozen
get	got	got
give	gave	given
go	went	been/gone
grow	grew	grown
have	had	had
hear	heard	heard
hold	held	held
hurt	hurt	hurt
keep	kept	kept
know	knew	known
lead	led	lead
learn	learned/learnt	learned/learnt

Verb	Past simple	Past participle
leave	left	left
let	let	let
lie	lay	lain
lose	lost	lost
make	made	made
mean	meant	meant
meet	met	met
pay	paid	paid
put	put	put
quit	quit	quit
read	read	read
ride	rode	ridden
run	ran	run
say	said	said
see	saw	seen
sell	sold	sold
send	sent	sent
shine	shone	shone
shoot	shot	shot
show	showed	shown
sing	sang	sung
sit	sat	sat
sleep	slept	slept
speak	spoke	spoken
spend	spent	spent
spill	spilled/spilt	spilled/spilt
stand	stood	stood
stick	stuck	stuck
swim	swam	swum
take	took	taken
teach	taught	taught
tell	told	told
think	thought	thought
throw	threw	thrown
understand	understood	understood
wake	woke	woken
wear	wore	worn
win	won	won
write	wrote	written

Pearson Education Limited
KAO Two
KAO Park
Hockham Way
Harlow, Essex
CM17 9SR
England
and Associated Companies throughout the world.

pearsonenglish.com/speakout3e

© Pearson Education Limited 2023

All rights reserved; no part of this publication may be reproduced, stored in a retrieval system, or transmitted in any form or by any means, electronic, mechanical, photocopying, recording, or otherwise without the prior written permission of the Publishers.

First published 2023
Seventh impression 2024

ISBN: 978-1-292-40746-3

Set in BBC Reith Sans

Printed in Slovakia by Neografia

Acknowledgements
Written by Frances Eales, Steve Oakes, Antonia Clare and JJ Wilson. The publishers and authors would like to thank the following people for their feedback and comments during the development of the material:
Burcu Çelik, Charlotte Gerard, Billie Jago, Rebecca Lennox, Dorota Walesiak.

Image Credits:
123RF.com: Aleksandr Ugorenkov 10, Juliane Jacobs 132, Nikkytok 10, pixelrobot 132, Sanga Park 8, Slavadumchev 27, Tarzhanova 10, teeraphat24 136, ueuaphoto 132; **Alamy Stock Photo:** Anthony Harvey/PA Images 44, Imaginechina Limited 74, Leon Werdinger 48, Oleg Upalyuk 74, Ray Rumbarger 68, RooM the Agency 83, 85; **BBC Studios:** 7, 16, 17, 19, 28, 29, 31, 40, 41, 43, 45, 52, 55, 64, 65, 67, 76, 79, 88, 89, 91, 100, 100-101; **Getty Images:** Angela Cappetta 35, Ariel Skelley 94, ArtMarie 27, Artur Debat 59, AsiaVision 146, bluejayphoto 102, Carlina Teteris 36, Catherine Falls Commercial 79, Circle Creative Studio 149, Comstock 95, Crispin la Valiente 129, Dejan Marjanovic 72, Dougal Waters 123, Dowell 25, Eightshot Studio 134, Elizabethsalleebauer 83, Elly Schuurman 83, EschCollection 52-53, Giselleflissak 36, Glenn Hill/SSPL 45, Glow Images 23, Grant Faint 73, HEX 36, Igor Alecsander 36, imamember 93, Jamroen Jaiman/EyeEm 132, Jetta Productions Inc 62, Joern Pollex 103, Jorg Greuel 71, Julien McRoberts 152, Kevin Mazur/WireImage 46, Kitti Boonnitrod 71, Klaus Vedfelt 84, 109, Lane Oatey 136, lechatnoir 43, leonovo 134, Liao Xun 76-77, Lisa5201 93, Luis Alvarez 14, 31, Mark Johnson 132, Marko Geber 156, Martin Novak 19, Martin-dm 8, 74, Maskot 20, 36, 42, 148, Michael Godek 26, Miquel Llop/NurPhoto 33, Mitch Diamond 83, MoMo Productions 93, 93, monkeybusinessimages 134, Monty Rakusen 134, Morsa Images 36, MStudioImages 92, Myriam Lima/EyeEm 8, Nednapa Chumjumpa/EyeEm 132, NeoPhoto 67, Neustockimages 38, Oliver Rossi 131, Oscar Wong 74, Paco Navarro 97, Peter Fleming 150-151, piranka 98, Rick Loomis/Los Angeles Times 73, Roine Magnusson 28-29, RWP UK 55, Sarote Pruksachat 35, sarra22 110, SDI Productions 86, 93, Sellwell 30, Sharon Lapkin 91, Simon Ritzmann 7, Skynesher 20, South_agency 37, 50, Stevica Mrdja/EyeEm 47, sturti 113, Tang Ming Tung 22, 136, Thamrongpat Theerathammakorn 154, Timothy A. Clary/AFP 46, Topical Press Agency 44, urbancow 130, vgajic 32, VichoT 83, ViewStock 130, VioletaStoimenova 56, Westend61 6, 12, 20, 20, 47, 80, 117, 135, Willie B. Thomas 149; **Shutterstock:** abumuslim1 25, 26, Alones 78, Amy Harris/Invision/AP 98, Ann Rheel 71, Cookie Studio 149, Eric Isselee 150, Felix Lipov 70, fizkes 136, gpointstudio 83, Granger 44, Joao Serafim 8, Jose AS Reyes 10, Labrador Photo Video 8, Lipskiy 132, Mangostar 8, Mariyana M 132, MGM/Eon/Danjaq/UPI/Kobal 119, Netflix/Moviestore 48, Pakhnyushchy 84, Photology1971 8, Planner 132, PotatoTomato 10, Prostock-studio 136, Rido 8, Robert Waltman 150-151, Shuang Li 69, Spiroview Inc 69, Sylv1rob1 8, tarasov 132, Tarzhanova 132, TonTectonix 11, Tzido Sun 134, Universal/Kobal 131, Venus Angel 132, Vladgrin 85

Cover Images:
Front: **Getty Images:** skynesher, Tara Moore, Tom Werner/DigitalVision, Westend61

Illustrated by
Liv Cleverley (NB Illustration) 13; Stephen Collins (Central Illustration Agency) 24, 60; Ben Hasler (NB Illustration) 22, 137; Sam Kalda (Folio) 34, Norbert Sipos (Beehive Illustration) 63, 142; Mark Willey (Designers Educational) 107